641.5 LAR
Larsen, Linda,
The everything potluck
cookbook /
1079916282 ORCO

WITHDRAWN
WORN, SOILED, OBSOLETE

D0128666

POTLUCK COOKBOOK

Dear Reader,

Peg Bracken, in her inimitable *I Hate to Cook Book* subtitled her chapter on Potluck Parties as "How to Bring the Water for the Lemonade." If it were only that easy! Potluck parties do take some work, but they are so much fun.

I think that any occasion can be cause for a party. A job promotion, a birthday, the beginning of the school year, the end of the school year, the holidays, or just a need to relax and eat with friends are all excellent reasons for a party.

With the economy struggling and everyone feeling the pinch of rising prices, we need to get together with family and friends more than ever. But hosting a party can be very expensive, and it takes a lot of energy and work. The solution? A potluck party. One of the best lessons I've learned in my life is to always bring something to a party. It could be a friendly smile, stories to share, a bouquet of flowers for the hostess, or food. A potluck party can be anything from a wedding celebration to a bridge party for four people. The underlying theme is always fellowship.

I find myself throwing potluck parties more and more these days. Not only is everyone so busy, but also with food costs skyrocketing, feeding even a group of four people a good meal can easily top $100. And that doesn't include all the time preparing the food.

Any way you choose to organize your party will be fine with your guests. With these tips, recipes, and information about throwing a potluck party, yours will be the best yet. Whether you ask guests to bring completed dishes or ask them to bring a few ingredients and cook together, you'll find that an informal potluck party is just plain fun.

Linda Larsen

Welcome to the EVERYTHING® Series!

These handy, accessible books give you all you need to tackle a difficult project, gain a new hobby, comprehend a fascinating topic, prepare for an exam, or even brush up on something you learned back in school but have since forgotten.

You can choose to read an *Everything®* book from cover to cover or just pick out the information you want from our four useful boxes: e-questions, e-facts, e-alerts, and e-ssentials.

We give you everything you need to know on the subject, but throw in a lot of fun stuff along the way, too.

We now have more than 400 *Everything®* books in print, spanning such wide-ranging categories as weddings, pregnancy, cooking, music instruction, foreign language, crafts, pets, New Age, and so much more. When you're done reading them all, you can finally say you know *Everything®*!

QUESTION

Answers to
common questions

FACT

Important snippets
of information

ALERT

Urgent
warnings

ESSENTIAL

Quick
handy tips

PUBLISHER Karen Cooper

DIRECTOR OF ACQUISITIONS AND INNOVATION Paula Munier

MANAGING EDITOR, EVERYTHING SERIES Lisa Laing

COPY CHIEF Casey Ebert

ACQUISITIONS EDITOR Katrina Schroeder

DEVELOPMENT EDITOR Brett Palana-Shanahan

EDITORIAL ASSISTANT Hillary Thompson

EVERYTHING SERIES COVER DESIGNER Erin Alexander

LAYOUT DESIGNERS Colleen Cunningham, Elisabeth Lariviere, Ashley Vierra, Denise Wallace

THE
EVERYTHING®

POTLUCK
COOKBOOK

Linda Larsen

BS in Food Science and Nutrition

Avon, Massachusetts

To my nieces and nephew,
Grace, Maddie, and Michael.

Copyright © 2009 by F+W Media, Inc. All rights reserved.
This book, or parts thereof, may not be reproduced
in any form without permission from the publisher; exceptions
are made for brief excerpts used in published reviews.

An Everything® Series Book.
Everything® and everything.com® are registered trademarks of F+W Media, Inc.

Published by Adams Media, a division of F+W Media, Inc.
57 Littlefield Street, Avon, MA 02322 U.S.A.
www.adamsmedia.com

ISBN 10: 1-59869-990-3
ISBN 13: 978-1-59869-990-6

Printed in the United States of America.

J   I   H   G   F   E   D   C   B   A

Library of Congress Cataloging-in-Publication Data
is available from the publisher.

This publication is designed to provide accurate and authoritative information with regard to the subject matter covered. It is sold with the understanding that the publisher is not engaged in rendering legal, accounting, or other professional advice. If legal advice or other expert assistance is required, the services of a competent professional person should be sought.

—From a *Declaration of Principles* jointly adopted by a Committee of the American Bar Association and a Committee of Publishers and Associations

Many of the designations used by manufacturers and sellers to distinguish their products are claimed as trademarks. Where those designations appear in this book and Adams Media was aware of a trademark claim, the designations have been printed with initial capital letters.

This book is available at quantity discounts for bulk purchases.
For information, please call 1-800-289-0963.

Contents

Introduction

POTLUCK PARTIES SEEM OLD-FASHIONED; just the name evokes an image of ladies wearing hats and gloves clustered in the kitchen, unwrapping their creations to the "oohs" and "aahs" of the others. They evolved from "covered-dish" dinners usually held by churches, back in the nineteenth century when just putting food on the table every day was a struggle. No one could afford to feed a crowd of people! Having each guest bring his or her most treasured recipe was an easy way to entertain even in the hardest times.

This type of party does take more organizing on the part of the host, but with lists and some attention to the details, you can have a great time at your own party. And you'll save money too.

There are two basic types of potluck parties: one where guests bring a completed or almost-completed dish, and one where guests bring individual ingredients and you cook together. Both are fun; choose the type that best fits your style of entertaining, temperament, and kitchen size.

And the party can be very free form; just ask guests to bring anything they want! You'll run the risk of having four desserts and two main dishes, but that's part of the fun. Or if you like to have more control, include the course or even the recipe you'd like the guest to bring along with the invitation.

A theme is important but not necessary for a potluck party. Some parties, especially those around the holidays, naturally evoke a theme. A Halloween party could revolve around pumpkin dishes and hearty meat stews, while a spring party could have a menu of cold salads, soups, and fruit muffins.

The most important part of a potluck party is making sure that the venue is clean and comfortable. Since you, as the host, don't have to focus as much on the food, put that energy into decorating the dining room and making sure that the kitchen is a cozy and welcoming place. You don't have to spend a fortune: a small lamp on the counter, some new dish towels and kitchen utensils, or a colorful rug on the floor add a warm and fresh feeling to any room.

Many of the recipes in this book are to be made ahead of the event, because that's the best type of food to transport any distance. You'll also find tips and hints for the best way to move food, and how to keep it safe. There are also last-minute recipes, just in case a guest's recipe doesn't turn out or if someone unexpectedly can't attend. You'll find ways to get organized, too, that will make the planning and execution of the party a breeze.

So join the crowd and make your next party a potluck. You're guaranteed a good time!

CHAPTER 1

All about Potluck Parties

The word *potluck* literally means "food you are lucky to find." A potluck party is a gathering where every invited guest brings something to the party. While rather an old-fashioned way of entertaining, potluck parties are becoming popular again. These parties are casual and informal. They give cooks and bakers a chance to shine, and even those who aren't comfortable in the kitchen can participate.

Why a Potluck Party?

In these days of ever-increasing food prices, most of us aren't even thinking about entertaining. Feeding our own families is becoming more difficult, so the thought of feeding six, eight, or more guests is quite daunting. The potluck party comes to the rescue! Not only are these parties fun, but they also spread the cost of food among all the guests. Potluck parties are quite the bargain. For the cost of one dish, each guest will be fed a meal worthy of any restaurant.

The Pluses of a Potluck

A potluck party is a wonderful way for experienced and new hosts to get together with friends. Parties don't have to have a purpose, but if they do, there's a built-in icebreaker. Coming to the door with a delicious dish in hand will help even the shyest guest feel involved in the party.

FACT

If you're feeling adventurous, try hosting a true potluck party. Just ask every guest to bring a favorite recipe. If you get five desserts and one main dish, so be it! You may want to have a backup plan of ordering pizza, just in case, but these types of parties are memorable and very fun.

Everyone is so busy these days. Just the thought of throwing a party can be exhausting. A typical party involves lots of planning, coordinating the menu, shopping for the food, cleaning the house, making all the recipes, serving, then cleaning up. Just the thought of that much work can put an end to entertaining. But a potluck party is different.

As the host, all you have to provide is a space for the party, and usually the main dish. The guests bring the rest! You can assign specific recipes to your guests, or just ask them to bring their favorite salad, potato side dish, dessert, appetizer, or whatever.

Spreading out the cost and the work this way is very efficient and, in these tough times, provides a way to get together with friends and family without prohibitive costs.

If you're hosting the party, of course, you'll need to have a presentable venue. But you don't have to host a potluck at your house! A beautiful park, the beach, or even your backyard can be the setting for a wonderful party.

ESSENTIAL

There are two types of potluck parties: where guests bring finished dishes that may need to be baked or reheated, and where guests bring ingredients and everybody cooks. If you have a large kitchen, or an outdoor kitchen with lots of room, a cooking potluck party can be lots of fun.

"Many hands make light work" is a common saying, and it's very true. You will probably find yourself hosting more parties if they are potluck parties, just because they are so easy. The communal experience of dining together is a basic part of every society, and it strengthens bonds between friends and family.

Finally, a potluck is a great way to save money. Because you don't have to provide every course of a dinner, you can splurge and make something a bit more expensive. You can serve steaks, use exotic cheeses, or provide out-of-season items like strawberries in January.

If You're the Host

As the host, you do still have the most responsibilities for the party. Make sure that the venue you choose is comfortable for all the guests, that you have serving pieces and eating utensils, and that there is enough food for everyone. But all of this effort doesn't have to be difficult; it just takes some planning. When you're prepared for the party, you can relax and enjoy it too.

The Theme

A theme always helps to get a party off the ground. It can be an obvious choice, like a birthday party or a holiday, or something more unusual, like a job promotion, housewarming, or the anniversary of an important date. If a theme doesn't readily suggest itself, think about having a bridge party, or a "Night at the Movies" fling.

POTLUCK PARTY IDEAS

- Potluck picnic
- Dessert party
- Oscar's party
- Big Game appetizer party
- Back-to-school gathering
- Celebrate summer party
- Wine and cheese party
- Housewarming
- Garden party
- Chocolate party

Other good ideas include a party to celebrate your nationality, where you bring a dish prepared in your grandparents' homeland, or an All-American potluck, with a plethora of American dishes like macaroni and cheese, Caesar salad, and brownies.

The Plan

As with any project, a party needs to be carefully planned. Make lists—lots of lists! List the guests you've invited, what each person is bringing to the party, the serving utensils and equipment you'll need, and a timetable for cooking.

It may help to keep all the information in a notebook or binder. You should have a guest list, the menu, shopping lists, timetable for cleaning and preparing the kitchen, and a plan for organizing the house as well as borrowing or buying any needed equipment.

When you're planning the menu, consider the number of dishes you are serving as well as the number of your guests. Each recipe has a general yield. Serving sizes may vary, but this is a general guide. The more dishes at the party, the more people each dish will serve. This is just human nature: if you're offered a choice of four entrees, you will take less than a regular serving size of each one.

SERVING SIZES AND AMOUNTS				
Food	**Per person**	**6 servings**	**12 servings**	**18 servings**
Appetizers	3	20	36	48
Drinks	16 ounces	80 ounces	192 ounces	288 ounces
Rolls	1	6	12	18
Main Dish	1 cup	1½ quarts	3 quarts	5 quarts
Salad	1 cup	1½ quarts	3 quarts	5 quarts
Vegetables	½ cup	3 cups	6 cups	2 quarts
Potatoes	1 cup	1½ quarts	3 quarts	5 quarts
Pies	⅛ pie	1 pie	2 pies	3 pies
Cakes	1/12 cake	½ cake	1 cake	2 cakes
Cookies	3 cookies	18 cookies	3 dozen cookies	4 dozen cookies

Guest List

A potluck party can be a gathering of old friends, or it can be a way to introduce people to each other. Since the party has an automatic built-in ice breaker, you don't have to worry about compatibility. There will always be something to talk about: the food!

Make sure that you don't invite more people than your house or venue can comfortably hold. Take bathroom facilities, available seating, and kitchen space into consideration too.

Invitations

Invitations can be as casual as a phone call or e-mail, or as fancy as mailed, handwritten invitations. If you're throwing a theme party, the invitations can match to set the stage. Handwritten invitations, especially when created and made by kids for a family party, can be very charming. You can include the food you'd like each participant to bring in the invitation.

Be sure to request a response, especially if you've asked that person to bring a specific dish. If you want control of the party, include one of the recipes from this book instead of requesting a general category of food.

Put It Together

Once you've settled on the theme, the guest list, and invitations, it's time to start planning the meal. Sometimes the theme will suggest the menu, as in a Hawaiian party or a Christmas brunch. Other times, you may want to serve a special new dish you have created and have your guests bring accompaniments.

Compose your menu with your guests' cooking skills in mind. If one of your guests is a great baker, ask him to bring a cake for dessert. If another loves to grill, ask her to bring a grilled appetizer. Be sure to balance the menu for color, texture, temperature, and flavors.

RECIPES FOR HEALTH-CONSCIOUS GUESTS TO BRING
- Vegetable salads
- Green salads
- Vegetarian main dishes
- Fruit desserts
- Whole-grain side dishes
- Fish and seafood main dishes
- Mediterranean dishes
- Low-fat soups and stews

Now you write, e-mail, or call your guests and tell them about the party. Make sure they can attend on the day of the party. Tell them the food you would like them to bring. Ask if they can make the recipe and if they're confident in their abilities. And be sure to ask if they have any special dietary needs or food allergies. Your party is on the way!

If You're the Guest

If you've been invited to a potluck party, get ready for a fun time! Dig out your best recipe for the food you're asked to bring, or practice the recipe the host gives you. Always bring something else to the potluck too: a good mood and a willingness to have a good time.

What to Bring

Whether the host asks you to bring a specific dish or one that falls into a general broad category, stick with what you know. Unless you're an experienced cook, make something you know turns out well and that you can make. This is not the time to experiment with a fancy new dish, especially if you're preparing it just before the party.

Tried-and-true recipes are your best choice. And bring what you like! If your family loves one of your dishes, chances are others will too. Everyone enjoys food prepared with love and care.

Be Open to Suggestions

If you're the guest at a potluck party, it's important that you cooperate as much as possible. Throwing a party, even a potluck party, still takes a lot of effort and energy. Offer to help beyond just bringing a dish. Always offer to help clean up, and ask if you can bring anything like serving utensils, beverages, or cooking equipment.

ESSENTIAL

If you're asked to bring a dish in a general category, pick your best recipe and serve it with pride. And be sure to bring the recipe, written out on several cards. Someone will be sure to ask for it. If the recipe is unusual or a family heirloom, be sure to make a note of that on the card.

Ask if you can bring serving dishes, utensils, even a grill if it's a cookout party. And do agree to the dish you're asked to bring, unless you have a moral or physical objection to it. In fact, if you're a good cook or have the time, ask if you can bring more than one dish.

Party Planning: Start Your Lists

Lists are essential to planning and organizing any event, and a potluck party is no exception. Make a list of the guests you invite, the food each person is bringing, what you have to provide, the shopping list, the cleaning list, and notes on how the party turned out.

One of the best lists to keep is a record of the party. After a few years of entertaining, you'll find you have a notebook full of great gatherings and ideas that you can repeat if you'd like. Always write down how each dish was liked, if there were any problems you could solve for next time, and ideas for new parties.

Guests' Likes and Dislikes

It's important to know what your guests like and don't like and what they will and won't eat when planning any party. With a potluck, you can be a little more adventurous, since there will be quite a lot of food. Still, be sensitive to the needs of vegetarians, those who keep kosher, and those who just plain don't like certain foods.

If a guest has a strong aversion to a food, seriously consider leaving it off the menu entirely. Some foods can upset people just with the aroma. The comfort and happiness of your guests is paramount.

Food Allergies

Most of all, be sure that you ask, every time, what food allergies your guests may have. These conditions can be life threatening, so if someone is allergic to peanuts, make sure that not only are peanuts or other nuts not on the menu, but that the food has been prepared in a peanut-free kitchen.

ALERT

If your party is fairly large, it's a good idea to make labels for each dish, with a note of what's in it. Be sure to make note of allergenic foods, which include nuts, wheat, milk, soy, seafood, and eggs, so those allergic to those ingredients can avoid it. Never use serving utensils to serve more than one food, to avoid cross-contamination.

If a guest is allergic to a food, be sure to ask about the severity of the allergy. That guest may want to bring more than one dish to be sure she has something she knows she can safely eat.

Choosing the Recipes

If you like to have lots of control, you can give a recipe to each guest and ask them to prepare it. Be sure to listen to your guests, though; a vegetarian wouldn't enjoy preparing a meat dish, while someone on a strict diet because of a health condition won't want to prepare a dish full of heavy cream and sugar.

Choose the recipes based on your tastes and on the types of dishes common to your area if you aren't throwing an ethnic party. Be sure to match the dish to the cooking and baking expertise of the guest.

Who Brings What?

Chances are you know at least a little bit about the people on your invitation list. If you know that one friend loves baking and is known for her fruit pies, ask her to bring one or two. If another friend is an expert at the grill, ask him to bring a recipe of his famous marinated grilled salmon. People will be happier bringing something they know is good and that they can cook.

If you don't know the kitchen experience of a guest, ask! If the guest says that she isn't a cook, ask her to bring something other than food, or come prepared to help you set up or clean up. A potluck is all about participating.

Roles for Non-Cooks

And what about people who can't cook or don't like to cook? They can still participate in a potluck, and if you are one of them, you can still host a potluck. Ask these people to provide other party essentials to take even more of the financial burden off you. The non-cook can even buy some of the ingredients if you're hosting a cooking potluck party.

CONTRIBUTIONS FOR THE NON-COOK
- Beverages
- Utensils and serving pieces
- Condiments
- Flowers for the table
- Party favors
- Food from the deli

- Serving on cleanup duty
- Bakery breads and desserts

Party and Cooking Techniques and Tips

It's best to plan the party and food so that only one or two dishes needs last-minute attention in the kitchen. If you have a small kitchen, think about using an outdoor grill (yours or borrowed) to take some of the pressure off the kitchen.

If some of your guests are bringing make-ahead casseroles, try to plan so they all bake at the same temperature, or are cooked in a slow cooker that can be transported in the car.

Organize Your Kitchen

Your kitchen has to be very organized with this type of party. The guests are probably going to see your entire kitchen, including inside the refrigerator and pantry. Clean out the oven, freezer, pantry, refrigerator, and drawers and cupboards before the party. Not only will this help you stock up on items you may be missing, but also you'll feel more comfortable knowing there's nothing to hide. Buy new dish towels and stock up on paper towels for easy cleanup.

Last-Minute Recipes

Just in case a recipe from a guest doesn't turn out, make sure that you have all of the ingredients for a backup recipe or two. There are several last-minute recipes in this book. Read through them and stock all of the ingredients. If there is a flop or someone decides at the last minute that they can't attend, you'll be able to fill the hole in the menu.

LAST-MINUTE RECIPES
- Ham Creole (page 78)
- Chicken and Pasta in Cheddar Sauce (page 113)
- Chicken Hawaiian (page 118)
- Beef Mornay (page 95)
- Grilled Red Snapper with Fruit Salsa (page 134)

- Sugar Snap Spinach Salad (page 193)
- Potluck Pita Pizzas (page 36)
- Swiss Fondue (page 40)
- Best Ever Garlic Bread (page 59)
- Grilled Herb Cheese Breadsticks (page 63)

Main dishes are usually the recipes you'll need to add at the last minute. Side dishes are easy: just boil some baby carrots and toss with butter, or put together a green salad. Have a bakery dessert or two on hand just in case.

Make-Ahead Tips

If you're providing the main dish (or two), as is traditionally the case for the host, pick one that can be made ahead of time. Casseroles are easy and delicious, and can be completed and refrigerated until the party begins. You just bake or microwave it until hot and bubbly.

For a small house or kitchen, or a party venue that doesn't have a complete kitchen, all of the food should be ready to eat, except for foods that can be grilled at the last minute. Make sure that the food stays cold or hot and that it's well wrapped against the elements.

Food Safety

Food safety is really the most important factor in a potluck party; any party, for that matter. If the food makes people sick, you will feel terrible too! Stress keeping hot food hot and cold food cold. Be sure to tell your guests to either completely cook a recipe or just assemble it and cook at the party. Never partially cook meats, then chill to finish at the destination.

Transporting Food

Transporting food, whether it's across the street or to another town, can be tricky. Follow suggestions in the recipes. If you're traveling a long distance, it's best to bring something that is done and can be served at room temperature, like a batch of cookies, roasted vegetables, bread or rolls, or a fruit pie.

If the host asks you to bring something like a hot dish or perishable appetizer, ask if you can bring a safe food instead. Or maybe there's a food you can make at home, pack into an insulated container, and bake or grill at the party.

Keep It Hot

Keeping food hot is more difficult than keeping it cold. Be sure to follow this ironclad rule: perishable foods can only be out of refrigeration for two hours, one hour if the ambient temperature is above 80°F.

That means that if you bake a meatball casserole, it can be transported in your car, then served at the party, within two hours. Be sure to take that timing into consideration when you're planning what to bring.

QUESTION

What's the danger zone in food temperature?
The temperature range you want to avoid is 40°F to 140°F. At these temperatures, bacteria can grow rapidly in perishable food. Even if you cook the food after it's been sitting at this temperature you can still get sick because some bacteria produce toxins that heat will not destroy.

The best way to keep hot foods hot is to use an insulated carrier. Many hardware stores and kitchenware stores have a nice supply of these items. If not, wrap the hot food in layers of newspaper, then in kitchen towels to hold in the heat.

Keep It Cold

Cold food is a bit easier to handle. First make sure that the food is thoroughly chilled or frozen before you transport it. Ice chests with frozen gel packs or bags of ice cubes can keep food cold for four to six hours. Follow that perishable rule again: two hours max out of refrigeration.

Cooking Together

Cooking together is a challenge. But after all, most party guests tend to congregate in the kitchen. Giving them a task to do is a great ice breaker and takes some of the pressure off you. With some planning, you can create great food together and have a wonderful time too.

For your party, it's best if you plan to have only one or two dishes that need to be baked or fried just before serving. Many dishes can be served cold or at room temperature. If possible, plan on a slow cooker dish, a refrigerated dish or two, one that should be grilled at the party, one finished on the stovetop, and one baked dish.

Basic Tips

Take a good look at your kitchen and decide how you can divide it up for the most efficiency. Even if you have a very small kitchen, you can designate one area for chopping, another for cleaning, and another for cooking. Then assign people to the areas, divide up the recipes, and get ready for fun.

FACT

> When you're inviting people to a cooking party, have a few appetizers ready and waiting for them. People will arrive hungry, and it's really nice to have some munchies and wine or other beverages available while they're cooking. There's nothing cozier than cooking in a nice kitchen, nibbling on snacks, and talking to friends.

Be sure that each cooking area has the recipe, utensils, tools, pots and pans, and ingredients all ready for the cooks. You don't want people having to stop and search for an item when they're getting into the swing of cooking.

You may want to divide up the recipes and ask each guest to bring a certain number of ingredients to defray the costs. This will require a lot of list making and double-checking to make sure all of the ingredients and utensils will be on hand.

How to Divide a Recipe

Take a look at a recipe, study it for a while, and you'll see how it naturally divides into several tasks. For instance, in a stir-fry recipe, the meat has to be prepped, the marinade prepared, and vegetables or fruits peeled, chopped, or diced. Then everything comes together in a few minutes on the stove.

So have a station where the meat is prepared, another for measuring and mixing ingredients for the marinade/stir-fry sauce, another for preparing and cooking the rice, and a fourth for the vegetable preparation. Then you, or another guest, will be the stir-fry master just before you want to eat.

ALERT

You want to make sure that all of these cooks aren't spoiling the broth. Tell everyone to wash hands before and after the preparation. Those working with raw ingredients like meats or eggs have to be very vigilant. Place containers of wet wipes around the kitchen so everyone keeps it clean.

Divide up the stations according to guest's cooking skills and what they like to do. You wouldn't give the task of cutting beef to a vegetarian, and a person with limited abilities because of arthritis perhaps wouldn't be comfortable handling a knife.

Recipe Stations

Model your kitchen after a professional kitchen. Each area of the kitchen, and each chef, is designated to produce one part of the meal. If you're preparing more than one dish, mix up the assignments so one person isn't stuck doing all the potato or onion peeling.

Make sure that there is enough space between each station so people can move freely without bumping into each other. Bring some stools or small chairs into the kitchen if there's room, so those who aren't working can rest for a while.

And designate a space to put dirty utensils, pots, and pans. A large container full of soapy water can be placed out of the way. As people work, they just drop the utensils into that container.

The Party

It's the day of your party! You should be excited and a little bit nervous, but very confident. You've planned well, and now it's time to enjoy the fruits of your labor. No matter what, be flexible and open to change. Nothing, short of the house burning down, is a disaster, so roll with the punches.

Timetable

The morning of your party, put the finishing touches on house cleaning. Get your family or friends to pitch in. Make sure that everything is ready well in advance of the starting time. The kitchen, especially, should be impeccably clean.

Do last-minute shopping for perishable items in the early afternoon. Read over your menu, check all of the food, and make sure that you have everything you need for the food you're preparing, as well as items like candles, flowers, serving utensils, and condiments.

FACT

A bulletin board is a great addition for any kitchen, and it can help you with a potluck party. Post all of your lists on the board, and check off tasks as they are accomplished. This will also help you keep track of the menu, so you see if there are holes and you have to bring in a last-minute recipe.

If you are preparing a make-ahead recipe, be sure to start it the night before if the recipe stipulates that. Many of the make-ahead recipes can be prepared a few hours before the party and spend time in the fridge before you bake or grill it to perfection.

Now take some time for yourself. Give yourself an hour or two to get ready: take a bubble bath, condition your hair, take a relaxing walk, or do something to pamper yourself. It's always a good idea to be ready and waiting for your guests. Try to have everything done at least half an hour before party time so you can sit and relax before the fun begins. Enjoy your clean house and the aroma of food drifting through the rooms.

Your Role

As the host, your role is to make sure that everyone is comfortable and having a good time. That starts with you! If the host is nervous or upset, everyone else at the party will feed that vibe and you'll have a big flop on your hands. If you're happy and confident, everyone else will be too.

If there are any disasters, like a recipe not turning out or something burning, don't panic. Just take it in stride and, if all else fails, just order in pizza and have a pizza party! The odds are that even if there's a failure, the guests won't even notice if you don't make a big deal out of it.

Now relax and enjoy the party. Remember that the guests take their cues from you, so be happy and really have fun. You've planned well and organized the event to perfection. Let's start cooking!

CHAPTER 2

Crowd-Pleasing Party Drinks

Lemon Sangria

Sangria is usually made with red wine.
This version is lighter and tastes just like a Lemon Drop cocktail, but it's easier to make.

EASILY DOUBLES

INGREDIENTS | **SERVES 10**

1 (6-ounce) can frozen lemonade concentrate

1 cup cold water

¼ cup limoncello

2 (750-milliliter) bottles chilled sparkling white wine

2 tablespoons lemon juice

2 cups chilled lemon-lime soda

1 lemon, thinly sliced

1. In large pitcher, combine concentrate with water and limoncello; mix until concentrate dissolves. At this point you can refrigerate until ready to serve.

2. Add wine, lemon juice, soda, and sliced lemon and stir gently. Serve immediately.

Limoncello

Limoncello is an Italian liqueur made from water, alcohol, lemon peel, and sugar. It's usually a gorgeous yellow color and has a fresh taste. You can find it at most liquor stores. If you can't, just add another 2 tablespoons lemon juice and 3 tablespoons vodka to the sangria.

Fruity Sangria

For the best flavor, this sangria should be made well ahead of time.
You can use any fresh fruits you'd like!

EASY

INGREDIENTS | **SERVES 12**

½ (12-ounce) can frozen orange juice concentrate

½ cup water

3 tablespoons sugar

½ cup peach schnapps

3 tablespoons lemon juice

2 bottles rose wine

1 cup pitted Bing cherries

1 peach, peeled and chopped

1 orange, thinly sliced

1 lime, thinly sliced

2 cups ginger ale

1. In large pitcher, mix concentrate, water, sugar, schnapps, and lemon juice and stir until concentrate and sugar dissolve. Stir in wine, cherries, peach, and orange and lime slices. Stir well, then cover and refrigerate overnight.

2. When ready to serve, stir in the ginger ale. Add ice cubes if you'd like, and serve immediately.

Pink Lemonade

Pink lemonade is perfect for a ladies' lunch or a child's birthday party.
Float more raspberries in the lemonade for a nice garnish.

HEALTHY

INGREDIENTS | SERVES 8

1 cup sugar
1 cup water
1 cup raspberries
1 lemon, thinly sliced
1 cup lemon juice
3 cups chilled sparkling water
4 cups cold still water

1. In small saucepan, combine sugar, 1 cup water, and raspberries. Bring to a boil. Reduce heat to low and simmer, stirring frequently, until sugar dissolves.

2. Add lemon slices to syrup and stir; let stand until cool. Cover and chill until cold.

3. When ready to serve, strain syrup and place in large pitcher. Add lemon juice, sparkling water, and 4 cups plain water. Stir well and serve immediately.

Cranberry Daiquiri

These pink daiquiris look like strawberry, but the taste is much more tart.
Garnish with sugared cranberries.

EASY

INGREDIENTS | SERVES 8

2 tablespoons lime juice
⅓ cup sugar
7 cups ice
2 cups cranberry juice cocktail
¼ cup lime juice
½ cup sugar
1 cup light rum
1 cup ginger ale

1. Dip the tops of eight daiquiri glasses in 2 tablespoons lime juice, then dip into ⅓ cup sugar to coat. Place on serving tray.

2. Combine remaining ingredients in blender. Cover and blend until smooth. Pour into prepared glasses and serve immediately.

Almond Smoothie

Smoothies are a great choice for a breakfast gathering,
and they can also be served as a quick and healthy snack.

QUICK

INGREDIENTS | SERVES 4

2 cups almond milk
2 cups vanilla yogurt
½ cup powdered sugar
½ teaspoon cinnamon
¼ teaspoon nutmeg
2 cups ice

Combine all ingredients in blender or food processor. Blend or process until smooth. Pour into glasses and serve immediately.

Keep It Healthy

You can find low-fat versions of almond milk and vanilla yogurt if you'd like. They should be the same thickness and consistency as the full-fat versions, so the recipe will turn out the same. Almond milk is a cholesterol-free product that is lower in calories than cow's milk.

Mango Margarita

These peach-colored margaritas are a nice change of pace
from the traditional lime variety.

EASILY DOUBLES

INGREDIENTS | SERVES 6

1 (12-ounce) can frozen lemonade concentrate
12 ounces tequila
2 cups cubed mango
2 ounces triple sec
6 cups ice cubes

1. In blender, combine concentrate, tequila, mango, and triple sec; blend until smooth.

2. Add ice cubes and blend until smooth. Pour into freezer container and freeze. When ready to serve, stir, then pour into margarita glasses.

Raspberry Sparkle Punch

*This beautiful punch has a nice flavor,
and it's not too sweet.*

INEXPENSIVE

INGREDIENTS | SERVES 14

1 (12-ounce) can frozen pink lemonade concentrate, thawed

1 (16-ounce) package frozen raspberries, thawed

1 cup water

2 tablespoons lemon juice

1 (64-ounce) bottle apple raspberry juice

½ cup chopped fresh mint

3 (12-ounce) cans ginger ale

3 cups raspberry sherbet

1. In blender or food processor, combine lemonade concentrate with raspberries; blend until smooth.

2. Mix with water, lemon juice, and apple raspberry juice in large pitcher. Cover and chill over night.

3. When ready to serve, chop mint and place in punch bowl. Add chilled mixture and ginger ale; stir gently and top with dollops of sherbet. Serve immediately.

Sherbet

Sherbet is a type of ice cream that is fat free or very low in fat. It's highly flavored and is the perfect ingredient to add to fruit punches. The sherbet keeps the punch cold and doesn't dilute the punch as it melts, as ice cubes, crushed ice, and ice rings do.

Orange Wine Cooler

*This wine cooler punch is fun to make and serve,
and it's really pretty too.*

EASY

INGREDIENTS | SERVES 8

1 (12-ounce) can frozen orange juice concentrate

1 cup water

1 (750-milliliter) bottle white wine

1 (48-ounce) bottle club soda

1. Combine concentrate with water and mix well. Add wine. Pour into ice cube trays and freeze until solid.

2. When ready to serve, place the cubes in a punch bowl and pour club soda over. Stir and let punch stand for 20 minutes, then serve.

Potluck Mocha Punch

Mocha is the combination of chocolate and coffee.
This easy and delicious punch is pretty too.

MAKE AHEAD

INGREDIENTS | SERVES 16

8 cups strong brewed coffee

1 cup sugar

1 (16-ounce) can chocolate syrup

2 teaspoons vanilla

1 quart whole milk

2 cups light cream

1 quart vanilla ice cream

1 quart chocolate ice cream

1. In large pitcher, combine coffee with sugar, syrup, and vanilla; mix well until sugar dissolves. Cover and chill for at least two hours.

2. When ready to serve, combine mixture in large punch bowl with milk and light cream; beat with wire whisk or eggbeater until smooth and frothy. Top with scoops of ice cream and serve immediately.

Keep It Healthy

You can use low-fat or no-fat ingredients in this punch to reduce calories. Use low fat vanilla and chocolate ice creams, nonfat light cream, and 1% or 2% milk. Chocolate syrup is already a low-fat food. If you like a strong mocha flavor, increase the amount of coffee and add 3–4 tablespoons of unsweetened cocoa powder in Step 1.

Lemon-Lime Soother

You can make this delicious drink alcoholic or not.
Just leave the tequila out if you want to serve this to kids.

EASY

INGREDIENTS | SERVES 12

1 (12-ounce) container frozen lemonade concentrate

1½ cups water

¼ cup lime juice

2 tablespoons lemon juice

1 cup tequila, if desired

1 (64-ounce) bottle lemon-lime carbonated beverage

1 lemon, thinly sliced

1 lime, thinly sliced

1 quart lime sherbet

1. In large pitcher, combine concentrate, water, lime juice, lemon juice, and tequila; mix well. Cover and chill for at least 4 hours.

2. When ready to serve, pour into punch bowl and add lemon-lime beverage. Stir well, then float lime and lemon slices in punch and add scoops of sherbet. Serve immediately.

Strawberry Cheesecake Smoothie

This tastes like a strawberry cheesecake in a glass!
You can substitute other frozen fruits; try peach or raspberry.

QUICK

INGREDIENTS | SERVES 8

1 (8-ounce) package cream cheese, softened

1 (14-ounce) can sweetened condensed milk

3 cups strawberry-flavored milk

1 (16-ounce) package frozen strawberries, thawed

2 tablespoons lemon juice

Combine all ingredients in large blender or food processor. Cover and blend or process until smooth. Serve immediately.

Party Fun

Garnish each glass with a strawberry for a fancy touch. Wash whole fresh strawberries with leaves and dry, then cut a small slit in the bottom. Pour the smoothie into the glass and balance the strawberry on the edge of the rim. Or you could make strawberry fans by slicing thin layers into the strawberry, keeping it whole at the leaves.

Tomato-Orange Cocktail

This super-refreshing cocktail is sweet, tart, and slightly spicy.
It's perfect for a summer party.

INEXPENSIVE

INGREDIENTS | SERVES 6

4 cups tomato juice

2 cups orange juice

2 tablespoons lemon juice

1 tablespoon honey

2 teaspoons minced red onion

¼ teaspoon salt

⅛ teaspoon white pepper

Mix together all ingredients and chill in refrigerator for 4–5 hours. When ready to serve, mix well, then strain and pour over crushed ice to serve.

Champagne Punch

Champagne punch is a great old-fashioned recipe.

EASILY DOUBLES

INGREDIENTS | SERVES 20

3 cups orange juice

1 cup lemon juice

4 cups pineapple juice

1 cup brandy

2 (750-milliliter) bottles champagne

1 (750-milliliter) bottle ginger ale

1 quart orange sherbet

1. In large pitcher, combine orange juice, lemon juice, pineapple juice, and brandy; mix well and chill for 4–5 hours.

2. Make sure champagne and ginger ale are chilled. When ready to serve, pour orange juice mixture into large punch bowl. Add champagne and ginger ale and stir gently. Top with scoops of sherbet and serve immediately.

Transport Tips

If you have a large pitcher with a tight, well-sealed top, you can transport this recipe to the party. Pack everything into a large cooler and add ice cubes in bags or frozen cooler packs. Be sure to bring the punch bowl, ladle, and cups. Assemble the punch at the party.

Fruited Tea Punch

Tea and fruit are so good for you, and when combined in this delicious punch they become a party in a glass.

HEALTHY

INGREDIENTS | SERVES 8–10

2 tablespoons loose tea leaves

2 cups boiling water

1 cup sugar

1 cup orange juice

½ cup lemon juice

2 oranges, thinly sliced

2 cups pitted Bing cherries

3 (12-ounce) cans ginger ale

6 cups cracked ice

1. Place tea leaves in bowl; add boiling water. Let steep for 3–4 minutes. Strain liquid into large pitcher; stir in sugar, orange juice, and lemon juice until sugar dissolves.

2. Add oranges and cherries; cover and chill for 4–5 hours. When ready to serve, pour into punch bowl. Add ginger ale and cracked ice and serve immediately.

Mulled Apple Cider

Mulling spices include cloves and cinnamon;
they add a spicy heat to apple cider.

HEALTHY

INGREDIENTS | SERVES 10–12

10 cups apple cider
1 cup orange juice
¼ cup honey
2 cinnamon sticks
1 orange
12 whole cloves
2 tablespoons lemon juice

1. Combine cider, orange juice, honey, and cinnamon sticks in 4-quart slow cooker.

2. Roll the orange on the countertop to soften. Stick the cloves into the whole orange and add to slow cooker. Cover and cook on low for 3–4 hours or until flavors blended and hot. Stir in lemon juice and serve.

Party Fun

This punch is really delicious in the late fall, which is the season for tiny apples called Lady Apples. If you can find them, they make a wonderful garnish for the punch. Place them in the slow cooker at the end of cooking time, and arrange some around the slow cooker too.

Grapefruit Cocktail

Pineapple adds a sweet touch to grapefruit in
this pretty and easy cocktail.

EASY

INGREDIENTS | SERVES 8

2 red grapefruit
5 cups grapefruit juice
1 (16-ounce) can pineapple tidbits, undrained
⅓ cup sugar
3 tablespoons lemon juice
2 cups ginger ale

1. Peel grapefruit and chop. Combine all ingredients except ginger ale in large pitcher; cover and chill for 2–3 hours.

2. Add ginger ale and stir. Strain into cocktail glasses and serve.

Hot Apricot Soother

*Apricots have a sweet-tart flavor and beautiful deep
orange-yellow color in this pretty and warming drink.*

MAKE AHEAD

INGREDIENTS | SERVES 10

8 cups apricot nectar

2 cups water

2 tablespoons honey

4 whole cloves

2 canned apricot halves

1 cinnamon stick

2 tablespoons lemon juice

1. In 3-quart slow cooker, combine nectar, water, and honey. Stick cloves into the apricot halves and add to slow cooker along with cinnamon stick.

2. Cover and cook on low for 4–5 hours or until mixture is blended and hot. Stir in lemon juice and serve immediately.

Party Fun

You can serve this mixture or any hot punch with cinnamon-stick stirrers. Just add a cinnamon stick to each cup or mug. This will release more cinnamon flavor into the drink, and it looks pretty too. Or you can sprinkle the top of the soother with ground cinnamon just before serving.

Milk Punch

*The combination of textures and flavors in this punch
tastes like a Creamsicle, that favorite kind of Popsicle.*

QUICK

INGREDIENTS | SERVES 18

1 (12-ounce) can frozen orange juice concentrate

6 cups cold whole milk

3 cups ginger ale

4 cups vanilla frozen yogurt

4 cups orange sherbet

1. In blender or food processor, combine concentrate with 1 cup milk; blend until smooth. Place in large punch bowl and stir in remaining milk.

2. Stir in ginger ale and mix, then add scoops of the frozen yogurt and sherbet. Stir gently and serve.

Coconut Eggnog

Eggnog can be served hot or cold; after cooking,
this mixture can be chilled for 4–5 hours; beat well again before serving.

EASILY DOUBLES

INGREDIENTS | SERVES 12

1 (14-ounce) can cream of coconut

2 (14-ounce) cans coconut milk

1 (14-ounce) can sweetened condensed milk

2 cups whole milk

Pinch salt

¾ cup white rum

¼ cup bourbon

1 teaspoon vanilla

1 teaspoon cinnamon

1. Combine all ingredients except rum, bourbon, vanilla, and cinnamon in 3½-quart slow cooker. Beat well with eggbeater. Cover and cook on low for 4–5 hours until hot.

2. Beat again, then add rum, bourbon, vanilla, and cinnamon. Stir well and serve. You can chill the nog at this point and serve cold.

Make It Healthy

Coconut oil, which makes coconuts taste rich, is actually good for you. It has saturated fat, but those fats are medium length, which the body digests easily, so it isn't stored in the liver. You could use low-fat sweetened condensed milk in this recipe to reduce calories a bit.

Banana-Orange Punch

There is a lot of vitamin C in this punch. The bananas add a
richness and smoothness to the mixture that is really delicious.

MAKE AHEAD

INGREDIENTS | SERVES 40

6 ripe bananas

1½ cups sugar

¼ cup lemon juice

1 (20-ounce) can crushed pineapple

2 cups orange sherbet

1 (12-ounce) can frozen orange juice concentrate

1 (12-ounce) can frozen lemonade concentrate

4 cups pineapple juice

3 liters ginger ale

1. In food processor, combine bananas, sugar, lemon juice, and crushed pineapple. Blend until smooth.

2. Pour into very large bowl. Add sherbet, concentrates, and pineapple juice and stir until blended.

3. Divide mixture into three 6-cup containers and freeze.

4. Take containers out of freezer 3 hours before serving; let stand in refrigerator to thaw slightly. Combine slush with 1 liter ginger ale in punch bowl and stir. Add remaining containers to punch bowl along with more ginger ale as needed to keep the bowl full.

Lemon Mint Punch

Stir in champagne instead of ginger ale to make this punch alcoholic.

INEXPENSIVE

INGREDIENTS | SERVES 12–14

2 cups sugar

6 cups water

3 cups fresh mint leaves

1 (12-ounce) can lemonade concentrate

½ cup lemon juice

1 liter ginger ale

1. In large saucepan, combine sugar and water; simmer over medium heat until sugar dissolves. Place mint leaves in large pitcher.

2. Pour hot syrup over mint leaves and muddle with a spoon. Cover and chill for 2–3 hours.

3. Strain mixture, discarding mint leaves. Add lemonade concentrate and lemon juice to mixture. Pour into punch bowl and add ginger ale; stir and serve.

Party Fun

Mint leaves are one of the best garnishes for drink or food. Pinch off the very end of the stem, rinse, and shake dry, then float some in the punch bowl. You can also garnish each glass with a sprig. There are several kinds of mint to choose from: plain mint, pineapple mint, and peppermint.

Frothy Hot Chocolate

This simple recipe for hot chocolate is rich, creamy, and smooth. And easy!

EASILY DOUBLES

INGREDIENTS | SERVES 4

4 cups milk

½ cup sugar

½ cup semisweet chocolate chips

⅓ cup cocoa powder

1 cup heavy cream

2 teaspoons vanilla

1. In large saucepan, combine milk, sugar, chocolate chips, and cocoa powder. Heat over low heat, stirring frequently with wire whisk, until chocolate melts and mixture is smooth.

2. While the mixture is heating, beat cream until soft peaks form. Remove chocolate mixture from heat and whisk in vanilla. Then whisk in cream.

3. Immediately pour into mugs and serve.

CHAPTER 3

Appetizers to Share

Orange Fruit Dip

*The tangy orange flavors mixed with the sweet
ingredients make this a tantalizing dip.*

EASY

INGREDIENTS | SERVES 12

1 (8-ounce) package cream cheese,
softened

1 (14-ounce) can sweetened condensed
milk

1 (7-ounce) jar marshmallow creme

3 tablespoons frozen orange juice
concentrate, thawed

⅓ cup orange marmalade

1 cup heavy whipping cream

¼ cup powdered sugar

1 teaspoon grated orange zest

Assorted fresh fruit

1. In large bowl, beat cream cheese until fluffy.
   Gradually add the sweetened condensed milk, beating
   until smooth. Add marshmallow creme, orange juice
   concentrate, and marmalade and beat well.

2. In small bowl, combine whipping cream with
   powdered sugar; beat until stiff. Fold into cream
   cheese mixture. Place in serving bowl and top with
   orange zest. Cover and chill for 2–3 hours before
   serving with fruit.

Roasted Garlic Spread

*Garlic becomes sweet and nutty when roasted. Serve as-is for a healthy spread,
or use in Swiss Fondue (page 40) or Bacon Potato Skins (page 44).*

INEXPENSIVE

INGREDIENTS | SERVES 6–8

3 whole garlic heads

2 tablespoons olive oil

1 tablespoon lemon juice

½ teaspoon salt

½ teaspoon dried thyme leaves

2 tablespoons butter

1. Preheat oven to 375°F. Cut the garlic heads in half,
   parallel to the root end. Remove excess papery skin
   from the heads. Place, clove side up, on heavy-duty
   foil.

2. Drizzle with olive oil and lemon juice and sprinkle
   with salt. Bring foil up around cloves. Place on cookie
   sheet. Bake for 45–55 minutes or until cloves are very
   soft.

3. Let cool for 20 minutes, then squeeze cloves out of the
   heads; discard skins. Place cloves in a small bowl and
   mash with thyme and butter. Serve as a spread or use
   as ingredient in recipes.

Glazed Pretzel Mix

Dried fruits are naturally sweet and have lots of fiber.
Use any type you'd like in this fun snack mix.

HEALTHY

INGREDIENTS | YIELDS 12 CUPS; SERVES 24

2 cups miniature pretzels
2 cups pretzel rods
2 cups pretzel sticks
2 cups small pecans
½ cup butter
½ cup honey
½ cup brown sugar
1½ cups dried blueberries
1½ cups dried cherries
1½ cups dried cranberries

1. Preheat oven to 300°F. Combine all the pretzels and the pecans on a large cookie sheet with a rim.

2. In medium saucepan, combine butter, honey, and brown sugar; cook and stir over medium heat until mixture blends. Drizzle over the pretzel mixture and toss to coat.

3. Bake for 35–40 minutes, stirring every 15 minutes, until mixture is glazed. Remove mixture to foil or a Silpat sheet and let cool. Break apart and mix with dried fruit; store in airtight container.

Tipsy Meatballs

Beer adds rich and smooth flavor to this updated appetizer recipe.

MAKE AHEAD

INGREDIENTS | SERVES 8–10

2 onions, chopped
1 (16-ounce) package frozen meatballs
1 (12-ounce) can beer
1 cup ketchup
½ cup chili sauce
2 tablespoons mustard
¼ cup pickle relish

1. Place onions in 4-quart slow cooker. Add meatballs. In medium bowl, combine remaining ingredients and pour into slow cooker.

2. Cover and cook on low for 5–7 hours until meatballs are hot and tender. Serve with toothpicks.

Keep It Healthy

The alcohol in the beer will not cook out of the sauce, even after hours of cooking. You can use nonalcoholic beer, but even that contains a tiny amount of alcohol. A nonalcoholic substitute would be 1½ cups beef broth. Be sure to tell your guests there is beer in this recipe.

Raspberry Fruit Dip

This pretty dip has a nice balance of flavors
because of the marshmallow crème and sour cream.

EASY

INGREDIENTS | SERVES 8–10

1 (8-ounce) package cream cheese, softened
1 (7-ounce) jar marshmallow crème
½ cup sour cream
1 cup frozen raspberries, thawed
½ cup raspberry preserves

1. In small bowl, beat cream cheese until fluffy. Gradually add marshmallow creme and sour cream, beating until smooth.

2. Stir in raspberries and place in serving dish. Top with raspberry preserves. Cover and chill for 3–4 hours before serving with fresh fruit and sugar cookies.

Keep It Healthy

You can easily substitute low-fat cream cheese and low-fat or nonfat sour cream in this recipe. Don't use all nonfat products, because the texture isn't as good. For best results, combine nonfat and low-fat products in any recipe. Serve this dip with apple and pear slices dipped in lemon juice, whole strawberries, and kiwi slices.

Potato Puffs

Crisp puff pastry is wrapped around smooth sour cream
potatoes in this inventive and easy appetizer recipe.

INEXPENSIVE

INGREDIENTS | YIELDS 16

1½ cups cooked potato flesh
2 tablespoons butter
2 tablespoons sour cream
½ teaspoon salt
½ teaspoon dried thyme leaves
½ teaspoon dried basil leaves
1 sheet frozen puff pastry, thawed
1 egg, beaten
1 cup chunky salsa

1. Heat potato flesh if it's cold. Stir in butter and sour cream and mix well. Add salt, thyme, and basil; let cool.

2. Roll puff pastry into a 12-inch square and cut into sixteen 3-inch squares. Place a generous 1 tablespoon potato mixture on each square. Gather all the edges together and seal to form puffs. Place, seam side down, on cookie sheet.

3. Brush with beaten egg. Bake at 350°F for 12–17 minutes until puffs are golden brown and hot. Serve with salsa.

Flaky Pâté Rolls

This appetizer is super-rich and perfect for a special occasion,
but it's easy to make.

EASY

INGREDIENTS | SERVES 12

1 cup Make-Ahead Pie Crust mix
(page 251)
2 tablespoons water
1 (7-ounce) can chicken liver pâté
1 egg
1 tablespoon milk

1. Preheat oven to 400°F. Combine Make-Ahead Pie Crust mix with water; mix with fork until dough forms. Roll out Crust between waxed paper to a 4" × 18" rectangle. Remove top layer of waxed paper. Gently spread one edge of the long side with the pâté, then roll up, using the waxed paper to help, but not rolling paper in with the pâté, starting with 18-inch side.

2. Pinch edges to seal and place on cookie sheet. Beat egg with milk in small bowl. Brush over roll. Bake for 15 minutes at 400°F, then reduce heat to 350°F and bake for 10–12 minutes longer until crust is golden brown.

3. Let stand for 5 minutes, then cut into ½-inch slices and serve.

Spicy Apricot Franks

Apricot preserves, tomato sauce, and some spices make a delicious sauce
for mini frankfurters in this easy slow cooker recipe.

EASY

INGREDIENTS | SERVES 8

⅔ cup apricot preserves
⅓ cup tomato sauce
2 tablespoons apple cider vinegar
1 onion, finely chopped
3 cloves garlic, minced
⅓ cup chicken broth
2 tablespoons soy sauce
½ teaspoon ground ginger
⅛ teaspoon white pepper
2 pounds mini cocktail franks

1. In 3- to 4-quart slow cooker, combine all ingredients except franks and mix well. Stir in franks.

2. Cover and cook on low for 7–8 hours, or on high for 3–4 hours, until sauce bubbles and franks are hot.

Edamame Guacamole

Edamame, or soybeans, are little green beans that have a rich, nutty taste.
They add fiber and nutrients to guacamole.

QUICK

INGREDIENTS | YIELDS 3 CUPS; SERVES 12

2 cups frozen shelled edamame

1 tablespoon olive oil

1 onion, finely chopped

1 jalapeño pepper, minced

3 tablespoons Roasted Garlic Spread (page 30)

2 avocados, peeled and chopped

½ cup sour cream

½ cup chunky salsa

2 tablespoons lime juice

½ teaspoon salt

⅛ teaspoon pepper

1. Cook edamame as directed on package; drain and place in food processor. Meanwhile, heat olive oil over medium heat and cook onion and jalapeño until tender, about 5 minutes.

2. Add to food processor along with remaining ingredients. Process until mostly smooth. Refrigerate for 2–3 hours, or serve immediately.

Make It Ahead

Like all guacamoles, this can be made ahead of time, as long as it is properly stored. Drizzle the top of the guacamole with lemon or lime juice, then press plastic wrap directly onto the surface. Refrigerate for up to 8 hours. Just stir before serving to mix the juice into the guacamole.

Fresh Tomato Salsa

Your own homemade salsa tastes nothing like salsa from a jar.
Serve this with any Tex-Mex recipe.

EASY

INGREDIENTS | YIELDS 4 CUPS; SERVING SIZE ½ CUP

4 red tomatoes, diced

3 nectarines, diced

2 avocados, peeled and diced

2 jalapeño peppers, minced

⅓ cup chopped green onion

3 tablespoons olive oil

1 teaspoon salt

⅛ teaspoon pepper

3 tablespoons lemon juice

¼ cup chopped parsley

¼ cup chopped cilantro

1. In large bowl, combine tomatoes, nectarines, avocados, jalapeños, and green onion; toss gently.

2. In small bowl, combine remaining ingredients; pour over tomato mixture. Cover and chill for 1–2 hours before serving.

Party Fun

For a big party, make several batches of salsa, each using different types of tomatoes. You can find many types and varieties of heirloom tomatoes in the market, especially at farmer's markets. Brandywine, Green Zebra, Big Rainbow, Jubilee, Mortgage Lifter, and Cherokee Purple are all heirloom tomatoes.

Shrimp Pizzettes

You can use crab, chopped chicken, or sausage in place of the shrimp in this easy pizza recipe.

QUICK

INGREDIENTS | YIELDS 20 PIZZETTES; SERVES 10.

1 tablespoon butter

4 green onions, chopped

2 cloves garlic, minced

1½ cups small frozen uncooked shrimp, thawed

1 (14-ounce) can refrigerated pizza dough

½ cup crumbled feta cheese

1 cup shredded Havarti cheese

1 teaspoon dried thyme leaves

¼ cup grated Parmesan cheese

1. Preheat oven to 450°F. In small skillet, melt butter over medium heat. Add green onions and garlic; cook and stir for 3 minutes. Add shrimp; cook and stir until shrimp turn pink. Remove from heat and drain.

2. Roll out pizza dough to 15" × 12" rectangle about ¼ inch thick. Cut into twenty 3-inch squares and place on cookie sheet.

3. Divide shrimp mixture among squares, then top with feta and Havarti cheeses. In small bowl, combine thyme and Parmesan cheese and sprinkle over Pizzettes.

4. Bake for 8–11 minutes or until crust is brown and cheese is melted and beginning to brown. Serve immediately.

Garlic Crackers

These crackers are saturated with garlic flavor, yet they're still crisp. They're a perfect complement to any soup.

EASILY DOUBLES

INGREDIENTS | YIELDS 35 CRACKERS

1 (4.3-ounce) package water crackers

⅓ cup butter

5 cloves garlic, minced

4 tablespoons Roasted Garlic Spread (page 30)

1 teaspoon dried basil leaves

1. Preheat oven to 350°F. Arrange crackers in single layer on large baking sheet.

2. Melt butter in small saucepan over low heat; add minced garlic and cook until garlic is fragrant, about 2–3 minutes.

3. Brush the butter mixture on the crackers. Mix Garlic Spread with basil leaves, then spread each cracker with ½ teaspoon of this mixture.

4. Bake for 4–6 minutes or until crackers are lightly browned. Immediately remove from baking sheet and let cool on wire racks.

Layered Taco Dip

This gorgeous dip has the best combination of flavors and textures.
You can also add shredded lettuce, sliced olives, and salsa.

EASILY DOUBLES

INGREDIENTS | SERVES 10–12

1 (15-ounce) can refried beans

2 chipotle peppers in adobo sauce, minced

2 tablespoons adobo sauce

1 (12-ounce) container prepared guacamole

2 avocados, minced

1 tablespoon lemon juice

1 (8-ounce) package cream cheese, softened

2 cups sour cream

1 (15-ounce) can black beans

2 cups chopped tomatoes

2 cups shredded pepper jack cheese

1. In medium bowl, combine refried beans with chipotle peppers and adobo sauce. Spread in a 13" × 9" glass baking dish.

2. In medium bowl, combine guacamole with avocados and lemon juice. Spread over beans in dish.

3. Beat cream cheese until fluffy; gradually add sour cream. Spread over guacamole. Drain and rinse black beans and sprinkle over sour cream mixture.

4. Add tomatoes and cheese; cover and refrigerate for 6–8 hours before serving with lots of taco chips.

Potluck Pita Pizzas

You can top these little pizzas any way you'd like.
Try refried beans, taco sauce, and shredded chicken,
or basil pesto, smoked turkey, and Havarti cheese.

LAST MINUTE

INGREDIENTS | SERVES 6

6 (4-inch) pita breads

1 tablespoon olive oil

2 tablespoons sun-dried tomato pesto

2 tablespoons tomato paste

⅓ cup pizza sauce

1 cup shredded part-skim mozzarella cheese

½ cup shredded sharp Cheddar cheese

1. Preheat oven to 400°F. Brush pita breads with olive oil and place on cookie sheet. Bake for 2 minutes, then remove and turn over.

2. In small bowl, combine pesto, tomato paste, and pizza sauce and mix well. Spread over pitas. Top with cheeses.

3. Bake pizzas for 5–8 minutes or until pitas are crisp and cheese is melted and beginning to brown. Let cool for 5 minutes and then serve.

Mom's Deviled Eggs

Deviled eggs are an old-fashioned favorite that everyone loves.
This one is a bit special, with toasted garlic and horseradish.

INEXPENSIVE

INGREDIENTS | SERVES 16

8 eggs
1 tablespoon butter
2 cloves garlic
5 tablespoons sour cream
2 tablespoons Dijon mustard
1 tablespoon prepared horseradish
½ teaspoon paprika

Party Fun

Pipe the egg yolk mixture into the whites for a fancy look. Just place a star tip in a cake bag and add filling, then pipe into the egg whites. You can also cut the eggs in half horizontally instead of lengthwise for a different look. Garnish the eggs with fresh herbs. Use a deviled-egg platter if you have one.

1. Place eggs in large saucepan and cover with cold water. Bring to a hard rolling boil over high heat. Cover and immediately remove from heat. Let stand for 12 minutes, then place pan in sink.

2. Run cold water into pan until eggs are cold. Then crack eggs gently against the sides of the pan under the water; let stand for 3 minutes. Peel eggs and refrigerate.

3. Melt butter in small saucepan. Toast garlic in butter for 4–5 minutes until golden. Remove and cool, then mash garlic into a paste.

4. Cut eggs in half and carefully remove yolks; place in small bowl. Add garlic, sour cream, mustard, horseradish, and paprika and beat for 4–5 minutes until very smooth. Stuff egg whites, then chill, covered, for 4–6 hours.

Bacon-Stuffed Tomatoes

*Place curly endive, curly parsley, or cilantro on the serving plate
to hold the little stuffed tomatoes upright.*

EASILY DOUBLES

INGREDIENTS | YIELDS 32 APPETIZERS

32 cherry tomatoes

8 slices bacon

1 onion, finely chopped

3 cloves garlic, minced

1 (3-ounce) package cream
cheese, softened

⅓ cup mayonnaise

⅓ cup grated Romano cheese

½ cup shredded Havarti cheese

Keep It Healthy

You can substitute turkey bacon for the
plain bacon, low-fat cream cheese and
mayonnaise for the full-fat versions. But
don't use low-fat cheeses, because they
don't have as much flavor. For even less fat,
use a fat-*free* version of the cream cheese
or the mayonnaise; the combination of
nonfat and low fat works well.

1. Cut tops off cherry tomatoes, remove seeds and jelly, and turn upside down on paper towel–lined cookie sheet.

2. Cook bacon in large skillet until crisp; remove, drain, and crumble. Drain skillet; do not wipe out. Add onion and garlic; cook and stir until onion starts to brown, about 12 minutes. Remove to food processor and let cool.

3. Add cream cheese and mayonnaise to food processor and process until smooth. Stir in bacon and cheeses.

4. Stuff cherry tomatoes with this mixture, then cover and refrigerate for 4–6 hours before serving.

Sausage Rolls

The spicier the sausage, the more flavorful these rolls will be.
They're perfect for a special occasion.

MAKE AHEAD

INGREDIENTS | SERVES 12–14

1 pound ground pork sausage

1 onion, chopped

3 cloves garlic, minced

1 red bell pepper, chopped

1 (8-ounce) package cream cheese, softened

½ cup low-fat sour cream

1 teaspoon dried thyme leaves

24 (9" × 15") sheets frozen phyllo dough, thawed

¼ cup butter, melted

1. In large pan, cook sausage, onion, and garlic until sausage is browned, stirring to break up meat. Add bell pepper; cook and stir for 3 minutes longer. Drain well and set aside to cool for 30 minutes.

2. In large bowl, beat cream cheese until fluffy; gradually beat in sour cream. Stir in sausage mixture and thyme.

3. Place one sheet phyllo on work surface; brush with butter. Layer another sheet of phyllo on top. Repeat, making a stack of six sheets. Place ¼ of sausage mixture on long side of stack. Roll up, then brush with butter. Place on cookie sheet.

4. Repeat with remaining phyllo, butter, and sausage mixture. At this point you can refrigerate the rolls for 18–24 hours.

5. Preheat oven to 375°F. Bake the rolls for 12–18 minutes or until browned and crisp. Remove from oven, let stand for 5 minutes, then cut into 1-inch rolls.

Swiss Fondue

Fondue is the perfect potluck appetizer.
The slow cooker will keep it at the perfect temperature without burning.

LAST MINUTE

INGREDIENTS | SERVES 8–10

2 cups shredded Gruyere cheese

2 cups shredded Havarti cheese

1 cup shredded baby Swiss cheese

2 tablespoons flour

2 tablespoons Roasted Garlic Spread (page 30)

2 cups dry white wine

2 teaspoons lemon juice

⅛ teaspoon white pepper

6 cups bread chunks

24 breadsticks

2 apples, sliced

24 cooked meatballs

Keep It Healthy

You can't substitute chicken broth or any other nonacidic liquid for the wine in this recipe; the cheese won't melt properly and you'll end up with a chunk of melted cheese in the broth. If you don't want to serve alcohol at your party, you'll need to make Updated Fondue (page 45).

1. In large bowl, toss cheeses with flour and set aside.

2. In large saucepan over low heat, combine Spread with 2 tablespoons wine; mix until combined. Add another ½ cup wine and stir until smooth. Add remaining wine and lemon juice and heat over low heat until bubbles start to rise.

3. Start adding the cheese/flour mixture, a handful at a time, stirring constantly. Continue until cheese melts and mixture is smooth. Stir in pepper and pour into 3-quart slow cooker, turned to "keep warm."

4. Serve immediately with chunks of bread, breadsticks, apple slices, and meatballs.

Salmon-Stuffed Mushrooms

Yes, even with the butter this is a healthy appetizer. Mushrooms have lots of vitamins and fiber, and salmon has healthy omega-3 fatty acids. Eat up!

HEALTHY

INGREDIENTS | SERVES 12

⅓ cup butter

4 cloves garlic, minced

½ pound salmon fillet

½ teaspoon salt

⅛ teaspoon white pepper

18 large mushrooms

1 cup shredded Havarti cheese

½ cup chopped parsley

1. Preheat oven to 325°F. In large saucepan, melt butter; add garlic and cook and stir for 2–3 minutes until fragrant.

2. Sprinkle salmon with salt and pepper and add to skillet. Cook, turning once, just until salmon flakes. Remove pan from heat and remove fish from pan.

3. Remove stems from mushrooms and save for another use. Drizzle the mushrooms with the garlic butter in the pan. Break salmon into small pieces and stuff into the mushroom caps.

4. Sprinkle each mushroom with some of the cheese. Bake for 11–16 minutes or until caps are tender and cheese melts. Sprinkle with parsley and serve immediately.

Ginger Turkey Meatballs

Fresh ginger root and ground ginger combine for some spicy heat in these easy meatballs.

HEALTHY

INGREDIENTS | SERVES 8–10

1 tablespoon olive oil

½ cup chopped onion

2 cloves garlic, minced

½ teaspoon salt

⅛ teaspoon pepper

½ teaspoon ground ginger

1 tablespoon grated ginger root

⅓ cup dry bread crumbs

1 egg

1 pound ground turkey

2 tablespoons olive oil

1 tablespoon butter

½ cup chicken broth

1 jar mango chutney

Make Ahead

You can make and form the meatballs ahead of time, cover, and store in the refrigerator for up to 24 hours. Cook the meatballs just before serving, then proceed with the recipe. You can also freeze the meatballs before cooking. Let them stand in the refrigerator overnight, then cook as directed.

1. In large saucepan, heat 1 tablespoon olive oil over medium heat. Add onion and garlic; cook and stir for 5 minutes. Remove from heat and place onion mixture in large bowl.

2. Add salt, pepper, ginger, ginger root, bread crumbs, and eggs and mix well. Add turkey and mix gently until combined.

3. Roll into 1½-inch balls, cover, and chill for 2–3 hours. When ready to eat, combine 2 tablespoons olive oil and butter in large saucepan. Cook meatballs, turning occasionally, until tender and golden brown, about 10–12 minutes.

4. Add broth and chutney to skillet and bring to a simmer. Place meatballs and sauce in chafing dish or slow cooker on warm.

Mini Mexican Pizzas

These little pizzas are packed full of flavor. You could add cooked chorizo, chopped chicken, or ground beef to the bean mixture if you'd like.

LAST MINUTE

INGREDIENTS | YIELDS 24

1 tablespoon olive oil
1 onion, chopped
2 jalapeño peppers, minced
1 (15-ounce) can refried beans
½ cup chunky salsa
2 teaspoons chili powder
6 (10-inch) corn tortillas
1 cup shredded sharp Cheddar cheese
½ cup shredded pepper jack cheese
¼ cup grated Cotija cheese
½ cup chopped cilantro leaves

Party Fun

Make these little pizzas using different flavors and colors of corn or flour tortillas. Red tortillas are flavored with red or cayenne pepper, while blue corn tortillas are really made from blue corn. Green tortillas are usually colored with spinach. This will give a festive and fun air to your party!

1. In large saucepan, heat olive oil over medium heat. Add onion; cook and stir for 5 minutes. Add jalapeño peppers; cook and stir for 2–3 minutes longer.

2. Remove from heat and stir in refried beans, salsa, and chili powder; mix well.

3. Preheat oven to 400°F. Place tortillas on two cookie sheets. Spread with the refried bean mixture and sprinkle with all of the cheeses.

4. Bake for 9–12 minutes or until tortillas are crisp and cheeses are melted and beginning to brown. Sprinkle with cilantro, then cut each pizza into four wedges and serve immediately.

Bacon Potato Skins

This gorgeous and filling appetizer could be served as an accompaniment to a green or pasta salad as the whole meal!

EASILY DOUBLES

INGREDIENTS | SERVES 8

4 russet potatoes, baked

6 tablespoons Roasted Garlic Spread (page 30)

6 slices bacon

1 onion, chopped

½ teaspoon paprika

¼ teaspoon pepper

1½ cups shredded Colby cheese

¼ cup grated Romano cheese

1 cup sour cream

¼ cup chopped flat-leaf parsley

Make-Ahead Hints

You can bake the potatoes ahead of time, scoop out the pulp, and spread with the Garlic Spread. Cook the bacon and onion, and combine the onion with seasonings and cheeses; refrigerate. Then bake the potato strips for 8–9 minutes, top with the cheese mixture and bake for 6–7 minutes longer, then serve.

1. Cut potatoes in half lengthwise, then in half again to make four strips each. Scoop out the pulp, and freeze it for later use, or use it in other recipes, like Potato Puffs (page 32). Make sure to leave about ¼-inch of the pulp on the skin. Spread each strip with some Roasted Garlic Spread.

2. Place the strips, skin side down, on cookie sheet. In large skillet, cook bacon until crisp; remove, drain, and crumble. Pour off drippings, but don't wipe out skillet. Add onion; cook and stir until tender.

3. Preheat oven to 450°F. Place onion in medium bowl and let cool for 15 minutes, then stir in paprika, pepper, and cheeses.

4. Bake the potato strips for 5 minutes, then remove from oven. Top with cheese mixture and return to oven; bake for 5–7 minutes longer or until cheeses melt and start to brown.

5. In small bowl, combine sour cream and parsley; serve with potato skins.

Updated Fondue

This dip can be served to everyone, including kids.
You can leave out the bacon if you'd like; add more shredded cheese.

EASILY DOUBLES

INGREDIENTS | SERVES 16

1 large round loaf sourdough bread

2 tablespoons butter

1 onion, minced

2 cloves garlic, minced

1 (8-ounce) package cream cheese, softened

½ cup sour cream

½ cup mayonnaise

1 cup shredded Cheddar cheese

1 cup shredded Gouda cheese

1 cup chopped Canadian bacon

18 soft breadsticks

2 cups baby carrots

3 apples, sliced

Transport Tips

You can make the filling for this dip in a 2-quart slow cooker then cook on low for 3–4 hours. When you're ready to go to the party, pack the slow cooker into a slow cooker holder and bring it along with the bread. When you get to the party, bake the hollowed-out bread until warm, about 10 minutes, then add the hot fondue mixture and serve.

1. Cut off top from the bread and set aside. Using a sharp knife, hollow out the bread, leaving a ¾-inch shell. Reserve bread for another use.

2. In small saucepan, melt 2 tablespoons butter over medium heat; add onion and garlic. Cook and stir until tender, about 6–7 minutes.

3. In large bowl, beat cream cheese until fluffy. Add sour cream and mayonnaise and beat until smooth. Stir in onion mixture, cheeses, and bacon. Spoon into bread shell.

4. Replace the top of the loaf, then wrap in heavy-duty foil. Place on cookie sheet. Bake in preheated 375°F oven for 55–65 minutes until the cheese mixture has melted and starts to bubble. Remove top and serve with breadsticks, carrot sticks, and apple slices.

Spiced-Nut Mix

*This spectacular recipe can be made with any whole nuts;
try cashews and almonds too.*

EASY

INGREDIENTS | SERVES 24

2 egg whites

½ cup sugar

½ cup brown sugar

1 teaspoon cinnamon

1 teaspoon ground ginger

⅛ teaspoon cayenne pepper

½ teaspoon salt

1 pound pecan halves

½ pound walnut pieces

¼ cup butter

1. Preheat oven to 300°F. In large bowl, beat egg whites until foamy. Gradually add sugar and beat until soft peaks form. Add brown sugar and beat until smooth. Add cinnamon, ginger, pepper, and salt and mix well.

2. Fold in pecans and walnuts. Melt butter in 15" × 10" jelly roll pan in the oven, then spoon nut mixture into butter.

3. Bake for 1 hour, stirring and turning nuts every 15 minutes, until the nuts are crisp and coating is brown. Spread on paper towels to drain and cool, then store in airtight container.

Party Fun

Serve these nuts, along with candies, in small nut cups placed on a buffet table. They're also great as gifts too; just package them into small containers and give to your guests as they leave. Pour about ⅓ cup of nuts into cellophane packets and tie with a ribbon that matches your party's theme.

Onion and Garlic Jam

This "jam" is naturally sweet because the sugars in the onions caramelize during long cooking times.

INEXPENSIVE

INGREDIENTS | SERVES 12

2 tablespoons olive oil

1 tablespoon butter

4 cups chopped onions

1 teaspoon salt

¼ cup brown sugar

3 tablespoons tarragon vinegar

2 teaspoons chopped fresh tarragon leaves

1 recipe Roasted Garlic Spread (page 30)

Party Fun

You can serve this condiment cold with crackers or crudités like baby carrots and zucchini slices, or warm it up in a saucepan and pour over any type of cheese. It also makes a great pizza topping or sandwich spread. Or you can stir it into soups or serve it as a condiment with roasted beef or grilled chicken.

1. In large heavy saucepan, melt olive oil and butter over medium heat. Add onions and salt. Cook mixture, stirring, until onions are translucent. Reduce heat to low and cook, stirring occasionally, until onions are deep golden brown.

2. Add sugar, vinegar, and tarragon leaves; cook and stir for another 10 minutes. Stir in Garlic Spread and remove from heat.

3. Pour into containers, cover, and refrigerate until cold. Store in refrigerator up to 4 days.

Super-Easy Pineapple Cheese Balls

There are so many recipes for cheese balls floating around.
This one is perhaps the easiest; perfect for the non-cook to make.

EASY

INGREDIENTS | YIELDS 48 BALLS

1 (8-ounce) can crushed pineapple, drained
2 cups grated sharp Cheddar cheese
⅓ cup mayonnaise
2 cups finely chopped pecans
⅓ cup finely chopped flat-leaf parsley

1. Drain pineapple very well, pushing on the fruit to extract the juice. In medium bowl, combine pineapple with the cheese and mix well. Stir in mayonnaise until well mixed.

2. Form into small balls about ¾ inch in diameter. Combine pecans with parsley and spread half on a plate.

3. Roll half of the balls in the pecan mixture and set on waxed paper. Repeat with remaining pecan mixture and remaining cheese mixture. Cover and chill for 3–4 hours before serving.

CHAPTER 4

Easy Bread Recipes

Irish Soda Rolls

Irish soda bread is a nice addition to almost any dinner,
but these rolls are easier to serve and are crustier than the bread.

QUICK

INGREDIENTS | YIELDS 12 ROLLS

¼ cup sugar
¼ cup brown sugar
3 cups all-purpose flour
1 cup whole wheat flour
2 teaspoons baking powder
½ teaspoon baking soda
2 eggs
1 cup buttermilk
1¼ cups sour cream
2 cups dried currants
2 tablespoons all-purpose flour

1. Preheat oven to 350°F. Line a cookie sheet with Silpat liner and set aside.

2. In large bowl, combine sugars, flours, baking powder, and baking soda and mix with a whisk until combined. In medium bowl, combine eggs, buttermilk, and sour cream and beat until combined. Add to the flour mixture and stir just until a dough begins to form.

3. Gently stir in currants. Drop mixture by scant ¼-cup amounts onto cookie sheets, making about 12 rolls. Partially smooth tops, then dust with flour.

4. Bake for 20–30 minutes or until rolls are light golden brown and set. Remove to wire rack and let cool for 15–20 minutes.

Cheese Herb Muffins

These muffins have the best flavor because of the combination of herbs and cheeses.

INEXPENSIVE

INGREDIENTS | YIELDS 12 MUFFINS

2 cups flour
1 tablespoon brown sugar
1½ teaspoons baking powder
½ teaspoon baking soda
½ teaspoon salt
1 tablespoon chopped chives
1 tablespoon chopped fresh thyme
2 eggs
⅔ cup buttermilk
⅓ cup butter, melted
2 tablespoons oil
1 cup diced Colby cheese
½ cup grated Parmesan cheese, divided

1. Preheat oven to 400°F. Spray 12 muffin cups with nonstick baking spray containing flour; set aside.

2. In large bowl, combine flour, brown sugar, baking powder, baking soda, salt, chives, and thyme and mix well.

3. In small bowl, combine eggs, buttermilk, melted butter, and oil and beat until combined. Add to dry ingredients and stir just until mixed. Fold in Colby cheese and half of Parmesan cheese.

4. Fill muffin cups ⅔ full and sprinkle with remaining Parmesan cheese. Bake for 20–25 minutes until muffins are light golden brown and firm. Cool on wire rack.

Cheese-Stuffed Rolls

These little rolls have to be served warm,
so the cheese inside each is soft and melty. Yum.

INEXPENSIVE

INGREDIENTS | YIELDS 24 ROLLS

1 recipe Refrigerator Rolls (page 54)
½ cup grated Parmesan cheese
1 teaspoon dried basil leaves
24 (½-inch) cubes Cheddar cheese
¼ cup butter, melted

Party Fun

Make the dough ahead of time, then have your guests have the fun of forming the rolls while the main entrée is cooking. The house will fill with wonderful aromas, and the "chore" is a great ice breaker for a party of relative strangers.

1. Prepare Refrigerator Rolls and chill the dough for at least 2 hours.

2. When ready to eat, grease 24 muffin cups with unsalted butter. Mix Parmesan cheese and basil on shallow plate. Divide dough into 24 balls. Press a cube of Cheddar cheese into the center of each ball. Dip tops in melted butter, then dip into Parmesan mixture.

3. Place in prepared muffin cups, buttered side up, cover, and let rise for 30 minutes. Preheat oven to 350°F. Bake rolls for 12–16 minutes until golden brown. Remove from cups immediately; let cool on wire rack. Serve warm.

Easy Walnut Boule

You could knead in dried cranberries, currants,
or raisins along with the walnuts if you'd like.

HEALTHY

INGREDIENTS | SERVES 16

1 recipe Whole Wheat Sourdough French Bread (page 52)
2 cups walnut pieces
3 tablespoons cornmeal
2 tablespoons flour

1. Prepare French Bread through first rising. Place on floured surface and knead in walnuts. Divide into two balls and roll on surface until smooth.

2. Grease two 8-inch rounds on a large baking sheet and sprinkle with cornmeal. Top with bread balls. Cut three slashes in top of each bread about ¼ inch deep and sprinkle with flour.

3. Cover and let rise for 45–55 minutes until doubled. Preheat oven to 400°F. Place pan of hot water on bottom rack. Bake breads on center rack for 25–30 minutes or until breads sound hollow when thumped with fingers. Cool on wire racks.

Whole Wheat Sourdough French Bread

Beer adds a great yeasty flavor to this bread and makes it even sourer.

EASILY DOUBLES

INGREDIENTS | YIELDS 2 LOAVES; SERVES 16

2 (0.25-ounce) packages active dry yeast

1 cup water

1 egg

½ cup beer

½ cup sour cream

2 cups whole wheat flour

1 teaspoon salt

3½–4 cups bread flour

3 tablespoons wheat germ

1. Combine yeast and water in large bowl; let stand for 15 minutes. Beat in egg, beer, and sour cream; mix with wire whisk.

2. Add 1 cup whole wheat flour and salt; beat to combine. Add remaining cup of whole wheat flour and 1 cup bread flour; beat well. Cover and let stand for 30 minutes.

3. Add enough bread flour to form a firm dough. Turn out onto floured surface and knead until elastic, about 6–7 minutes. Place in greased bowl, turning to grease top.

4. Cover and let rise for 1 hour. Punch down dough, turn out onto floured surface, cover with bowl, and let rest for 10 minutes. Divide dough in half. Roll or pat out each half to a 12" × 8" rectangle. Tightly roll up, starting with longer side.

5. Place on lightly greased cookie sheets. Slash top of dough with a sharp knife. Cover and let rise for 30–40 minutes until double.

6. Preheat oven to 375°F. Bake bread for 40–50 minutes or until golden brown and bread sounds hollow when tapped with finger. Let cool on wire rack.

Parmesan Bread

This simple pan bread is made from a batter, not a dough, so you don't need to knead the dough. It's easy, savory, and perfect for a spaghetti dinner.

INEXPENSIVE

INGREDIENTS | YIELDS 2 LOAVES; SERVES 16

2 (0.25-ounce) packages active dry yeast

½ cup warm water

2 tablespoons sugar

½ cup whole milk

½ cup butter

1 teaspoon salt

2 eggs

3–3½ cups all-purpose four

1 cup grated Parmesan cheese

1 tablespoon chopped flat-leaf parsley

1 teaspoon fresh thyme leaves

2 tablespoons butter, melted

Party Fun

You can use this batter in several different ways. Spoon it into greased muffin cups to make little rolls. Top it with more cheese and herbs just before baking to make a cheesy herb crust. Whichever form they take, be sure to serve this recipe warm! Reheat the bread by wrapping it in foil and heating in a 400°F oven for 5–10 minutes.

1. Place yeast in small bowl; add water and let stand for 5 minutes. Meanwhile, combine sugar, milk, butter, and salt in small saucepan; heat until butter melts. Pour into large bowl; let cool to lukewarm.

2. Spray two 8-inch round cake pans with nonstick baking spray containing flour and set aside. Add eggs to milk mixture, beating well. Stir in yeast mixture. Add flour, beating until a stiff batter forms. Fold in cheese, parsley, and thyme.

3. Divide batter into prepared pans. Cover and let rise for 30–40 minutes until doubled in size. Preheat oven to 375°F. Bake bread for 20–30 minutes until deep golden brown. Brush with melted butter, then remove from pans and let cool on rack for 5 minutes before serving.

Refrigerator Rolls

This batter can be refrigerated up to 36 hours, so it's a great choice for a party.
Bake them as you need them!

HEALTHY

INGREDIENTS | YIELDS 24 ROLLS

1 (0.25-ounce) package active
dry yeast

¼ cup warm water

¼ cup butter

½ teaspoon salt

2 tablespoons sugar

¼ cup orange juice

¾ cup water

1 egg

1 cup whole wheat flour

2–2½ cups all-purpose flour

¼ cup butter, melted

1. In small bowl, combine yeast with ¼ cup warm water; set aside. Combine butter, salt, sugar, orange juice, and ¾ cup water in large microwave-safe bowl; microwave on high for 1–2 minutes until butter melts. Set aside until lukewarm.

2. Beat egg into orange juice mixture, then add yeast. Add whole wheat flour and beat well, then add enough all-purpose flour to make a soft dough; knead for 5 minutes.

3. Place in greased bowl, turning to grease top. Cover tightly and chill for 2–36 hours in refrigerator.

4. When ready to bake, preheat oven to 350°F. Grease muffin tins with unsalted butter. Pinch off about 3 tablespoons of the dough and place in each cup. Brush with melted butter, and let rise for 30 minutes.

5. Bake for 10–15 minutes until rolls are light and golden brown. Remove from muffin cups immediately and let cool on wire rack.

Southern Bacon Corn Bread

Real southern corn bread is baked in a cast-iron skillet greased with bacon grease.
No sugar is used, but it's served with lots of butter!

LAST MINUTE

INGREDIENTS | SERVES 9

5 slices bacon
2 tablespoons butter
2 cups cornmeal
2 cups all-purpose flour
1 teaspoon salt
2 teaspoons baking powder
1 teaspoon baking soda
2 eggs, beaten
½ cup butter, melted
2½ cups buttermilk
½ cup sour cream

Party Fun

You can bake corn bread batter in lots of different forms. Divide the batter into greased muffin cups, filling them about ⅔ full, and bake for 18–23 minutes. Or use corn bread stick pans, which are shaped to look like little ears of corn. You can also add other ingredients to the batter, like chopped green onion or grated Cheddar cheese.

1. In large cast-iron skillet, cook bacon until crisp. Remove bacon from pan, crumble, and set aside. Add 2 tablespoons butter to skillet and remove from heat.

2. Preheat oven to 400°F. In large bowl, combine cornmeal, flour, salt, baking powder, and baking soda and mix well. In medium bowl, combine eggs, ½ cup melted butter, buttermilk, and sour cream. Add to dry ingredients and mix just until blended, then stir in crumbled bacon.

3. Return skillet to medium heat and carefully swirl bacon grease and butter around. Pour in batter and immediately place in oven. Bake for 35–45 minutes until deep golden brown. Immediately remove from skillet and serve.

Mini Whole Wheat Cheesy Breads

Again, serve these little breads warm from the oven,
so the soft cheese enhances the crisp crust.

INEXPENSIVE

INGREDIENTS | SERVES 12

1 recipe Whole Wheat Sourdough French Bread (page 52)

6 tablespoons butter, melted

2 cups shredded Havarti cheese

¼ cup cornmeal

Party Fun

These little breads are so fun to serve. Place one between each place serving, along with some softened butter and a sharp little knife. Two people share one loaf, cutting it into slices and spreading with butter. You can sprinkle the breads with more shredded cheese before serving for a crisp crust.

1. Prepare bread dough through first rising. Spray two 9" × 5" loaf pans with nonstick baking spray containing flour. Divide dough into six portions. Roll each out on floured surface to a 4" × 8" rectangle. Brush each with melted butter and sprinkle with cheese.

2. Roll each up, starting with 4-inch side. Seal edges by pinching edges together. Dip bottoms of each roll in cornmeal and place three rolls, crosswise, in each pan. Brush with more melted butter.

3. Cover and let rise in warm place for 45–50 minutes. Preheat oven to 375°F. Bake bread for 35–45 minutes until golden brown. Immediately remove from pans; cool on rack for 10 minutes, then serve.

Dinner-Size Herbed Popovers

Most popovers are really large, about 5–6 inches tall, really too big for a dinner roll. These are just the right size.

LAST MINUTE

INGREDIENTS | YIELDS 20 POPOVERS

2 cups all-purpose flour

½ teaspoon salt

1 tablespoon chopped flat-leaf parsley

½ teaspoon dried thyme leaves

1 teaspoon dried basil leaves

½ teaspoon dried oregano leaves

1 cup skim milk

1 cup whole milk

5 large eggs

3 tablespoons butter, melted

4 tablespoons unsalted butter, melted

1. In large bowl, combine flour, salt, and herbs and mix together. In medium bowl, combine milks, eggs, and 3 tablespoons melted butter and beat well. Add to flour mixture and whisk until thoroughly combined.

2. Cover tightly and refrigerate for at last 24 hours. Batter can be made ahead up to three days. You can also bake the popovers immediately.

3. Preheat oven to 425°F. Grease 24 muffin cups with unsalted butter. Fill each cup half full of batter. Bake for 20 minutes, then reduce heat to 350°F and bake for 15–25 minutes longer until popovers are puffed and deep golden brown. Remove from cups and serve immediately.

Thick Whole Wheat Pizza Crust

Your own pizza crust has a depth of flavor you can't get from frozen or canned.

EASILY DOUBLES

INGREDIENTS | YIELDS 2 CRUSTS;
SERVES 16

1 (0.25-ounce) package active
dry yeast

1¼ cups warm water

1 teaspoon honey

¼ cup orange juice

1 teaspoon salt

2 tablespoons olive oil

1½ cups whole wheat flour

1½–2 cups bread flour

Make-Ahead Hints

This type of pizza crust is baked with the toppings on it, so the insides are fairly soft. You can't prebake this type of crust, as you can with Classic Pizza Crust (page 70). But you can make the dough ahead of time and refrigerate it until it's time to make and bake the pizzas. Just let it stand at room temperature for 30 minutes, and go ahead.

1. In large bowl, combine yeast, water, and honey; stir well and let stand for 5 minutes. Add orange juice, salt, and olive oil. Add the whole wheat flour and beat for 2 minutes.

2. Gradually stir in enough bread flour to make a soft dough. Turn dough out onto floured surface and knead for 9–10 minutes until smooth and elastic. Place in greased bowl, turning to grease top. Cover and let rise for 1 hour.

3. Punch dough down and divide into two parts. Let rest for 5 minutes. Roll out each half to a 12-inch circle.

4. Grease two round pizza pans with shortening and sprinkle with cornmeal. Top with crusts. Let rise for 30 minutes. Preheat oven to 400°F. Top crusts and bake for 20–25 minutes until crust is golden and cheese is melted and browning.

Best Ever Garlic Bread

Garlic bread is the perfect accompaniment to Ham Tetrazzini (page 75) or Italian Chicken Medallions (page 121).

Garlic bread is the perfect accompaniment to Ham Tetrazzini (page 75) or Italian Chicken Medallions (page 121).

LAST MINUTE

INGREDIENTS | YIELDS 12

12 slices Whole Wheat Sourdough Bread (page 52)

2 tablespoons mayonnaise

⅓ cup butter, softened

¼ cup grated Parmesan cheese

½ teaspoon grated lemon zest

¼ teaspoon garlic powder

3 cloves garlic, minced

½ teaspoon dried thyme leaves

¼ teaspoon dried oregano leaves

¼ teaspoon garlic pepper

1. Preheat oven to broil. Place Bread slices on broiler pan; broil on one side until golden brown. Turn over.

2. In small bowl, combine all remaining ingredients and mix well. Spread over the bread. Broil until topping bubbles and begins to brown. Serve immediately.

Orange Cashew Pear Bread

This tender bread is rich, with brown sugar, orange juice, and cashews.
It's perfect for a brunch or even for breakfast on the run.

HEALTHY

INGREDIENTS | YIELDS 2 LOAVES;
SERVES 16

1 (16-ounce) can pears
⅔ cup orange juice, divided
½ cup butter, softened
¼ cup vegetable oil
½ cup brown sugar
¾ cup sugar
3 eggs
2¼ cups all-purpose flour
¾ cup whole wheat flour
1½ teaspoons baking powder
½ teaspoon baking soda
½ teaspoon salt
⅛ teaspoon nutmeg
¾ cup ground cashews
⅓ cup sugar

1. Preheat oven to 350°F. Spray two 8" × 4" loaf pans with nonstick baking spray containing flour; set aside. Drain pears, discarding juice; puree pears until smooth. Add ⅓ cup orange juice and set aside.

2. In large bowl, combine butter, oil, brown sugar, and ¾ cup sugar and beat until smooth. Add eggs, one at a time, beating well after each addition.

3. In medium bowl, combine all-purpose flour, whole wheat flour, baking powder, baking soda, salt, and nutmeg. Add to butter mixture alternately with pear mixture. Fold in cashews.

4. Divide batter among prepared pans. Bake for 40–50 minutes or until breads are golden brown and firm. In small bowl, combine remaining ⅓ cup orange juice with ⅓ cup sugar. Pour over breads. Remove breads from pans and let cool on wire rack.

Cranberry Almond Rolls

*These little rolls can be served with breakfast or brunch,
or as an accompaniment to Thanksgiving or Christmas dinner.*

EASY

INGREDIENTS | SERVES 12–14

24 frozen dinner rolls

¼ cup butter, melted

1 cup whole berry cranberry sauce

1 tablespoon brown sugar

⅓ cup chopped toasted almonds

Party Fun

To dress up these little rolls for breakfast or brunch, drizzle frosting on them. Combine 2 tablespoons melted butter with 1½ cups powdered sugar and 1 tablespoon cranberry juice. Using the tip of a spoon, drizzle the frosting back and forth over the completely cooled rolls, then let stand until set.

1. Thaw dinner rolls as directed on package. Grease two cookie sheets or line with Silpat liners. Preheat oven to 350°F.

2. Place 12 rolls on each cookie sheet. Flatten with palm until the dough is about 3 inches in diameter. Brush with melted butter.

3. In small bowl, combine cranberry sauce, brown sugar, and almonds and mix to blend. Make a deep depression in the center of each roll and fill with a generous tablespoon of the cranberry mixture. Let rolls rise for 30–40 minutes.

4. Bake rolls for 20–30 minutes or until golden brown. Remove from cookie sheets and let cool on wire racks.

Italian-Herbed Bread

If you can't find fresh rosemary, don't use dried because it's too intense.
Substitute ½ teaspoon dried thyme leaves, ½ teaspoon dried basil leaves,
and ½ teaspoon dried oregano leaves.

EASILY DOUBLES

INGREDIENTS | YIELDS 1 LOAF;
SERVES 8–10

1 (0.25-ounce) package active dry yeast

½ cup warm water

1 teaspoon sugar

½ cup milk

1 tablespoon olive oil

2 tablespoons butter, melted

1 teaspoon salt

2 tablespoons chopped fresh rosemary

½ teaspoon dried Italian seasoning

2¼–2¾ cups bread flour

3 tablespoons butter, melted

⅓ cup grated Romano cheese

1. In large bowl, combine yeast, warm water, and sugar; mix and let stand for 5 minutes. Add milk, olive oil, 2 tablespoons melted butter, salt, rosemary, and Italian seasoning and mix well.

2. Gradually beat in enough flour to make a soft dough. Knead on floured surface for 8–9 minutes until smooth and elastic. Place in greased bowl, turning to grease top. Cover and let rise for 1 hour.

3. Spray a 9" × 5" loaf pan with nonstick baking spray containing flour. Punch down dough and let rest for 5 minutes. Roll out to 7" × 12" rectangle. Brush with 3 tablespoons melted butter and sprinkle with cheese. Roll up tightly, sealing ends.

4. Place in prepared pan, cover, and let rise for 30–40 minutes. Preheat oven to 375°F. Bake bread for 35–45 minutes or until bread is golden brown and sounds hollow when tapped. Remove from pan and let cool on wire rack.

Grilled Herb Cheese Breadsticks

These flavorful breadsticks have the ingredients of pesto, just deconstructed!

LAST MINUTE

INGREDIENTS | SERVES 10–12

1 loaf French bread
½ cup butter, melted
½ cup olive oil
2 teaspoons dried basil leaves
1 teaspoon dried oregano leaves
¼ teaspoon garlic powder
¾ cup grated Parmesan cheese

Party Fun

When you're serving a main dish cooked on the grill, make these breadsticks too. You can cut the bread into the sticks ahead of time; just keep in an airtight container. Make the butter mixture, then have one or two of the guests coat the sticks. The grill master can be in charge of grilling the flavorful sticks until crisp.

1. Cut bread into three equal sections, then cut each section into six breadsticks, making eighteen in all.

2. In shallow bowl, combine butter, olive oil, basil, oregano, and garlic powder and mix well. Brush over all sides of breadsticks, then sprinkle breadsticks with cheese. Use all of the butter mixture and all of the cheese.

3. Grill over direct medium heat for 4–6 minutes, turning frequently, until golden brown. Serve immediately.

Caramelized Onion Scones

Scones are a quick bread with a tender texture similar to biscuits, but a bit heavier.
This well-flavored version is perfect for any dinner party.

INEXPENSIVE

INGREDIENTS | SERVES 12

1 cup butter
2 onions, chopped
3 cloves garlic, minced
3 cups all-purpose flour
1 cup whole wheat flour
¼ cup brown sugar
2 teaspoons baking powder
1 teaspoon baking soda
½ teaspoon salt
1½ teaspoons dried thyme leaves
⅛ teaspoon white pepper
1 cup sour cream
⅓ cup buttermilk
1 egg, beaten
2 tablespoons butter, melted

1. In large skillet, melt butter over medium heat. Add onion and garlic; cook and stir until tender, about 5 minutes. Lower heat to low and continue to cook onions and garlic, stirring frequently, until onions are light golden brown, about 15–20 minutes longer. Remove from heat and place in small bowl.

2. In large bowl, combine flours, brown sugar, baking powder, baking soda, salt, thyme, and pepper and mix well. Add sour cream, buttermilk, and egg to onion mixture and beat well.

3. Preheat oven to 400°F. Stir onion mixture into flour mixture just until combined. Divide into two balls and place on ungreased cookie sheet. Flatten balls with hand to ½-inch thick. Cut each ball into 6 wedges and separate slightly.

4. Bake scones for 14–18 minutes until golden brown. Remove to wire rack and brush with melted butter. Serve warm.

Pesto Focaccia

Focaccia can be topped with everything from sautéed onions to red bell peppers to olives; take your pick!

INGREDIENTS | SERVES 12–14

2 (0.25-ounce) packages active dry yeast

2 cups warm water

1 tablespoon sugar

1½ teaspoons salt

1 teaspoon dried basil leaves

½ cup purchased basil pesto

2 cups all-purpose flour

2½–3½ cups bread flour

3 tablespoons olive oil

½ cup grated Parmesan cheese

3 cloves garlic, minced

1 teaspoon dried thyme leaves

Party Fun

Focaccia is definitely a party bread. You can make two smaller focaccia breads if you'd like; just divide the dough in half. This bread is made for sharing; cut into large pieces and place in baskets, then let people just tear off what they want with their hands. Keep the dough soft; that's what gives the bread its characteristic texture.

1. In large bowl, combine yeast with water and sugar; stir and let stand for 10 minutes. Add salt, basil, and pesto and stir to combine. Add all-purpose flour and beat for 2 minutes.

2. Add enough bread flour to make a soft and slightly sticky dough. Knead on floured surface until smooth and elastic, about 8–9 minutes. Place in greased bowl, turning to grease top. Cover and let rise for 1 hour.

3. Punch down dough. Spray a large baking sheet with nonstick baking spray containing flour. Sprinkle with cornmeal. Punch down dough and place on baking sheet; let rest for 10 minutes. Roll and press dough to cover sheet.

4. Using your fingers, push into the dough to dimple it. Drizzle with the olive oil, then the cheese, garlic, and thyme leaves. Let rise for 30 minutes. Preheat oven to 400°F.

5. Bake bread for 18–23 minutes or until golden brown. Remove from baking sheet and let cool on wire rack for 10 minutes, then serve.

Thyme Cream Scones

The cream replaces the butter or shortening used in these scones, so don't be afraid of using it. There is no substitute for the real thing.

EASY

INGREDIENTS | YIELDS 12 SCONES

3 cups flour
1 tablespoon baking powder
1 teaspoon baking soda
1 teaspoon salt
½ cup grated Romano cheese
2 teaspoons dried thyme leaves
1½ cups heavy whipping cream
½ cup buttermilk
2 tablespoons milk
¼ cup grated Parmesan cheese

1. Preheat oven to 400°F. In large bowl, combine the flour, baking powder, baking soda, salt, cheese, and thyme leaves; mix with wire whisk.

2. Add cream and buttermilk all at once; stir until a soft dough forms. Gather dough together on lightly floured surface and gather into a large ball. Cut into two balls.

3. Place dough on greased cookie sheet and form into two 8-inch circles. Cut each circle into six wedges and separate slightly. Brush with milk and sprinkle with Parmesan cheese. Bake for 16–19 minutes or until scones are golden. Remove to wire rack to cool for 5 minutes before serving.

Banana Almond Muffins

Banana muffins are delicious and easy to make.
The fragrant nut topping makes them special.

HEALTHY

INGREDIENTS | YIELDS 12 MUFFINS

1 cup brown sugar, divided
2 tablespoons flour
1½ teaspoons cinnamon, divided
½ cup chopped almonds
3 tablespoons butter, melted
1¾ cups all-purpose flour
⅓ cup ground oatmeal
1 teaspoon baking soda
1 teaspoon baking powder
⅛ teaspoon cardamom
½ teaspoon salt
3 ripe bananas, mashed
¼ cup buttermilk
⅓ cup oil
½ cup sugar
1 egg, beaten
1 teaspoon vanilla

1. Preheat oven to 375°F. Spray 12 muffin cups with nonstick baking spray containing flour and set aside.

2. In small bowl, combine ½ cup brown sugar, 2 tablespoons flour, ½ teaspoon cinnamon, and almonds and mix well. Stir in 3 tablespoons melted butter until crumbly; set aside.

3. In large bowl, combine 1¾ cups flour, ground oatmeal, baking soda, baking powder, ½ teaspoon cinnamon, cardamom, and salt. In medium bowl combine ½ cup brown sugar, mashed bananas, buttermilk, oil, sugar, egg, and vanilla and beat.

4. Add banana mixture to dry ingredients and mix just until moistened. Divide among muffin cups and top with nut mixture.

5. Bake for 18–23 minutes or until muffins spring back when lightly touched. Remove to wire rack to cool.

Make-Ahead Tip

Muffins are great quick breads to make ahead of time. Like all quick breads, their flavor and texture get better a day after baking. They're easy to warm up too. Just place muffins on a microwave-safe serving tray, cover with paper towel, and microwave on high for 6–7 seconds per muffin. Let stand for 3 minutes, then serve.

Spicy Apple Muffins

This ingredient list is long, but the muffins go together quickly.
The aroma while baking is incredible!

INEXPENSIVE

INGREDIENTS | YIELDS 12 MUFFINS

1 cup brown sugar, divided
2 tablespoons flour
½ cup quick cooking oatmeal
1½ teaspoons cinnamon, divided
11 tablespoons melted butter, divided
1½ cups grated apples
2 tablespoons lemon juice
½ cup sugar
1¾ cups all-purpose flour
½ cup whole wheat flour
1 teaspoon baking powder
½ teaspoon baking soda
½ teaspoon salt
¼ teaspoon nutmeg
⅓ cup applesauce
2 eggs
2 teaspoons vanilla

Party Fun

As with any muffin batter, you can convert it to bread tins. Try making this recipe with tiny bread tins that are about 4" × 2". Put a little more batter into each tin; you should get 8 breads with this recipe. Then each person gets his or her own little loaf of bread.

1. Preheat oven to 350°F. Spray 12 muffin cups with nonstick baking spray containing flour and set aside.

2. In small bowl, combine ½ cup brown sugar, 2 tablespoons flour, oatmeal, and ½ teaspoon cinnamon and mix well. Add 3 tablespoons butter and mix until crumbly; set aside. In another small bowl, place apples. Sprinkle with lemon juice and sugar; let stand while making batter.

3. In large bowl, combine flour, whole wheat flour, baking powder, baking soda, salt, 1 teaspoon cinnamon, and nutmeg and mix well. In medium bowl, combine remaining melted butter, ½ cup brown sugar, applesauce, eggs, and vanilla.

4. Add butter mixture to dry ingredients along with apple mixture; mix just until combined. Place into prepared muffin cups and sprinkle with oatmeal mixture.

5. Bake for 22–28 minutes or until muffins spring back when lightly touched with finger. Remove to wire rack to cool.

Anadama Rolls

These hearty rolls have such a rich taste and perfect texture.
Serve them warm with more melted butter.

INEXPENSIVE

INGREDIENTS | YIELDS 12 ROLLS

1 tablespoon cornmeal
⅔ cup yellow cornmeal
3 tablespoons butter
¾ cup boiling water
⅓ cup light molasses
1 teaspoon salt
1 (0.25-ounce) package active dry yeast
¼ cup orange juice
1 egg, beaten
1 cup whole wheat flour
1½–2 cups all-purpose flour
½ cup dried currants
2 tablespoons melted butter

Keep It Healthy

Anadama bread, with its combination of corn meal and molasses, is already a very healthy bread. This recipe makes it healthier by replacing some of the white flour with whole wheat. Orange juice is added to offset some of the bitter flavors of the whole wheat flour and molasses; and it adds vitamin C.

1. Spray 12 muffin cups with nonstick baking spray containing flour and sprinkle with 1 tablespoon cornmeal; set aside. In large bowl, combine cornmeal, butter, boiling water, molasses, and salt and mix until butter melts. Let stand until lukewarm.

2. Add yeast and stir; let stand for 10 minutes. Add orange juice and egg and beat well; beat in whole wheat flour.

3. Beat in enough all-purpose flour to make a stiff batter, then stir in currants. Place batter in prepared muffin cups. Let rise in warm place until batter reaches tops of muffin cups.

4. Preheat oven to 375°F. Bake rolls for 18–24 minutes or until they sound hollow when tapped with fingers. Remove to wire rack, brush with melted butter, and let cool for 15 minutes before serving.

Classic Pizza Crust

This crust can be used for any homemade pizza recipe.
Try it with Black Bean Pizza (page 160) or invent your own toppings.

EASILY DOUBLES

INGREDIENTS | YIELDS 1 CRUST;
SERVES 6

1 (0.25-ounce) package active dry yeast

1 cup warm water

2 tablespoons olive oil

½ teaspoon salt

2–2½ cups bread flour

¾ cup yellow cornmeal

1 tablespoon solid shortening

2 tablespoons yellow cornmeal

1. In large bowl, mix yeast with water; let stand for 10 minutes. Add oil and salt, then add 1 cup bread flour and cornmeal; beat well.

2. Gradually add enough remaining bread flour to form a stiff dough. Knead on floured surface for 8–10 minutes, then place in greased bowl, turning to grease top. Cover and let rise for 1 hour.

3. Punch down dough and let rest for 10 minutes. Grease a cookie sheet with solid shortening and sprinkle with 2 tablespoons cornmeal. Roll out dough directly on cookie sheet to 12 inches round or square. Let rise for 20 minutes.

4. Preheat oven to 400°F. Bake pizza crust for 10 minutes, then remove and let cool. Wrap and store for 2–3 days. When ready to bake, top pizza as directed and bake for 20–25 minutes until crust is golden.

CHAPTER 5

Easy Pork Recipes

Ham Loaf with Mustard Sauce

This classic old-fashioned recipe has the best flavor.
Serve it with some cooked green beans and a fruit salad.

EASY

INGREDIENTS | SERVES 8

1 pound ham, ground

1 pound spicy bulk pork sausage

½ cup finely minced onion

3 garlic cloves, minced

2 eggs, beaten

1 cup soft bread crumbs

½ cup milk

2 tablespoons Dijon mustard

2 tablespoons honey

⅛ teaspoon ground nutmeg

1 recipe Mustard Sauce (page 174)

1. Preheat oven to 350°F. In large bowl, combine ham, sausage, onion, garlic, eggs, bread crumbs, milk, 2 tablespoons mustard, honey, and nutmeg; mix well.

2. Form into a large loaf and place on a broiler rack. Bake for 65–75 minutes or until meat thermometer registers 160°F. Cover and let stand for 10 minutes, then slice loaf and serve with Mustard Sauce.

Party Fun

For a comfort food party, this recipe and Stuffed Meatloaf Pinwheels (page 92), along with Creamy Cheesy Potatoes (page 181) would be fabulous. Serve with some gelatin salads, like Frozen Cranberry Salad (page 196) or Orange Fluff Salad (page 204) and for a retro finish, Raspberry Dream Cake (page 249). Yum!

Curried Pineapple Ham

Serve this excellent dish over hot cooked brown or wild rice along with a green salad,
some cooked baby carrots, and warmed rolls.

LAST MINUTE

INGREDIENTS | SERVES 8

2 tablespoons butter

1 tablespoon olive oil

1 onion, chopped

3 cloves garlic, minced

1 tablespoon curry powder

3 tablespoons flour

½ teaspoon dried tarragon leaves

½ teaspoon salt

⅛ teaspoon pepper

3 cups chicken broth

4 cups diced ham

1 (15-ounce) can pineapple tidbits, drained

¼ cup light cream

1. In large saucepan, combine butter and olive oil over medium heat. Add onion and garlic; cook and stir until tender, about 5 minutes. Add curry powder; cook and stir for 1 minute longer.

2. Add flour, tarragon, salt, and pepper; cook and stir until bubbly. Add remaining ingredients except cream; bring to a simmer. Simmer for 10–12 minutes until mixture has thickened. Stir in cream and serve.

Party Fun

Serve a selection of skillet dishes with different types of cooked rice and pasta for a great buffet. Keep everything warm by placing the skillet dishes into slow cookers; turn to warm and set on the table next to the rice.

Deviled Ham Sandwiches

Make these sandwiches ahead of time and refrigerate.
Then when you want to eat, just bake, adding another 5–10 minutes until hot.

MAKE AHEAD

INGREDIENTS | SERVES 8

3 cups finely chopped ham
4 hard-cooked eggs, chopped
½ cup minced red onion
3 tablespoons chopped sweet pickle
1 cup grated Colby cheese
½ cup mayonnaise
¼ cup honey mustard salad dressing
2 tablespoons Dijon mustard
⅛ teaspoon cayenne pepper
8 Hoagie buns, split

1. Preheat oven to 400°F. In medium bowl, place ham; break up with fork. Add remaining ingredients except the Hoagie buns and mix well.

2. Use mixture to fill the Hoagie buns. Wrap in heavy-duty foil. Place on a baking sheet and bake for 15–20 minutes until sandwiches are hot. Open the foil for the last 5 minutes to crisp the top of the buns.

Walnut Pork Chops

Walnuts cooked in syrup are also called "wet walnuts," and are often used in desserts.
They're a wonderful addition to tender pork chops.

EASILY DOUBLES

INGREDIENTS | SERVES 6

6 (1-inch thick) pork loin chops
1 teaspoon salt
¼ teaspoon pepper
3 tablespoons flour
2 tablespoons butter
2 tablespoons olive oil
1 cup walnut pieces
1 onion, chopped
4 cloves minced garlic
⅓ cup honey
½ cup chicken broth

1. Sprinkle chops with salt and pepper, then sprinkle with flour. Melt butter with olive oil in large skillet; add walnut pieces and cook and stir until fragrant. Remove walnuts to plate.

2. Add onion and garlic to skillet and cook for 5 minutes, then add pork chops. Cook on first side until well browned, then turn and brown for 3 minutes on second side.

3. Preheat oven to 350°F. Place chops in greased baking dish and sprinkle with walnuts. Add honey and chicken broth to skillet. Bring to a boil, then pour over chops. Cover and bake chops for 40–50 minutes until chops are done and lightly pink in center.

Ham and Cheese Soufflé

This soufflé is easier to serve than others, because it will stand without falling.

MAKE AHEAD

INGREDIENTS | SERVES 6

3 cups cubed French bread

2 cups chopped cooked ham

2 (4-ounce) cans sliced mushrooms, drained

2 cups shredded Havarti cheese

1 cup shredded Cheddar cheese

6 eggs, beaten

2 cups milk

½ cup sour cream

½ teaspoon salt

1 teaspoon dry mustard

¼ cup Dijon mustard

3 tablespoons flour

¼ cup melted butter

¼ cup grated Parmesan cheese

1. The day before, spray a 9" × 13" glass baking dish with nonstick cooking spray. Combine bread, ham, mushrooms, and both cheeses in the dish and toss to mix; spread into an even layer.

2. In large bowl, beat eggs with milk, sour cream, salt, dry mustard, Dijon mustard, flour, and melted butter until combined. Pour over bread and cheese mixture. Cover and refrigerate for 8–24 hours.

3. When ready to bake, preheat oven to 350°F. Sprinkle with Parmesan cheese and bake for 50–60 minutes until puffed and deep golden brown.

Make-Ahead Tips

This type of soufflé is more like a strata, or layered bread and cheese topped with an egg custard. You can make several of them ahead of time if you're serving a crowd, then bake them one after the other so a hot soufflé is always available. Flavor them in different ways: chicken and peas or sausage and green bell pepper are good combinations.

Ham Tetrazzini

You can make this one ahead; just chill after sprinkling the whole thing with cheese.
Add 10–15 minutes to the baking time.

MAKE AHEAD

INGREDIENTS | SERVES 6

¼ cup butter
1 onion, chopped
3 cloves garlic, minced
1 (8-ounce) package sliced mushrooms
¼ cup flour
½ teaspoon salt
⅛ teaspoon pepper
1 teaspoon dried thyme leaves
1 (14-ounce) can chicken stock
1½ cups milk
1 cup sour cream
1 cup shredded Havarti cheese
3 cups chopped ham
1 (16-ounce) package spaghetti
2 tablespoons butter
¼ cup grated Parmesan cheese
¼ cup grated Romano cheese

1. Bring a large pot of water to a boil. Spray a 9" × 13" glass baking dish with nonstick cooking spray and set aside.

2. In large saucepan, melt ¼ cup butter. Cook onion, garlic, and mushrooms until tender, about 6–7 minutes. Sprinkle with flour, salt, pepper, and thyme; cook until bubbly.

3. Stir in chicken stock and milk; cook and stir until thickened. Remove from heat and stir in sour cream, Havarti cheese, and ham; set aside.

4. Preheat oven to 350°F. Cook spaghetti until al dente according to package directions. Drain and return to pot; toss with butter and Parmesan cheese. Stir in 1 cup of the ham sauce.

5. Arrange spaghetti along the outside edges of the baking dish. Pour remaining ham mixture inside, then sprinkle with Romano cheese. Bake for 35–45 minutes until casserole is bubbly and cheese is browned.

Pork and Asparagus Casserole

This elegant casserole is delicious and easy to make. Substitute your own favorite cheese for the Havarti if you'd like.

MAKE AHEAD

INGREDIENTS | SERVES 6

1 pound asparagus
1 cup long-grain brown rice
2 cups chicken stock
1 pound pork tenderloin, cubed
2 tablespoons flour
½ teaspoon dried tarragon
½ teaspoon salt
⅛ teaspoon pepper
2 tablespoons butter
1 (16-ounce) jar Alfredo sauce
1 cup milk
1½ cups shredded Havarti cheese
½ cup grated Parmesan cheese, divided

Make-Ahead Tips

Most meat casseroles can be made ahead of time, refrigerated, and then baked before serving. Add 10–15 minutes to the baking time so the dish is bubbly and hot. There's one caveat to this rule: make sure that the meat is completely cooked before you refrigerate the dish. You can't partially cook meat and hold it for later cooking.

1. Break ends off asparagus and cut into 2-inch pieces. Drop into boiling water for 3 minutes, remove and drop into ice water to stop the cooking.

2. In medium saucepan, combine rice and stock; simmer for 15–20 minutes until rice is almost cooked; set aside.

3. Preheat oven to 400°F. Toss pork with flour, tarragon, salt, and pepper. Brown in butter on all sides. Add Alfredo sauce and milk to pork; bring to a simmer. Simmer for 5–8 minutes until pork is just cooked.

4. Remove from heat and add asparagus and cooked rice. Fold in Havarti cheese and half of Parmesan cheese. Place in 2-quart casserole.

5. Top with remaining Parmesan cheese and bake for 25–35 minutes until casserole is bubbling and top is browned. Serve immediately.

Sausage and Fruit Turnovers

These little turnovers are fun to make and eat.
Sausage and fruit is a natural combination.

EASILY DOUBLES

INGREDIENTS | SERVES 4

½ pound spicy pork sausage
1 onion, chopped
½ cup dried cranberries
1 cup frozen sliced peaches, thawed
1 cup shredded Havarti cheese
1 (14-ounce) can refrigerated pizza dough

1. In medium skillet, cook sausage with onion until sausage is browned, stirring to break up meat. Drain well and place in medium bowl. Add cranberries.

2. Cut peaches into small pieces and add to sausage mixture along with cheese; mix well.

3. Preheat oven to 425°F. Unroll dough onto lightly floured surface and cut into four pieces. Pat each piece into a 6-inch square and place on two greased baking sheets.

4. Divide pork mixture among squares. Fold one corner over to the opposite corner; seal edges with a fork. Bake for 18–22 minutes until turnovers are golden brown. Serve immediately.

Ham Creole

Creole food begins with a mixture of onion, celery, and green bell pepper.
Spices and meat complete this classic dish.

LAST MINUTE

INGREDIENTS | SERVES 8–10

¼ cup olive oil

3 tablespoons flour

2 onions, chopped

4 cloves garlic, minced

1 cup chopped celery

¼ cup chopped celery leaves

2 green bell peppers, chopped

2 (14.5-ounce) cans diced tomatoes, undrained

1 cup chili sauce

1 cup vegetable juice cocktail

1 teaspoon dried thyme leaves

½ teaspoon salt

½ teaspoon cayenne pepper

1 bay leaf

4 cups chopped ham

1. In large saucepan, heat olive oil and flour over medium heat, stirring frequently, until the mixture turns light brown. Add onions and garlic; cook and stir for 5–6 minutes until tender. Add celery, celery leaves, and bell peppers; cook and stir for 4 minutes longer.

2. Add tomatoes, chili sauce, vegetable juice cocktail, thyme, salt, pepper, cayenne pepper, and bay leaf. Stir well and bring to a simmer; simmer for 35–40 minutes until blended. Add ham; simmer for 10–15 minutes longer. Remove bay leaf and serve over hot cooked rice.

Party Fun

A Southern potluck is a great idea for a party. Search out Southern recipes in old church cookbooks and online, then gather for a fabulous meal. Serve this Ham Creole along with foods like Black-Eyed Pea Salad (page 159), hot corn bread served with whipped honey, jambalaya, and a coconut cake for dessert.

Asian Pork Tenderloin

Pork tenderloin marinates beautifully;
the meat absorbs flavors and becomes very tender and juicy.

EASY

INGREDIENTS | SERVES 6

½ cup low-sodium soy sauce

2 tablespoons hoisin sauce

2 tablespoons honey

3 cloves garlic, minced

1 cup chicken broth, divided

1 tablespoon brown sugar

1 tablespoon grated ginger root

¼ teaspoon pepper

2 (1-pound) pork tenderloins

2 tablespoons butter

1. In large ziplock bag, combine soy sauce, hoisin sauce, honey, garlic, ½ cup broth, brown sugar, ginger root, and pepper. If necessary, pull the silver skin off the pork and discard.

2. Add pork to bag, close, and squish bag to mix marinade into pork. Place in casserole dish and refrigerate for 12–24 hours.

3. When ready to eat, pour tenderloin and marinade into a greased ovenproof skillet. Bake, uncovered, at 425°F for 20–30 minutes until meat thermometer registers 155°F.

4. Remove pork and cover to keep warm. Place pan on stovetop and add ½ cup chicken broth; boil 3 minutes, scraping to remove pan drippings. Add 2 tablespoons butter, swirl to coat, and pour over pork; serve immediately.

Grilled Greek Pork Tenderloin

A cool cheese, tomato, and olive topping is the perfect finishing touch to these tender and juicy tenderloins.

MAKE AHEAD

INGREDIENTS | SERVES 6

½ cup fresh lemon juice
⅓ cup olive oil
8 cloves garlic, divided
1 teaspoon salt
2 tablespoons fresh oregano leaves
⅛ teaspoon cayenne pepper
2 (1-pound) pork tenderloins
½ cup crumbled feta cheese
1 cup chopped tomatoes
⅓ cup sliced Kalamata olives
¼ cup minced flat-leaf parsley
½ teaspoon grated lemon zest

Transport Tips

Make sure that there's a grill ready and waiting for this recipe if you're taking it to the party. Pack the tenderloin, still in the marinade, in an ice chest with lots of frozen gel packs or bags of ice. Pack the tomato topping in a small, hard-sided container and add to the ice chest. Then just grill, slice, and serve at the party!

1. In large ziplock bag, combine lemon juice, oil, 4 cloves minced garlic, salt, oregano, and pepper.

2. Cut slits in the pork tenderloin. Cut the remaining four cloves garlic into thin slivers and insert into slits in the tenderloin. Add to bag with marinade, seal, and knead to coat. Refrigerate for 8–12 hours.

3. When ready to eat, prepare and preheat grill. In small bowl, combine feta cheese, tomatoes, olives, parsley, and lemon zest; set aside.

4. Drain tenderloin, reserving marinade. Grill for 20–25 minutes, turning twice and basting occasionally with marinade, until pork registers 155°F. Remove from heat and cover; discard marinade.

5. Slice pork crosswise and serve with feta cheese mixture.

Avocado-Stuffed Pork Chops

*Smooth, buttery avocado makes an excellent stuffing for tender pork chops.
This one's a winner!*

EASILY DOUBLES

INGREDIENTS | SERVES 6

6 (1-inch thick) boneless
pork loin chops
1 teaspoon salt
⅛ teaspoon pepper
1 avocado, mashed
2 tablespoons lemon juice
2 tablespoons butter
3 cloves garlic
1 avocado, diced
¼ cup flour
2 tablespoons butter
1 tablespoon olive oil

1. Preheat oven to 350°F. Cut a deep pocket into the side of the pork chops, making a small entrance hole and moving the knife back and forth to enlarge the pocket. Be careful you don't poke through the other side. Sprinkle with salt and pepper.

2. In bowl, combine mashed avocado, lemon juice, butter, and garlic and mix well. Stir in diced avocado. Using a small spoon, fill the pockets in the pork chops with this mixture. Secure with toothpick and sprinkle chops with flour.

3. Melt butter with olive oil in a large ovenproof skillet and add chops; brown on both sides. Transfer to oven.

4. Bake for 20–30 minutes until a meat thermometer registers 155°F. Let stand for 5 minutes, then serve.

Baked Pork Chops

The secret to this recipe is to get the coating on the chops really crisp so it will stand up to the cream sauce.

EASY

INGREDIENTS | SERVES 6

6 boneless (1-inch) pork loin chops
1 teaspoon seasoning salt
⅛ teaspoon pepper
2 beaten eggs
2 tablespoons flour
2 cups panko bread crumbs
2 teaspoons dried Italian seasoning
2 tablespoons butter
2 tablespoons olive oil
1 onion, chopped
1 (8-ounce) package sliced mushrooms
2 (10-ounce) containers Alfredo sauce
½ cup dry white wine
¼ cup light cream

Keep It Safe

You no longer have to cook pork to well done. Medium-well, or 155°F, is perfectly safe with the newer methods of raising pork. That means the pork will still be slightly pink on the inside. You can't make this recipe ahead of time and chill it because the meat isn't completely cooked in the first step, so this recipe should be made at the party.

1. Preheat oven to 350°F. Sprinkle chops with salt and pepper on both sides. In shallow bowl, beat eggs with flour; and combine bread crumbs and Italian seasoning on plate.

2. Dredge chops in egg mixture, then press into bread crumbs to coat. Set aside on wire rack.

3. In large skillet, melt butter with olive oil over medium heat. Add chops; brown well on first side until crisp. Turn and brown on second side, about 8–10 minutes total. Remove to glass baking dish.

4. Add onion and mushrooms to pan; cook and stir until tender. Add Alfredo sauce, wine, and cream and bring to a simmer.

5. Pour this mixture over the chops. Bake for 35–45 minutes until the chops register 155°F. Let stand for 5 minutes, then serve.

Ham and Apple Curry

This easy curry has lots of flavor. You could substitute leftover cooked cubed pork for the ham if you'd like.

QUICK

INGREDIENTS | SERVES 6

3 tablespoons butter
1 onion, chopped
3 cloves garlic, minced
1 tablespoon curry powder
3 apples, peeled, cored, and sliced
3 tablespoons flour
½ teaspoon salt
⅛ teaspoon pepper
2 cups apple juice
½ cup light cream
3 cups cubed ham
½ cup mango chutney
4 cups hot cooked rice

1. In large saucepan, melt butter over medium heat. Add onion and garlic; cook and stir until tender, about 5 minutes. Add curry powder and apples; cook and stir for 4 minutes longer.

2. Sprinkle with flour, salt, and pepper; cook and stir until bubbly. Add apple juice and light cream; cook and stir until sauce thickens.

3. Add ham; simmer for 6–7 minutes until ham is hot. Then add chutney and remove from heat. Serve over hot cooked rice.

Tamale Pie

This hearty casserole feeds a crowd. The spicier the sausage, the spicier the casserole. If you like it really hot, add more jalapeño peppers.

INEXPENSIVE

INGREDIENTS | SERVES 8

2 cups chicken broth

1 cup water

1 cup yellow corn meal

1½ pounds spicy pork sausage

2 onions, chopped

4 cloves garlic, minced

2 jalapeño peppers, minced

1 green bell pepper, chopped

1 red bell pepper, chopped

2 (14-ounce) cans diced tomatoes

1 (15-ounce) can black beans, drained

1 tablespoon chili powder

1 teaspoon cumin

½ teaspoon salt

⅛ teaspoon pepper

1 cup shredded Muenster cheese

¼ cup grated Cotija cheese

1. In medium saucepan, bring broth and water to a boil Add corn meal; bring to a simmer, then lower heat, cover, and simmer for 15–20 minutes, stirring frequently, until thick. Set aside.

2. In large saucepan, cook sausage with onion, garlic, and jalapeño peppers until sausage is brown. Drain well, then add bell peppers; cook for 5 minutes longer.

3. Add tomatoes, beans, chili powder, cumin, salt, and pepper; simmer for 15 minutes. Preheat oven to 400°F.

4. Stir Muenster cheese into cornmeal mixture. Place half of the cornmeal mixture in bottom of greased 3-quart casserole dish. Top with sausage mixture, then remaining cornmeal mixture. Sprinkle with Cotija cheese.

5. Bake for 30–40 minutes or until casserole is bubbling and cornmeal topping is golden brown. Let stand for 5 minutes, then serve.

Easy Baked Pork Kiev

Like Chicken Kiev, but using pork cutlets! This easy recipe is a winner.

EASILY DOUBLES

INGREDIENTS | SERVES 6

6 (6-ounce) boneless pork loin chops, butterflied

¾ cup dry bread crumbs

½ cup grated Romano cheese

1 teaspoon dried oregano leaves

1 teaspoon seasoned salt

⅛ teaspoon white pepper

7 tablespoons butter, softened

2 tablespoons minced flat-leaf parsley

½ teaspoon dried basil leaves

6 ounces Muenster cheese

6 tablespoons butter, melted

Make-Ahead Tips

You can make the Pork Kiev ahead of time. Just pound, fill, and roll the chops and refrigerate, covered, until it's time to cook. Then dip in butter, roll in bread crumbs, and bake until done. If you coat the bundles ahead of time, the bread mixture will get soggy.

1. Place the chops in a heavy-duty plastic bag, one at a time, and pound them until about ¼-inch thick. Sprinkle with seasoned salt and pepper and set aside. On plate, combine bread crumbs, Romano cheese, and oregano; mix well.

2. In small bowl, combine softened butter, parsley, and basil; mix well. Preheat oven to 400°F.

3. Place pork chops on work surface. Spread each with some of the butter and herb mixture. Cut cheese into 12 thin strips. Place two strips on each pork chop; roll up, folding in sides to enclose. Secure with toothpicks.

4. Dip each filled chop in melted butter, then roll in bread crumb mixture to coat. Place in 9" × 13" glass baking dish and drizzle with any remaining butter. Bake for 25–30 minutes or until pork is 155°F. Serve immediately.

Ham and Potato Casserole

This comforting, homey casserole is perfect for a cold winter's night.
Serve with a spinach salad, some cooked carrots, and a fruit pie for dessert.

EASY

INGREDIENTS | SERVES 8

2 tablespoons butter
2 tablespoons olive oil
1 onion, chopped
2 cloves garlic, minced
¼ cup flour
½ teaspoon salt
⅛ teaspoon pepper
1 teaspoon dried dill weed
2 cups milk
1 cup grated Colby cheese
3 cups frozen Southern-style hash brown potatoes, thawed
3 cups cubed cooked ham
2 cups frozen baby peas
3 hard-cooked eggs, sliced
¼ cup dried bread crumbs
2 tablespoons grated Parmesan cheese
2 tablespoons melted butter

1. Preheat oven to 350°F. Spray a 3-quart casserole dish with nonstick cooking spray and set aside.

2. In large skillet, melt 2 tablespoons butter with olive oil over medium heat. Add onion and garlic; cook and stir until tender, about 5 minutes. Add flour, salt, pepper, and dill weed; cook and stir until bubbly.

3. Add milk and cook and stir until thickened. Remove from heat and add Colby cheese; stir until melted.

4. Layer one-third of the potatoes, ham, peas, and eggs in prepared dish. Pour over $\frac{1}{3}$ of the sauce. Repeat layers, ending with sauce.

5. In small bowl, combine bread crumbs, Parmesan cheese, and 2 tablespoons melted butter; sprinkle over casserole. Bake for 45–50 minutes until casserole is bubbly and top is browned.

Lip-Smackin' Ribs

This barbecue sauce is wonderful on just about any meat.
You can make a few batches and freeze them for grilling anytime.

MAKE AHEAD

INGREDIENTS | SERVES 10

5 pounds country-style pork ribs
2 tablespoons chili powder, divided
1 teaspoon seasoned salt
2 tablespoons butter
1 tablespoon olive oil
1 onion, chopped
5 cloves garlic, minced
¼ cup chopped celery leaves
½ cup chili sauce
½ cup ketchup
¼ cup Dijon mustard
3 tablespoons brown sugar
3 tablespoons red wine vinegar
1 teaspoon Tabasco sauce
½ teaspoon salt
¼ teaspoon pepper

1. Preheat oven to 350°F. Place ribs in a large roasting pan and sprinkle with 1 tablespoon chili powder and 1 teaspoon seasoned salt. Bake for 1½ hours.

2. Meanwhile, heat butter and olive oil in large saucepan. Add onion and garlic; cook and stir until tender, about 6 minutes. Add celery leaves, chili sauce, ketchup, mustard, brown sugar, vinegar, Tabasco sauce, salt, and pepper. Bring to a simmer; reduce heat and simmer for 15 minutes. Remove from heat.

3. When ribs are done, drain well. Return to pan and pour sauce over. Spread the sauce around on the ribs, turning them with tongs, to coat completely.

4. Return ribs to oven and bake for 30–40 minutes longer, basting occasionally with sauce, until sauce has glazed.

Transport Tips

You can easily transport these ribs after they have been made, but don't do that after the 1½ hours of baking time, before the ½-hour finishing time. The ribs will stay hot for a good two hours after baking if they are properly wrapped and packaged. You can make extra sauce and toss them on the grill for a few minutes if you'd like.

Grilled Peach Tenderloin

*This flavorful marinade adds great flavor and tenderizes
the pork so you can cut it with a fork.*

EASY

INGREDIENTS | SERVES 8

¼ cup lime juice

3 tablespoons reduced-sodium soy sauce

⅓ cup peach preserves

1 tablespoon grated fresh ginger root

4 cloves garlic, minced

¼ teaspoon cayenne pepper

2 (1-pound) pork tenderloins

Party Fun

You could use this delicious all-purpose marinade for any type of meat at all. In fact, use it to marinate chicken breasts, pork chops, and a flank steak. Grill all of them, then slice and offer a buffet to your party guests. Offer the meat along with fixings to make fajitas for a wonderful dinner.

1. In bowl, combine lime juice, soy sauce, preserves, ginger root, garlic, and pepper; mix well.

2. Remove the skin from the tenderloin if necessary. Pierce all over with a fork and add to marinade. Turn to coat, then cover and refrigerate for 12–24 hours.

3. When ready to eat, prepare and preheat grill. Drain tenderloins, reserving marinade. Grill tenderloins, covered, over direct medium heat for 15–20 minutes, turning several times and brushing occasionally with marinade, until 155°F. Let stand for 5 minutes before slicing to serve. Discard remaining marinade.

Thai Grilled Pork

Peanut butter, soy sauce, and curry powder sound like an improbable combination, but they add great flavor and tenderness to pork tenderloin.

MAKE AHEAD

INGREDIENTS | SERVES 6–8

1 tablespoon olive oil
1 onion, chopped
2 cloves garlic, minced
¼ cup peanut butter
¼ cup low-sodium soy sauce
2 tablespoons lemon juice
2 tablespoons honey
1 tablespoon curry powder
¼ teaspoon cayenne pepper
2 (1-pound) pork tenderloins
1 cup chopped honey roasted peanuts

1. In microwave-safe bowl, combine olive oil with onion and garlic; microwave on high for 2–3 minutes. Stir, then microwave for 1–2 minutes longer until very tender.

2. Remove bowl from microwave and add remaining ingredients except pork and chopped peanuts; mix well.

3. Cut pork tenderloin into 1½-inch cubes. Add to peanut butter mixture and toss; cover and refrigerate for 18–24 hours.

4. When ready to grill, thread tenderloin on skewers. Grill for 8–11 minutes, turning once, until meat thermometer registers 155°F. As pork cooks, remove to a plate coated with peanuts; roll to coat, then serve.

CHAPTER 6

Beef Entrees

Stuffed Meatloaf Pinwheels

This delicious make-ahead recipe has a beautiful presentation.
Serve with some simmering pasta sauce if you'd like.

MAKE AHEAD

INGREDIENTS | SERVES 8–10

2 eggs

1 (10.75-ounce) can tomato soup

4 cloves garlic, minced

¼ cup grated Parmesan cheese

2 pounds lean ground beef

2 tablespoons olive oil

1 onion, chopped

1 green bell pepper, chopped

2 cups soft whole wheat bread crumbs

2 tablespoons Dijon mustard

1 cup shredded Cheddar cheese

½ cup shredded Swiss cheese

1. In large bowl, beat eggs with half of the soup, garlic, and Parmesan cheese. Add ground beef and mix until combined.

2. Place meat mixture onto waxed paper; pat into a 14" × 10" rectangle and refrigerate.

3. In small saucepan, heat olive oil over medium heat. Add onion and bell pepper; cook and stir until tender, about 5 minutes. Place in medium bowl and add remaining soup, bread crumbs, and mustard; mix well. Stir in cheeses.

4. Spread bread crumb mixture over the meat. Roll up meat, enclosing filling, starting with short side. Do not roll waxed paper into meat. Cover and chill meat mixture for 8–24 hours.

5. When ready to eat, preheat oven to 325°F. Line a 9" × 13" baking dish with foil. Cut the meat roll into 1½-inch slices. Place cut side down in prepared baking dish. Bake for 45–55 minutes until meat is thoroughly cooked.

Shepherd's Pie

A Shepherd's pie is a rich meat mixture baked with a creamy and cheesy potato crust.
It's a healthy version of a main dish pie.

HEALTHY

INGREDIENTS | SERVES 10

1½ pounds ground beef

2 onions, chopped

3 cloves garlic, minced

3 tablespoons flour

1 teaspoon dried marjoram leaves

⅛ teaspoon pepper

3 tablespoons Worcestershire sauce

1 cup beef broth

½ cup chili sauce

¼ cup ketchup

1 (10-ounce) package frozen peas and carrots

1 (10-ounce) package frozen green beans

1 (24-ounce) package refrigerated mashed potatoes

⅓ cup sour cream

1 cup shredded Cheddar cheese

1. Preheat oven to 375°F. In large skillet, cook ground beef with onion and garlic until beef is browned. Drain, then return to heat and add flour, marjoram, and pepper. Cook and stir for 4 minutes, then add Worcestershire sauce, beef broth, chili sauce, and ketchup.

2. Simmer for 10 minutes, then add frozen vegetables. Pour into a 2½-quart casserole and set aside.

3. In large bowl, combine potatoes with sour cream and cheese; beat until combined. Spread over meat mixture.

4. Bake for 35–40 minutes or until casserole is bubbling and potatoes are brown and slightly crisp on top.

Keep It Healthy

Make your own mashed potatoes instead of using the refrigerated variety. Just peel and cube 5 potatoes. Boil until tender, then drain and mash with 2 tablespoons butter, salt, pepper, and about ½ cup milk. Use low-fat sour cream and Cheddar cheese too. And you can add more vegetables to the beef mixture.

Potato Caraway Meatballs

Potatoes add moisture, texture, and great flavor to these simple meatballs.

INEXPENSIVE

INGREDIENTS | SERVES 6

1 cup frozen hash brown potatoes, thawed

½ teaspoon salt

⅛ teaspoon pepper

½ teaspoon grated lemon zest

1 teaspoon caraway seeds, divided

1 egg

½ cup minced onion

2 garlic cloves, minced

1 pound ground beef

2 tablespoons olive oil

1 onion, chopped

3 cups beef broth

¼ cup tomato paste

2 tablespoons cornstarch

¼ cup tomato juice

1. Drain the potatoes and place on work surface. Cut into finer pieces. Then combine in large bowl with salt, pepper, lemon zest, ½ teaspoon caraway seed, egg, minced onion, and garlic. Mix well, then work in ground beef.

2. Form into 2-inch meatballs and chill for 2–3 hours. When ready to eat, heat skillet and add olive oil. Add 1 chopped onion; cook and stir until tender. Add meatballs and brown for 5 minutes, turning frequently.

3. In small bowl, combine 1 cup beef broth with tomato paste; stir until blended. Add to skillet along with remaining broth. Cover and simmer for 25–30 minutes until meatballs are tender.

4. In small bowl, combine cornstarch and tomato juice. Stir into skillet along with remaining ½ teaspoon caraway seed and simmer for 5–10 minutes until sauce thickens. Serve over hot mashed potatoes.

Beef Mornay

This rich dish can also be served over baked puff pastry shells or hot cooked rice.

LAST MINUTE

INGREDIENTS | SERVES 6–8

1 pound beef round steak
2 tablespoons lemon juice
¼ cup flour
½ teaspoon salt
⅛ teaspoon pepper
4 tablespoons butter
1 onion, chopped
2 cloves garlic, minced
1 (8-ounce) package sliced mushrooms
1 red bell pepper, sliced
1 (12-ounce) can evaporated milk
½ cup light cream
1½ cups beef broth
1½ cups grated Gruyere cheese
⅓ cup grated Parmesan cheese
8 English muffins, split and toasted

Party Fun

Choose a few skillet dishes and offer a variety of foods to serve them over. Baked puff pastry squares, puff pastry shells, toasted English muffins, hot cooked wild rice, mashed potatoes, or pasta tossed with a little olive oil can all be offered as a comfort food buffet. Keep everything warm in slow cookers and on warming trays.

1. Slice beef into ¼" x 4" strips and toss with lemon juice; let stand for 10 minutes. Drain, sprinkle with flour, salt, and pepper and set aside.

2. In large skillet, melt butter over medium heat. Add beef strips; cook and stir until browned, about 5–6 minutes. Remove beef from skillet and add onions and garlic. Cook and stir for 5 minutes.

3. Add mushrooms; cook and stir for 4 minutes longer. Add red bell pepper; cook for 3 minutes. Add evaporated milk, cream, and beef broth and return beef to skillet.

4. Simmer for 4–5 minutes until sauce has thickened. Stir in cheeses until melted. Serve over toasted English muffins.

Beef-Stuffed Peppers

Bell peppers are usually stuffed with a mixture of vegetables and rice or chicken.
Beef adds a hearty touch to this classic recipe.

EASILY DOUBLES

INGREDIENTS | SERVES 6

6 bell peppers, various colors
1 pound lean ground beef
1 onion, chopped
3 cloves garlic, minced
3 tablespoons butter
3 tablespoons flour
½ teaspoon salt
⅛ teaspoon pepper
1 teaspoon dried marjoram leaves
1 cup beef broth
½ cup light cream
1 tablespoon Worcestershire sauce
1½ cups cooked rice
1½ cups shredded Swiss cheese
1 cup water
⅓ cup grated Romano cheese

1. Cut the tops off the peppers and carefully remove membranes and seeds. Blanch the peppers in boiling water for 2 minutes; remove and drain.

2. In large skillet, cook ground beef with onion and garlic until beef is browned, stirring to break up meat. Drain well, then add butter to skillet; let melt.

3. Sprinkle with flour, salt, pepper, and marjoram; cook and stir until bubbly. Add beef broth, cream, and Worcestershire sauce; cook and stir until thickened.

4. Add rice and Swiss cheese; cook and stir until cheese is melted. Use this mixture to fill peppers.

5. Set stuffed peppers in baking dish large enough to hold them snugly upright. Pour water around peppers. Sprinkle peppers with Romano cheese and bake for 35–45 minutes until peppers are tender and tops are browned.

Beef Burgundy

Beef Burgundy is a classic recipe that everyone will love. It's a good choice for serving a crowd.

EASY

INGREDIENTS | SERVES 8

1¼ cups Burgundy wine

¼ cup olive oil

3 tablespoons low-sodium soy sauce

3 tablespoons oyster sauce

4 cloves garlic, minced

1 teaspoon dried marjoram leaves

2 pounds sirloin strip steak, cubed

3 tablespoons butter

2 onions, chopped

1 (8-ounce) package sliced mushrooms

2 tablespoons flour

⅛ teaspoon pepper

1½ cups beef broth

Keep It Healthy

Wine, in moderation, is very good for you. Most, but not all of the alcohol will burn off in the high heat of the stovetop. Keep this in mind if you have any recovering alcoholics on the guest list. And use a Burgundy wine that you would drink. The flavor is concentrated during cooking, and you want the best flavor in your recipes.

1. In large bowl, combine wine, olive oil, soy sauce, oyster sauce, garlic, and marjoram leaves; mix well. Add steak; cover and refrigerate for 4–6 hours.

2. When ready to cook, drain meat, reserving marinade. Melt butter in large skillet and add beef; cook until browned on all sides, about 5–6 minutes. Remove meat from pan.

3. Add onions and mushrooms to pan; cook, stirring frequently to remove pan drippings, for 10 minutes. Sprinkle with flour and pepper; cook and stir until bubbly.

4. Add beef broth, reserved marinade, and steak to skillet; cook and stir until mixture starts to simmer. Reduce heat to low, cover, and simmer for 1 hour, stirring occasionally. Serve over hot cooked rice.

Old-Fashioned Meatball Casserole

Meatballs, pasta, and cheese bake in a rich mushroom vegetable sauce in this classic casserole.

INEXPENSIVE

INGREDIENTS | SERVES 8

2 tablespoons butter

1 onion, chopped

3 cloves garlic, minced

1 green bell pepper, minced

1 (8-ounce) can sliced mushrooms, drained

1 (15-ounce) jar Alfredo sauce

½ cup milk

1 teaspoon dried basil

3 cups uncooked egg noodles

1 (16-ounce) package frozen cooked meatballs, thawed

2 cups cottage cheese

2 cups shredded Colby cheese

½ cup grated Parmesan cheese

1. Preheat oven to 350°F. Bring a large pot of salted water to a boil. In large saucepan, melt butter over medium heat. Add onion and garlic; cook and stir until tender, about 5 minutes.

2. Add bell pepper and mushrooms; cook and stir for 3 minutes longer. Add Alfredo sauce, milk, and basil; simmer for 5 minutes, then remove from heat.

3. Cook egg noodles until almost al dente according to package directions. Drain and add to sauce mixture.

4. In greased 3-quart casserole dish, layer ⅓ of the meatballs, cottage cheese, Colby cheese, and sauce. Repeat layers, ending with sauce. Sprinkle with Parmesan cheese. Bake for 45–55 minutes until casserole is bubbly and top is browned.

Orange Pot Roast

This hearty one-dish meal is satisfying and rich.
Add more vegetables to the roast if you'd like.

HEALTHY

INGREDIENTS | SERVES 10

1 (3-pound) beef rump roast
¼ cup flour
1 teaspoon salt
¼ teaspoon pepper
3 tablespoons olive oil
2 onions, chopped
4 cloves garlic, minced
1 cup orange juice
1 teaspoon grated orange rind
2 tablespoons honey
1 teaspoon dried marjoram leaves
2 tablespoons Worcestershire sauce
½ cup beef broth
3 sweet potatoes, peeled and cubed
5 carrots, cut into chunks
2 tablespoons butter

1. Preheat oven to 350°F. Sprinkle roast with flour, salt, and pepper. Heat olive oil in large skillet and brown beef on all sides. Place beef in large roasting pan and set aside.

2. Add onions and garlic to skillet; cook and stir, scraping up drippings, until tender, about 5 minutes. Add orange juice, rind, honey, marjoram, Worcestershire sauce, and beef broth; bring to a simmer. Simmer for 5 minutes.

3. Meanwhile, place potatoes and carrots around beef. Pour orange sauce over and cover tightly. Roast for 2½ hours until meat and vegetables are tender.

4. Remove beef and vegetables from pan and cover to keep warm. Pour drippings into saucepan. Bring to a boil; boil for 3 minutes, then swirl in butter and serve with roast.

Party Fun

This recipe makes an excellent centerpiece for a holiday meal. Buy or borrow a very large serving platter and set the roast in the center. Surround it with the vegetables roasted with the meat, then drizzle some sauce over everything. Serve the rest of the sauce on the side. Garnish the platter with fresh herb sprigs and sliced oranges.

Flat Iron Steak

Flat Iron steak is a fairly new cut, made from trimmed top blade steaks.
The cut is tender and juicy and very well flavored.

¼ cup red wine vinegar
¼ cup minced onion
3 cloves garlic, minced
1 teaspoon dried marjoram leaves
1 teaspoon dried basil leaves
1 teaspoon salt
¼ teaspoon pepper
2 tablespoons olive oil
2 pounds flat iron steaks
¼ cup butter, softened
¼ cup basil pesto
½ cup crumbled feta cheese
1 cup grape tomatoes, halved

1. In zip-top bag, combine vinegar, onion, garlic, marjoram, dried basil, salt, pepper, and olive oil. Add steaks, seal bag, and knead to coat. Refrigerate for at least 1 hour, up to 24 hours.

2. Prepare and preheat grill. Meanwhile, combine butter, pesto, feta, and tomatoes; mix well and refrigerate.

3. Drain steak, discarding marinade. Grill steak over direct medium heat for 5–7 minutes per side until desired doneness. Remove from grill and let stand for 5 minutes, then serve with butter mixture.

Cal-Mex Meatloaf

A rich and hearty meatloaf is always welcome.
This one is full of texture, flavor, and color.

HEALTHY

INGREDIENTS | SERVES 8

2 tablespoons olive oil
½ cup diced red onion
½ cup diced red bell pepper
½ cup diced yellow bell pepper
2 cloves garlic, minced
2 jalapeño peppers, minced
2 eggs, beaten
¾ cup chili sauce, divided
½ cup quick-cooking oatmeal
1 teaspoon dried basil leaves
1 teaspoon dried thyme leaves
1 teaspoon salt
¼ teaspoon cayenne pepper
1 pound ground beef
½ pound ground pork
2 tablespoons brown sugar
3 tablespoons Dijon mustard

1. Preheat oven to 350°F. Spray a broiler pan with nonstick cooking spray and set aside.

2. In large saucepan, heat olive oil over medium heat. Add red onion, all the bell peppers, garlic, and jalapeño peppers; cook and stir for 6–7 minutes until tender. Remove from heat and place in large bowl.

3. Add eggs, ½ cup chili sauce, oatmeal, basil, thyme, salt, and cayenne pepper and mix well. Add beef and pork and mix well.

4. Form into a loaf and place on broiler pan. In small bowl, combine remaining ¼ cup chili sauce, brown sugar, and mustard; pour over loaf. Bake for 60–75 minutes until internal meat thermometer registers 160°F.

5. Cover meatloaf and let stand for 10 minutes before slicing to serve.

Keep It Healthy

Use 90% ground beef in this recipe for less fat. You can use this type of beef without fear of the meatloaf being dry because there are so many other ingredients in the recipe. The vegetables, eggs, and chili sauce add moisture as well as flavor. And because there's so much flavor, you can cut the salt in half.

Mushroom Steak

*Swirling butter into a sauce at the last minute thickens it slightly,
makes it velvety, and adds great flavor.*

LAST MINUTE

INGREDIENTS | SERVES 6

6 (5-ounce) beef tenderloin steaks
1 teaspoon steak seasoning
¼ teaspoon pepper
2 tablespoons butter
1 tablespoon olive oil
1 onion, chopped
3 cloves garlic, minced
1 cup sliced cremini mushrooms
1 cup sliced button mushrooms
½ cup dry red wine
½ cup beef broth
1 tablespoon fresh thyme leaves
2 tablespoons butter

1. Make sure you have all of the vegetables prepared before you start this recipe. Sprinkle steaks with steak seasoning and pepper on both sides. Let stand at room temperature while you heat 2 tablespoons butter and olive oil in a large skillet.

2. Add steaks; cook 9–12 minutes, turning once, for medium. Remove to a warm platter and cover to keep warm. You can put the steaks in a 250°F oven while you make the sauce.

3. Add onion and garlic to pan; cook for 3 minutes. Then add mushrooms; cook and stir for 3 minutes longer. Add wine, beef broth, and thyme leaves; bring to a boil. Boil hard over high heat for 2–3 minutes until sauce reduces slightly.

4. Remove pan from heat and swirl in 2 tablespoons butter. Immediately pour over the steaks and serve.

Brie Meatloaf

Brie adds incredible flavor to this special meatloaf.
Garnish it with some fresh thyme sprigs and place a few
slices of Brie on top to melt into the loaf before serving.

EASY

INGREDIENTS | SERVES 6–8

½ cup crushed cracker crumbs

2 eggs, beaten

¼ cup buttermilk

½ teaspoon onion powder

1 teaspoon dried thyme leaves

1 teaspoon seasoned salt

⅛ teaspoon pepper

¼ cup steak sauce, divided

1 pound 85% lean ground beef

½ pound ground pork

⅔ cup diced Brie cheese, without rind

2 tablespoons brown sugar

2 tablespoons coarse brown mustard

1 tablespoon honey

1. Preheat oven to 350°F. Spray a 9" × 5" loaf pan with nonstick cooking spray and set aside.

2. In large bowl, combine crumbs, eggs, buttermilk, onion powder, thyme, seasoned salt, pepper, and 2 tablespoons steak sauce and mix well.

3. Mix in beef and pork with your hands just until combined. Gently mix in Brie cheese pieces. Press into prepared loaf pan.

4. In small bowl, combine remaining 2 tablespoons steak sauce, brown sugar, mustard, and honey; pour over meatloaf. Bake for 50–60 minutes until internal temperature reads 160°F. Drain meatloaf, cover, let stand for 10 minutes, then remove from pan and slice.

Transport Tips

Meatloaf is easy to transport to the party. Just wrap it in an insulated carrier and bring with you in the car. As long as you eat the food within two hours of removing it from the oven, it will be wholesome. You could also bake the meatloaf and cool it, then serve it cold in sandwiches at the party.

Ragu Bolognese

Ragu Bolognese usually contains lots of different types of meat.
This easier version is still rich and delicious.

INEXPENSIVE

INGREDIENTS | SERVES 8

3 slices bacon

2 tablespoons butter

1 onion, chopped

4 cloves garlic, minced

½ cup chopped carrots

½ cup chopped celery

½ teaspoon salt

⅛ teaspoon pepper

1¼ pounds ground beef

1 (26-ounce) jar pasta sauce

¼ cup dry red wine

½ cup beef stock

1 (16-ounce) package linguine

½ cup heavy cream

1. In large saucepan, cook bacon until crisp. Drain on paper towel, crumble, and set aside. Drain fat from pan but do not wipe out.

2. Add butter to pan; cook onions, garlic, carrots, and celery until tender, about 6–7 minutes. Add salt and pepper.

3. Add beef and bacon; cook and stir to break up meat, until meat is browned. Drain mixture. Add pasta sauce, wine, and stock to pan; bring to a simmer. Simmer, stirring frequently, for 30–40 minutes.

4. Bring a large pot of salted water to a boil. Add linguine; cook until al dente according to package directions. Add cream to meat sauce and simmer.

5. Drain pasta and place on serving plate and top with meat mixture. Serve immediately.

Teriyaki Steak

This marinade can be used for other meats as well.
Try it with pork chops or boneless, skinless chicken thighs.

MAKE AHEAD

INGREDIENTS | SERVES 4

¼ cup teriyaki sauce

¼ cup low-sodium soy sauce

2 tablespoons minced ginger root

2 tablespoons brown sugar

2 teaspoons sesame oil

2 tablespoons peanut oil

1 tablespoon bourbon

4 (6-ounce) rib-eye steaks

Keep It Safe

Whenever you brush a marinade that has been in contact with raw meat on meat that's cooking, be sure that you "cook off" the marinade. That means that the side that was just exposed to the marinade faces the heat for at least 1 minute. The uncooked marinade isn't safe to eat without boiling.

1. In ziplock bag, combine all ingredients except the steaks and mix. Add steaks, close bag and knead to combine.

2. Place bag in dish and refrigerate for 12–24 hours. When ready to eat, prepare and preheat grill. Drain steaks, reserving marinade.

3. Grill steaks for 5–7 minutes per side, brushing occasionally with reserved marinade, until desired doneness. Let steaks stand, covered, for 5 minutes before serving. Discard remaining marinade.

Steak and Bean Enchiladas

This excellent recipe for enchiladas is rich and delicious.

MAKE AHEAD

INGREDIENTS | SERVES 8–10

1 pound round steak

1 tablespoon chili powder

½ teaspoon cumin

2 tablespoons butter

1 tablespoon oil

1 onion, chopped

3 cloves garlic, minced

2 jalapeño peppers, minced

1 (15-ounce) can refried beans

14 (8-inch) flour tortillas

2 cups shredded Cheddar cheese, divided

1 (18-ounce) can enchilada sauce

1 cup salsa

1 cup shredded pepper jack cheese

1. Spray 13" × 9" glass baking dish with nonstick cooking spray and set aside. Preheat oven to 350°F. Slice round steak against the grain into ½" × 3" strips. Sprinkle with chili powder and cumin. Melt 2 tablespoons butter and 1 tablespoon oil in large saucepan. Add steak; brown on all sides, about 5 minutes, and remove from pan.

2. Cook onion, garlic, and jalapeño in saucepan until tender, about 6 minutes. Add refried beans and steak to pan; heat until mixture simmers.

3. Spread mixture onto flour tortillas; top each with 2 tablespoons Cheddar cheese. Roll up and place in prepared pan.

4. In saucepan, combine enchilada sauce and salsa; bring to a simmer. Pour over enchiladas. Top with remaining ¼ cup Cheddar cheese and pepper jack cheese.

5. Bake for 30–45 minutes until the casserole is bubbly and cheese on top melts and begins to brown. Serve immediately with sour cream, salsa, and avocados.

Curried Meatballs

Curry powder is sweet, spicy, warm, and hot, all at the same time.
Along with chutney, it adds fabulous flavor to these easy meatballs.

QUICK

INGREDIENTS | SERVES 8

1 tablespoon olive oil
⅓ cup minced peeled apple
¼ cup minced onion
3 cloves garlic, minced
1 tablespoon curry powder
½ teaspoon salt
⅛ teaspoon cayenne pepper
1 egg, beaten
1 (12-ounce) bottle mango chutney, divided
1 pound ground beef
1 (16-ounce) jar Alfredo sauce
1 green bell pepper, chopped
½ cup celery, chopped
2 teaspoons curry powder

Make-Ahead Tips

You can make the meatballs ahead of time and place on a plate. Cover and refrigerate until it's time to eat. Prepare the bell pepper and celery as well, cover and refrigerate. Then proceed with the recipe as directed. Start the rice cooking when you're forming the meatballs so it will be ready when the recipe is.

1. In large saucepan, heat olive oil over medium heat. Add apple, onion, and garlic; cook and stir until tender, about 5 minutes. Add curry powder; cook and stir for 1 minute longer.

2. Remove from heat and place in large bowl. Add salt, cayenne pepper, egg, and ½ cup chutney; mix well. Add beef and mix gently with your hands until combined.

3. Form into 1-inch meatballs. Return saucepan to heat and add butter. Brown meatballs on all sides, shaking pan occasionally, about 4–5 minutes. Drain off excess fat.

4. Return saucepan to heat and stir in Alfredo sauce, green pepper, celery, and 2 teaspoons curry powder. Bring to a simmer; reduce heat to low, cover, and simmer for 12–18 minutes until meatballs are thoroughly cooked. Stir in remaining chutney and serve over hot cooked rice.

Beef with Black Bean Sauce

*Fermented black beans are a very concentrated flavoring agent in
Chinese cooking. This wonderful recipe is beautiful too.*

LAST MINUTE

INGREDIENTS | SERVES 4

1 pound flank steak

2 tablespoons cornstarch

3 tablespoons low-sodium soy sauce

2 tablespoons rice wine vinegar

4 cloves garlic, minced

2 tablespoons fermented black beans, rinsed

2 tablespoons peanut oil

1 onion, chopped

1 tablespoon minced fresh ginger root

1 red bell pepper, sliced

1 green bell pepper, sliced

1 cup beef broth

1. Cut flank steak into ½" × 2" strips against the grain. Combine cornstarch, soy sauce, rice wine vinegar, and garlic in large bowl and add steak; cover and marinate in refrigerator for 25 minutes.

2. Meanwhile, drain black beans and finely mince; set aside. Drain meat, reserving marinade.

3. Heat oil in large skillet or wok. Add meat; stir-fry until browned, about 3–4 minutes. Remove from wok. Add onion, ginger root, and black beans; stir-fry for 3–4 minutes.

4. Add bell peppers to wok; stir-fry for 2–3 minutes longer. Add beef broth to reserved marinade; stir and pour into wok along with beef. Stir-fry for 4–5 minutes until sauce boils and thickens. Serve immediately.

Indian Steak

These spices add spectacular flavor to flat iron steaks, and the lime juice tenderizes them. Serve this recipe with roasted potatoes and a green salad.

EASY

INGREDIENTS | SERVES 6

2 tablespoons butter

1 onion, minced

3 cloves garlic, minced

1 tablespoon curry powder

2 tablespoons beef broth

1 tablespoon lime juice

½ teaspoon ground cumin

½ teaspoon mustard powder

1 teaspoon salt

¼ teaspoon pepper

⅛ teaspoon cayenne pepper

6 (5-ounce) flat-iron steaks

1. In small saucepan, combine butter with onion and garlic over medium heat. Cook and stir until tender, about 6 minutes. Add curry powder; cook and stir for 1–2 minutes longer until fragrant.

2. Remove from heat and add remaining ingredients except steak. Let cool for 10 minutes, then rub over steaks.

3. Cover and refrigerate for 12–24 hours. When ready to cook, prepare and preheat grill. Grill steaks over medium direct heat for 8–12 minutes, turning once, until desired doneness. Let steaks stand for 5–10 minutes, then serve.

Party Fun

Make several different types of marinade and marinate steaks, chicken, and pork chops. Grill them and set up a buffet. If you want to give your guests a choice before cooking, use grill charms to mark the meat before they go on the grill. Charms are little metal pieces you stick onto meat before grilling.

Smothered Steak

To double this recipe, use two slow cookers.
Serve over hot cooked rice or cooked pasta to soak up all the sauce.

EASILY DOUBLES

INGREDIENTS | SERVES 6

2 onions, chopped

2 cloves garlic, minced

1 pound bottom round steak

3 tablespoons flour

½ teaspoon salt

⅛ teaspoon pepper

1 teaspoon dried marjoram leaves

1 (14.5-ounce) can diced tomatoes, undrained

2 tablespoons Worcestershire sauce

1 cup beef broth

¼ cup tomato paste

1 (8-ounce) can sliced mushrooms, drained

1. Place onions and garlic in bottom of 4-quart slow cooker. Cut steak into strips ½" × 3" across the grain. Toss with flour, salt, pepper, and marjoram. Place on top of onions in slow cooker.

2. Open tomatoes and drain ¾ of can into slow cooker. Add Worcestershire sauce, beef broth, and tomato paste to remaining tomatoes in can and mix well; pour over meat. Add mushrooms.

3. Cover and cook on low for 8–10 hours until beef and vegetables are tender. Stir well and serve over hot cooked rice or noodles.

CHAPTER 7

Chicken Entrees

Poached Chicken

*When a recipe calls for sliced or chopped cooked chicken, this is the recipe to use.
Poach a lot of chicken, chop and freeze, and you'll be ready for anything.*

EASY

INGREDIENTS | YIELDS 8 BREASTS; 6
CUPS CHOPPED COOKED CHICKEN

1 cup chicken broth

1 cup water

3 tablespoons lemon juice

2 sprigs fresh thyme

8 boneless, skinless chicken breasts

1. Combine broth, water, lemon juice, and thyme in large skillet; bring to a simmer over medium-high heat.

2. Add chicken; reduce heat to low. Cover and simmer for 20–25 minutes or until chicken registers 160°F.

3. Remove chicken from skillet and place in glass baking dish. Pour poaching liquid over. Cover and chill until chicken is cold. Then slice or chop and use in recipes. Can be stored in refrigerator for 3 days or frozen for up to 3 months.

Chicken Baked with Creamy Salsa

*The salsa mixture insulates the chicken as it
cooks and adds moisture and flavor.*

EASY

INGREDIENTS | SERVES 8

8 boneless, skinless chicken breasts

1 teaspoon salt

¼ teaspoon pepper

1 teaspoon paprika

1 cup chunky salsa, drained

1 (4-ounce) can chopped green chilies, drained

½ cup low-fat sour cream

⅓ cup mayonnaise

1 tablespoon chili powder

1. Preheat oven to 375°F. Place chicken breasts between two sheets of waxed paper. Flatten with meat mallet or rolling pin to ¼-inch thickness. Remove top sheet and sprinkle chicken with salt, pepper, and paprika. Place chicken in baking dish.

2. In medium bowl, combine remaining ingredients and mix well. Spoon this mixture over the chicken.

3. Bake chicken, uncovered, for 15–25 minutes until chicken is thoroughly cooked. Serve with hot cooked rice.

Chicken and Pasta in Cheddar Sauce

Pasta is usually served with a tomato sauce or a mozzarella cheese sauce.
This one is different—and delicious!

LAST MINUTE

INGREDIENTS | SERVES 6

4 Poached Chicken breasts (page 112), cubed
2 tablespoons olive oil
1 onion, chopped
3 cloves garlic, minced
1 (16-ounce) package fettuccine
½ pound asparagus, cut into 2-inch pieces
2 cups frozen baby peas
1 (16-ounce) jar Alfredo sauce
1½ cups shredded sharp Cheddar cheese
⅓ cup grated Romano cheese

1. Bring a large pot of water to a boil. Cube Chicken Breasts and set aside. In large skillet, heat olive oil over medium heat. Add onion and garlic; cook and stir until tender, about 5 minutes.

2. Cook fettuccine according to package directions. Meanwhile, add asparagus and peas to skillet; cook and stir for 3–4 minutes until asparagus is crisp tender. Add chicken and Alfredo sauce to skillet; bring to a simmer.

3. Drain pasta when al dente. Add to skillet along with Cheddar cheese; cook and stir over medium heat for 2–3 minutes until chicken is hot and sauce is blended. Sprinkle with Romano cheese and serve.

Scalloped Chicken

This recipe is a great way to use up leftover chicken
or turkey from Thanksgiving.

EASY

INGREDIENTS | SERVES 6

2 tablespoons butter
1 onion, chopped
4 cloves garlic, minced
4 cups chicken stock
3 eggs, beaten
4 cups cooked cubed chicken
2 cups frozen baby peas
3 cups soft whole wheat bread crumbs
1 cup grated Parmesan cheese

1. Preheat oven to 350°F. Spray a 3-quart shallow baking dish with nonstick cooking spray and set aside.

2. In large saucepan, melt butter over medium heat. Add onion and garlic; cook and stir until tender, about 6 minutes. Remove from heat and add chicken stock, then beat in the beaten eggs; set aside.

3. In bowl, combine chicken and peas and mix. In another bowl, combine crumbs with cheese and mix well. Layer crumb mixture with chicken mixture in prepared casserole, beginning and ending with crumb mixture.

4. Pour chicken stock mixture slowly into casserole. Bake for 55–65 minutes until casserole is brown and bubbly.

Chicken in Phyllo

This elegant recipe is perfect for entertaining.
Serve it with a spinach salad and a sweet fruit salad.

MAKE AHEAD

INGREDIENTS | SERVES 8–10

6 boneless, skinless chicken breasts
½ cup honey mustard salad dressing
1 tablespoon olive oil
1 tablespoon butter
1 onion, chopped
4 cloves garlic, minced
1 cup chopped mushrooms
1 teaspoon dried tarragon leaves
⅛ teaspoon pepper
36 (9" × 15") sheets frozen phyllo dough, thawed
½ cup butter, melted
½ cup grated Parmesan cheese
2 cups Fresh Tomato Salsa (page 34)

1. Cut each chicken breast in half lengthwise. Place in casserole dish and cover with salad dressing; let stand for 15 minutes.

2. In small saucepan, combine oil and butter over medium heat. Add onion, garlic, and mushrooms; cook and stir until tender and liquid evaporates. Add chicken breasts; cook on both sides until brown, about 5-6 minutes. Add tarragon and pepper and remove from heat.

3. Place one sheet phyllo dough onto work surface; brush sparingly with butter and sprinkle with cheese. Repeat layers until you have a stack of three.

4. Place one chicken tender near 9" side of phyllo; top with a spoonful of the mushroom mixture. Roll up, starting with 9" side, folding in sides. Place on cookie sheet, seam side down; brush with more butter.

5. Repeat with remaining phyllo, butter, cheese, chicken, and filling. Bake for 18–23 minutes or until chicken registers 160°F and phyllo is crisp and brown. Serve immediately with salsa.

Chicken with Crisp Potato Crust

*The combination of potato chips and bread crumbs
gives the crust a deep flavor and wonderful crispness.*

EASILY DOUBLES

INGREDIENTS | SERVES 6

6 boneless, skinless chicken
breasts

¼ cup apple juice

⅓ cup Dijon mustard

2 tablespoons lemon juice

2 tablespoons butter, melted

2 cups plain potato chips, crushed

½ cup panko bread crumbs

Transport Tips

This is an easy recipe to transport. Just
place the chicken, still in its marinade, in a
cooler packed with ice. Combine the
potato chips and crumbs and place in small
plastic bag. When you get to the party,
broil the chicken as directed, then turn and
add topping; broil until chicken reaches
160°F.

1. Place chicken breasts in ziplock bag. Add apple juice, mustard, lemon juice, and butter; seal bag and squish to knead. Place in casserole dish, cover, and refrigerate for 8–24 hours.

2. When ready to eat, remove chicken from marinade. Place on broiler pan. In medium bowl, combine potato chips and bread crumbs.

3. Broil chicken 6 inches from heat source for 8 minutes. Turn chicken and top with potato chip mixture, pressing in gently to secure topping. Broil for 2–3 minutes longer until topping is crisp and dark golden brown. Serve immediately.

Chicken-Stuffed Apples

This recipe is like an inside-out stuffed chicken.
Each person gets 2–3 apple halves to enjoy.

HEALTHY

INGREDIENTS | SERVES 5–6

6 large baking apples
3 tablespoons lemon juice
1 cup crushed croutons
2 cups diced cooked chicken
½ cup dried currants
¼ cup finely chopped walnuts
½ teaspoon salt
1 teaspoon dried thyme leaves
⅛ teaspoon pepper
¼ cup butter, melted
1 cup chicken broth, divided
½ cup apple juice

1. Cut apples in half and remove core. Carefully remove apple flesh, leaving a ½-inch shell. Chop the removed flesh and place in medium bowl. Drizzle with 2 tablespoons lemon juice. Brush shells with 1 tablespoon lemon juice.

2. Add croutons, chicken, currants, and walnuts to apples and mix well. Sprinkle with salt, thyme, and pepper, then drizzle with butter and 3 tablespoons chicken broth and toss to coat.

3. Cut thin slice off bottoms of apple shells so they will sit without tipping. Fill each shell with some of the chicken mixture, piling it up. Arrange in 2-quart baking dish. Preheat oven to 400°F.

4. Pour remaining chicken broth and apple juice into pan and cover. Bake for 35–45 minutes, basting apples occasionally with the liquid in pan, until apples are tender.

Hot Chicken Sandwiches

A large sandwich can make a party!
You can double or triple this recipe for a crowd.

EASILY DOUBLES

INGREDIENTS | SERVES 6

1 large loaf Italian bread

4 tablespoons butter, melted, divided

2 cups chopped Poached Chicken (page 112)

½ cup diced celery

1 red bell pepper, diced

2 tablespoons pickle relish

2 tablespoons mustard

½ cup sour cream

1 cup diced Havarti cheese

¼ cup chopped green onion

Keep It Healthy

You can use low-fat sour cream and low-fat cheese in this recipe. Or reduce the cheese and add more chopped vegetables; chopped mushrooms or zucchini would be nice additions. Olive oil can be substituted for the butter for coating the insides and outsides of the bread shell.

1. Preheat oven to 400°F. Slice the bread in half lengthwise. Scoop out some of the bread from both halves, leaving a ¾-inch shell. Save bread for making bread crumbs. Brush insides of loaves with 2 tablespoons butter and place on cookie sheet. Toast for 10 minutes, then remove and let cool.

2. In large bowl, combine remaining ingredients and mix well. When bread has cooled, fill one half with chicken mixture, then place top on bread. Brush with remaining melted butter.

3. Wrap loaf in aluminum foil and bake for 30–35 minutes until sandwiches are hot. To serve, unwrap foil and slice loaf into six pieces.

Chicken Hawaiian

*A creamy chicken mixture spiked with pineapple and orange
is served over rice in this easy recipe.*

LAST MINUTE

INGREDIENTS | SERVES 6

4 boneless, skinless chicken breasts, cubed
2 tablespoons flour
½ teaspoon salt
⅛ teaspoon pepper
1 tablespoon butter
2 tablespoons olive oil
1 onion, chopped
3 cloves garlic, minced
1 jalapeño pepper, minced
1 green bell pepper, chopped
1 (15-ounce) can pineapple tidbits, drained
1 (16-ounce) jar Alfredo sauce
2 tablespoons orange juice
1 tablespoon low-sodium soy sauce
⅓ cup chopped cilantro
4 cups cooked long-grain brown rice

1. Sprinkle chicken with flour, salt, and pepper. In large skillet, heat butter and olive oil over medium heat. Add chicken; cook and stir until almost cooked, about 5–6 minutes. Remove chicken from skillet.

2. Add onion, garlic, jalapeño pepper, and green pepper to skillet; cook and stir until tender, about 5 minutes. Return chicken to skillet with pineapple, Alfredo sauce, orange juice, and soy sauce.

3. Bring to a simmer; simmer for 10–15 minutes until chicken is thoroughly cooked. Stir in cilantro and serve over hot cooked rice.

Apple-Orange Baked Chicken

Don't serve the onions and oranges that are under the chicken;
they are there to provide lots of flavor and cushion the chicken from the oven's heat.

HEALTHY

INGREDIENTS | SERVES 8

2 (4-pound) chickens, cut up

1 teaspoon salt

¼ teaspoon white pepper

1 teaspoon paprika

2 oranges, sliced

1 onion, peeled and sliced

¼ cup butter, melted

1 cup applesauce

⅓ cup orange marmalade

½ cup frozen orange juice concentrate, thawed

1 tablespoon olive oil

1. Preheat oven to 375°F. Remove skin from the chicken; sprinkle with salt, pepper, and paprika. Line roasting pan with orange and onion slices and top with chicken. Drizzle chicken with melted butter and set aside.

2. In bowl, combine remaining ingredients and mix well. Pour over chicken.

3. Cover pan with foil and bake for 55 minutes, basting once with the orange mixture. Uncover and bake for 40–50 minutes longer, basting frequently with orange mixture, until chicken is thoroughly cooked.

Keep It Healthy

You could use all bone-in, skin-on chicken breasts in this recipe. In that case, the baking time should be cut to ½ hour covered, ½ hour uncovered. That would cut the fat in this recipe, while keeping all the flavor. Chicken cooked with the skin on is moister, but if you just don't eat the skin, the fat content is greatly reduced.

Bacon Blue Cheese–Stuffed Chicken

This delicious recipe is packed full of flavor.
Serve it with a gelatin salad and a lemon pie for dessert.

MAKE AHEAD

INGREDIENTS | SERVES 8

8 boneless, skinless chicken breasts

1 teaspoon salt

¼ teaspoon pepper

5 slices bacon

1 onion, chopped

2 (3-ounce) packages cream cheese, softened

3 tablespoons Dijon mustard

½ cup minced fresh basil leaves

⅔ cup crumbled Gorgonzola cheese

⅓ cup flour

¼ cup ground walnuts

½ teaspoon seasoned salt

2 eggs, beaten

3 tablespoons butter

Make Ahead

You can make the chicken rolls ahead of time and chill in the refrigerator until you're ready to cook the dish. Prepare the flour and walnut mixture, but don't beat the egg until the last minute. Then dredge the chicken as directed, brown in the skillet, and bake in the oven until done.

1. Place chicken breasts between two sheets of waxed paper and pound until ¼ inch thick. Remove top sheet, sprinkle chicken with salt and pepper, and set aside.

2. In large skillet, cook bacon until crisp; drain on paper towels, crumble, and set aside. Drain bacon fat from skillet; do not wipe. Add onion to skillet; cook and stir until tender, about 5 minutes.

3. In medium bowl, beat cream cheese with mustard until smooth. Add crumbled bacon, cooked onions, basil leaves, and Gorgonzola and mix well. Spread this mixture on the chicken breasts.

4. Roll up chicken and fasten edges with toothpicks. On plate, combine flour, walnuts, and seasoned salt. Dredge chicken rolls in egg, then in the flour mixture. Melt butter in same skillet and brown chicken on all sides, turning frequently. Place chicken in 13" × 9" baking dish. Preheat oven to 350°F.

5. Bake chicken rolls for 15–20 minutes or until chicken is thoroughly cooked.

Italian Chicken Medallions

Chicken medallions cook very quickly and are very tender.
Be sure not to overcook them in the first step.

HEALTHY

INGREDIENTS | SERVES 6–8

6 chicken breasts
⅓ cup flour
1 teaspoon salt
⅛ teaspoon pepper
2 teaspoons dried Italian seasoning
2 tablespoons olive oil
1 onion, chopped
3 cloves garlic, minced
1 red bell pepper, sliced
1 green bell pepper, sliced
1 (26-ounce) jar pasta sauce
1 (16-ounce) package spaghetti pasta
½ cup grated Romano cheese

Keep It Safe

When handling raw chicken, be sure to keep it away from uncooked foods and foods that have finished cooking. Wash your hands, utensils, cutting boards, and anything else that has come in contact with the raw poultry in hot soapy water. Never thaw chicken at room temperature, and promptly refrigerate leftovers.

1. Cut chicken breasts into 1-inch pieces crosswise. Place chicken on waxed paper, cut side up, cover with another sheet of waxed paper, and gently pound until ¼-inch thick. Combine flour, salt, pepper, and Italian seasoning on plate; dredge chicken in this mixture; set aside.

2. Bring a large pot of water to boil. Meanwhile, in large skillet, heat olive oil over medium heat. Add chicken in three batches; sauté quickly on each side, about 2 minutes. Remove from heat and place on plate.

3. Add onion and garlic to skillet; cook and stir to release pan drippings, about 4 minutes. Add bell peppers and pasta sauce; bring to a simmer. Simmer for 10 minutes.

4. Cook pasta as directed on package. When pasta has 2 minutes to go, return chicken to skillet. Drain pasta and add to skillet; cook and stir for 1–2 minutes until chicken is thoroughly cooked. Sprinkle with cheese and serve.

Chicken Salpicon

*Salpicon is a salad with all of the ingredients chopped or diced to about
the same size so you get a perfect combination of flavors in every mouthful.*

MAKE AHEAD

INGREDIENTS | SERVES 6

5 Poached Chicken breasts (page 112), diced

⅓ cup orange juice

1 teaspoon dried thyme leaves

2 tablespoons butter

3 cups frozen Southern-style hash brown potatoes, thawed

½ cup honey mustard salad dressing

3 tablespoons olive oil

½ cup orange juice

½ teaspoon salt

⅛ teaspoon pepper

3 avocados, diced

5 tomatoes, seeded and chopped

1 red onion, diced

1 (8-ounce) package Monterey jack cheese, diced

1. In large bowl, combine Poached Chicken with ⅓ cup orange juice and thyme leaves; toss well so chicken starts to absorb juice; refrigerate.

2. In large pan, melt butter over medium heat. Add thawed and drained potatoes; cook and stir until potatoes are browned and starting to crisp. Remove to paper towels to drain.

3. In small bowl, combine salad dressing, olive oil, ½ cup orange juice, salt, and pepper and mix well.

4. Pour dressing over chicken mixture and stir to blend. Add potatoes, avocados, tomatoes, red onion, and cheese and mix well. Cover and refrigerate for 2–3 hours to blend flavors.

Chicken Calzones

Calzones are stuffed pizzas. You can fill them with anything you'd like.
This rich chicken mixture is delicious.

INEXPENSIVE

INGREDIENTS | YIELDS 8 CALZONES

1 loaf frozen bread dough, thawed

1 tablespoon butter

1 onion, chopped

3 cloves garlic, minced

1 red bell pepper, chopped

1 (8-ounce) package cream cheese, softened

2 Poached Chicken breasts (page 112), chopped

1 cup shredded Havarti cheese

¼ cup chopped flat-leaf parsley

1 egg, beaten

2 tablespoons milk

Make-Ahead Hints

You can make the chicken filling ahead of time; just cover it and refrigerate until you want to assemble the calzones. The bread dough, if defrosted in the refrigerator, should be just fine until it's time to eat. You may want to let the dough stand at room temperature for 30–50 minutes before assembling if the package directions specify that.

1. Divide bread dough into eight pieces and cover with kitchen towel; set aside.

2. In small skillet, melt butter over medium heat. Add onion, garlic, and bell pepper; cook and stir until tender, about 6 minutes. Remove from heat and beat into cream cheese in large bowl. Add Chicken Breasts, Havarti cheese, and parsley to cream cheese mixture.

3. Preheat oven to 400°F. Roll out each ball of dough to an 8-inch circle. Top with ½ cup of the chicken mixture. Fold dough over filling, making a half round. Seal edges and flute. In small bowl, combine egg with milk; brush over calzones.

4. Bake for 25–35 minutes or until calzones are browned and hot. Let cool on wire racks for 5 minutes, then serve.

Chicken Newburg

Chicken and shrimp combine in a delicious recipe flavored with cheese and onion.

EASILY DOUBLES

INGREDIENTS | SERVES 6

5 boneless, skinless chicken breasts
⅓ cup flour
1 teaspoon paprika
1 teaspoon salt
⅛ teaspoon pepper
3 tablespoons butter
1 onion, chopped
3 cloves garlic, minced
1 (12-ounce) can evaporated milk
1 (3-ounce) package cream cheese
1 teaspoon dried tarragon leaves
1 pound raw shrimp, shelled
2 tablespoons lemon juice
1 cup shredded Monterey jack cheese
1 cup shredded sharp Cheddar cheese
3 cups cooked long-grain rice

1. Cut chicken breasts into 1-inch pieces. On plate, combine flour, paprika, salt, and pepper. Toss chicken in this mixture to coat.

2. In large skillet, melt butter over medium heat. Add chicken; cook and stir until browned, about 4–5 minutes. Remove chicken from skillet.

3. Add onion and garlic to skillet; cook and stir to remove pan drippings. Add milk, cream cheese, and tarragon; cook and stir until cream cheese melts and sauce thickens.

4. Add shrimp, lemon juice, and chicken to skillet; cook and stir until shrimp curl and turn pink. Stir in cheeses; cook and stir until cheese melts. Serve over hot cooked rice.

Transport Tips

You should not partially cook meat and then chill or freeze it; this encourages the growth of bacteria. So it wouldn't be possible to partially cook this recipe and transport it. Prepare all of the ingredients: cube the chicken, shred the cheese, chop the onion and garlic, and transport everything in an ice chest to the party.

Pear Brie–Stuffed Chicken

Brie and pears combine in tender chicken rolls for an excellent stuffing.
The cereal and nut coating adds a crunchy crust.

MAKE AHEAD

INGREDIENTS | SERVES 6

6 boneless, skinless chicken breasts
1 teaspoon salt
⅛ teaspoon pepper
2 pears, peeled and chopped
2 tablespoons lemon juice
8 ounces Brie cheese, chopped
½ cup sour cream
2 eggs, beaten
1 cup corn flakes, crushed
½ cup ground walnuts
¼ cup flour
2 teaspoons dried thyme leaves
2 tablespoons butter
2 tablespoons olive oil

1. Place chicken breasts between sheets of waxed paper; pound until ¼ inch thick. Remove top sheet and sprinkle chicken with salt and pepper; set aside.

2. In medium bowl, combine pears, lemon juice, Brie, and sour cream and mix well. Divide among chicken. Roll up chicken, folding in sides, to enclose filling; secure with toothpicks.

3. Place eggs in shallow bowl; combine corn flakes, walnuts, flour, and thyme on plate. Dip chicken bundles in eggs, then in corn flake mixture, pressing to coat. Let stand on wire rack to 10 minutes, or refrigerate up to 4 hours.

4. Preheat oven to 375°F. Melt butter with oil in saucepan. Add chicken bundles; brown on all sides. Place in baking dish. Bake for 15–20 minutes until chicken is thoroughly cooked.

Chicken in Parchment

This healthy and delicious one-dish meal can be made with your favorite vegetables and cheese.

HEALTHY

INGREDIENTS | SERVES 8

2 (4-ounce) packages wild rice mix
2 tablespoons olive oil
1 onion, chopped
3 cloves garlic, minced
1 red bell pepper, chopped
1 cup chopped mushrooms
1 cup diced Havarti cheese
½ teaspoon salt
⅛ teaspoon pepper
8 boneless, skinless chicken breasts
1 teaspoon thyme
1 tablespoon grated lemon zest
¼ cup lemon juice
¼ cup chicken broth

Transport Tips

This dish can be easily transported. Just cook the rice, sauté the vegetables, and combine; let cool, then stir in cheese, salt, and pepper. Place in large bowl, cover, and refrigerate. Bring this mixture, foil, the chicken, lemon zest, juice, and chicken broth to the party; assemble the packets there and proceed with the recipe.

1. Cook rice mix as directed on package, using chicken broth in place of water; set aside.

2. In medium skillet, heat olive oil over medium heat. Add onion and garlic; cook and stir until tender, about 5 minutes. Stir in bell peppers and mushrooms; cook and stir for 3 minutes longer. Remove from heat and stir in rice mixture, then add cheese, salt, and pepper.

3. Preheat oven to 400°F. Tear off eight sheets of foil, 12" × 18". Divide rice mixture between foil sheets. Top each with a chicken breast. Sprinkle chicken breasts with thyme and lemon zest; rub into chicken.

4. Mix lemon juice and broth; drizzle over chicken. Fold up packets, using double folds in foil, leaving room for heat expansion.

5. Place packets on a jelly roll pan and bake for 20–30 minutes until chicken is thoroughly cooked. Remind guests to be careful of steam when opening packets.

Tuscan Chicken

A crispy seasoned bread and cheese topping helps keep the chicken moist as it bakes.

HEALTHY

INGREDIENTS | SERVES 6

6 boneless, skinless chicken breasts
1 teaspoon salt
⅛ teaspoon pepper
2 tomatoes
6 slices provolone cheese, cut in half
1 cup dry bread crumbs
¼ cup grated Parmesan cheese
3 tablespoons olive oil
3 cloves garlic, minced
1 teaspoon dried basil leaves
½ teaspoon dried oregano leaves
1 teaspoon dried thyme leaves
1 cup chicken broth

1. Preheat oven to 400°F. Place chicken breasts in 9" × 13" glass baking dish; sprinkle with salt and pepper.

2. Slice tomatoes. Place one half slice cheese on each chicken breast, then two tomato slices. Top with remaining cheese slices. In small bowl, combine remaining ingredients except broth and mix well; sprinkle over chicken. Pour chicken broth into pan around chicken.

3. Bake, covered, for 25 minutes. Then uncover chicken and bake for 15–20 minutes longer until chicken is thoroughly cooked. You can broil the chicken after cooking to brown the bread crumbs, if you'd like.

Stir-Fried Chicken Pizza

A stir-fried topping adds great flavor and texture to an unusual pizza.

EASY

INGREDIENTS | SERVES 6

3 boneless, skinless chicken breasts

1 teaspoon salt

⅛ teaspoon pepper

1 teaspoon dried marjoram leaves

2 tablespoons olive oil

1 onion, chopped

2 cloves garlic, minced

1 red bell pepper, chopped

¼ cup apple jelly

2 tablespoons mustard

¼ cup sour cream

1 focaccia bread or thick baked pizza crust

1 cup shredded Gouda cheese

½ cup shredded mozzarella cheese

3 tablespoons grated Parmesan cheese

1. Preheat oven to 425°F. Cut chicken into cubes and sprinkle with salt, pepper, and marjoram. Heat olive oil in large skillet; stir-fry chicken until done, about 5–6 minutes.

2. Remove chicken from skillet. Add onion and garlic; stir-fry until tender, about 4 minutes. Add red bell pepper; stir-fry for 2 minutes longer. Drain mixture, then add jelly, mustard, and sour cream. Remove from heat and stir to blend.

3. Spread onion mixture on focaccia bread; top with chicken. Sprinkle with cheeses. Bake for 12–17 minutes or until pizza is hot and cheese melts and begins to brown.

Party Fun

Have different types of pizza crust available, provide some toppings like the classic tomato sauce and pepperoni, this chicken mixture, and ground beef with Tex-Mex seasonings, and have yourself a pizza party. Let guests assemble their own masterpiece; all you have to do is bake them until done.

Savory Roast Chicken Dinner

*This one-dish meal is easily doubled or tripled to serve a crowd;
just use more roasting pans.*

EASILY DOUBLES

INGREDIENTS | SERVES 4

¼ cup salt

¼ cup sugar

2 quarts water

1 (3–4 pound) whole chicken

1 teaspoon salt

3 cloves garlic, minced

¼ teaspoon pepper

1 tablespoon fresh thyme leaves

2 teaspoons fresh oregano leaves

2 tablespoons olive oil

1 lemon, sliced

1 onion, quartered

3 sprigs fresh thyme

2 tablespoons butter, melted

1 (16-ounce) package baby carrots

3 russet potatoes, cubed

1 cup chicken broth

1. Brine chicken by combining ¼ cup salt, sugar, and water in large bowl. Add chicken and add a plate to keep the chicken under the brine. Refrigerate for 1–4 hours. Rinse the chicken, discarding brine, and pat it dry.

2. Preheat oven to 350°F. In small bowl, combine 1 teaspoon salt and garlic; rub into a paste. Add pepper, 1 tablespoon fresh thyme, oregano, and olive oil and mix well. Rub half of this mixture inside the chicken cavity, and the rest on top.

3. Stuff chicken with lemon, onion, and thyme sprigs. Brush melted butter on bottom of roasting pan. Place chicken on wire rack in roasting pan and surround with carrots and potatoes. Pour broth into pan.

4. Roast chicken and vegetables, uncovered, for 2 to 2½ hours, basting chicken occasionally with liquid in pan, until chicken is thoroughly cooked. Cover and let stand for 10 minutes before serving.

Potluck Bacon Chicken

*Fresh basil leaves along with bacon and cream cheese add fabulous
flavor to stuffed chicken rolls in this classic dish.*

EASILY DOUBLES

INGREDIENTS | SERVES 6

10 slices bacon

1 onion, chopped

4 cloves garlic, minced

6 boneless, skinless chicken breasts

½ teaspoon salt

⅛ teaspoon pepper

1 cup fresh basil leaves

2 (3-ounce) packages cream cheese, softened

1 cup sour cream, divided

1 teaspoon dried thyme leaves

1 (16-ounce) jar Alfredo sauce

1 (8-ounce) jar sliced mushrooms, drained

⅓ cup milk

Keep It Healthy

You can substitute low-fat cream cheese, nonfat sour cream, and low-fat Alfredo sauce for the regular versions in this delicious recipe. Turkey bacon would also be a lower-fat alternative than regular bacon. Add more vegetables to the sauce; some frozen thawed carrot slices or bell peppers add nutrition, color, and flavor.

1. Partially cook 6 slices of the bacon until much of the fat is rendered out but it is still pliable. Refrigerate. Drain fat, then cook remaining four slices of bacon until crisp. Drain bacon, crumble, and set aside.

2. Drain fat from skillet; do not wipe out. Add onion and garlic; cook and stir until tender, about 5 minutes.

3. Pound chicken breasts until ¼-inch thick. Sprinkle with salt and pepper, then cover chicken with a layer of basil leaves.

4. In medium bowl, beat cream cheese with ⅓ cup sour cream until smooth. Stir in crumbled crisp bacon and onion mixture. Spread this mixture over the basil leaves; roll up chicken and secure with toothpicks. Wrap partially cooked bacon around chicken.

5. Place chicken in baking dish. In same bowl, combine remaining ⅔ cup sour cream, thyme, Alfredo sauce, mushrooms, and milk. Pour over chicken.

6. Bake for 55–65 minutes or until chicken and bacon are thoroughly cooked. Serve over hot cooked couscous or rice.

Wendy's Chicken

*The combination of cranberries and Jarlsberg cheese
turns chicken into a gourmet dish. Yum.*

LAST MINUTE

INGREDIENTS | SERVES 6

2 pounds boneless, skinless
chicken breasts

3 tablespoons lemon juice

3 tablespoons flour

1 teaspoon salt

⅛ teaspoon white pepper

2 tablespoons butter

1 tablespoon olive oil

4 cloves garlic, minced

1½ cups heavy cream

1 cup shredded Jarlsberg cheese

¾ cup dried cranberries

2 teaspoons chopped fresh dill

Keep It Healthy

You can substitute 2 (12-ounce) cans
evaporated skim milk for the heavy cream
if you'd like, but you really have to use the
butter, olive oil, and Jarlsberg cheese for
this dish to work. Or substitute 1 (16-
ounce) jar reduced-fat Alfredo sauce for
the cream. But try it just once with the
real thing!

1. Cut each chicken breast into four pieces crosswise.
   Place on plate and toss with lemon juice; let stand for
   10 minutes, then drain. Combine flour, salt, and
   pepper and sprinkle over chicken pieces; toss to coat.

2. In large skillet, melt butter into olive oil over medium
   heat. Add garlic; cook for 2 minutes. Then add
   chicken; cook, stirring, for 6–8 minutes or until
   chicken is just done. Remove chicken from skillet and
   cover.

3. Add cream to skillet and turn heat to high. Simmer for
   6–7 minutes until cream is reduced, scraping bottom
   to loosen pan drippings. Stir in cheese and
   cranberries; cook and stir until cheese melts.

4. Return chicken to pan and heat (do not simmer) for
   1–2 minutes to blend sauce. Sprinkle with dill and
   serve immediately.

CHAPTER 8

Elegant Seafood Entrees

Salmon Cream Enchiladas

This mild dish is suitable for any crowd.
If your crowd likes it spicy, add chili powder and cayenne pepper to the tomato mixture.

EASILY DOUBLES

INGREDIENTS | SERVES 6

2 tablespoons olive oil
1 onion, chopped
2 cloves garlic, minced
1 (4-ounce) can chopped green chilies, undrained
1 cup salsa
1 (8-ounce) can tomato sauce
1 (12-ounce) pouch salmon, drained
1½ cups sour cream
1½ cups shredded Monterey jack cheese
8 (10-inch) flour tortillas
¼ cup grated Cotija cheese

1. Preheat oven to 350°F. In large saucepan, heat olive oil over medium heat. Add onion and garlic; cook and stir until tender, about 5 minutes. Add chilies, salsa, and tomato sauce; bring to a simmer.

2. Meanwhile, in medium bowl combine salmon, sour cream, and Monterey jack cheese.

3. Dip tortillas, one at a time, into tomato sauce and place on work surface. Top with a spoonful of the salmon mixture and roll up; place in baking dish.

4. Repeat with remaining sauce, tortillas, and filling. Pour the sauce over filled tortillas and sprinkle with Cotija cheese. Bake for 25–35 minutes.

Grilled Red Snapper with Fruit Salsa

Grilled fish has a delicious smoky flavor.
Top it with a cold fruit salsa for an easy and elegant recipe.

QUICK

INTRODUCTION | SERVES 6

1 cup raspberries
1 cup blueberries
1 cup chopped strawberries
¼ cup minced red onion
2 tablespoons lime juice
1 jalapeño pepper, minced
⅛ teaspoon cayenne pepper
6 red snapper fillets
2 tablespoons olive oil
1 teaspoon paprika
1 teaspoon dried thyme leaves
1 teaspoon salt
⅛ teaspoon pepper

1. In medium bowl, combine all berries with red onion, lime juice, jalapeño pepper, and cayenne pepper; mix gently, cover, and refrigerate. Salsa can be made up to 2 hours ahead.

2. When ready to cook, prepare and preheat grill. Rub fillets with olive oil. In small bowl, combine paprika, thyme, salt, and pepper; sprinkle over fish and rub in.

3. Grill fish over direct heat for 2–4 minutes per side, turning once, until fish flakes when tested with fork. Serve with fruit salsa.

Pecan-Crusted Fish Fillets

Pecans and bread crumbs make a crisp topping on
mild white fish fillets in this delicious recipe.

EASILY DOUBLES

INGREDIENTS | SERVES 6

¼ cup honey mustard
3 tablespoons butter, melted
1 cup chopped pecans
½ cup soft bread crumbs
1 teaspoon dried dill weed
2 tablespoons chopped fresh parsley
6 (6-ounce) orange roughy fillets
2 tablespoons lemon juice
½ teaspoon salt
⅛ teaspoon pepper

1. Preheat oven to 375°F. Grease a cookie sheet with rims with butter and set aside. In small bowl, combine honey mustard and butter. On shallow plate, combine pecans, bread crumbs, dill, and parsley.

2. Arrange fillets on prepared sheet and drizzle with lemon juice. Sprinkle with salt and pepper. Spread honey mustard mixture over fish, then top with pecan mixture, patting to coat.

3. Bake fish for 8–13 minutes or until fish flakes when tested with a fork. Serve immediately.

Potato Salmon Pie

This hearty pie is good for a cold winter night.
You can use leftover mashed potatoes; use about 4 cups.

INEXPENSIVE

INGREDIENTS | SERVES 8

2 tablespoons olive oil
1 onion, chopped
3 cloves garlic, minced
1 green bell pepper, chopped
1 cup frozen baby peas
1 (23-ounce) package refrigerated mashed potatoes
3 eggs, beaten
½ teaspoon salt
⅛ teaspoon pepper
½ cup grated Romano cheese
1 (14-ounce) can red salmon, drained and flaked
1 recipe Easy Paste Pastry (page 266)
2 tablespoons butter

1. Preheat oven to 350°F. In small skillet, heat olive oil over medium heat. Add onion and garlic; cook and stir until tender, about 5 minutes. Add bell pepper and peas; cook and stir until tender, about 4–5 minutes longer.

2. Place potatoes in a large bowl; beat in eggs, salt, pepper, and cheese. Add onion mixture and salmon. Place in pie crust. Top with second crust and cut slits in crust.

3. Place little pieces of the butter into the slits in the pie crust. Bake for 55–65 minutes until crust is brown. Let stand for 10 minutes, then slice to serve.

Shrimp Provençal

This easy meal, with a twist from France, is full of flavor and it's good for you too.

EASY

INTRODUCTION | SERVES 6

1 tablespoon olive oil
3 tablespoons butter
2 onions, chopped
4 cloves garlic, minced
1 (14-ounce) can diced tomatoes, undrained
1 (8-ounce) can tomato sauce
¼ cup dry sherry, if desired
½ teaspoon fennel seeds
1 teaspoon sugar
½ teaspoon salt
⅛ teaspoon cayenne pepper
1 teaspoon dried thyme leaves
1½ pounds raw medium shrimp, shelled
3 cups hot cooked brown rice
½ cup crumbled goat cheese

1. In large saucepan, combine olive oil and butter over medium heat. Add onion and garlic; cook and stir for 5–6 minutes until tender.

2. Add all remaining ingredients except shrimp, rice, and cheese. Bring to a simmer, stirring frequently. Reduce heat to low, partially cover, and simmer for 50 minutes, stirring occasionally.

3. Just before serving, stir in shrimp; cook and stir until shrimp curl and turn pink, about 3–4 minutes. Serve over rice and sprinkle with cheese.

Shrimp and Wild Rice Pilaf

Bacon and shrimp are natural partners.
Pair them with onion-flavored wild rice in a creamy sauce
and you have an easy and delicious main dish.

MAKE AHEAD

INTRODUCTION | SERVES 8

6 slices bacon

1 tablespoon butter

2 tablespoons olive oil

1 onion, chopped

1 leek, chopped

3 cloves garlic, minced

2 cups uncooked wild rice

4 cups chicken broth

1 (16-ounce) jar four-cheese Alfredo sauce

2 cups baby frozen peas

2 pounds medium frozen cooked shrimp, thawed

¼ cup grated Parmesan cheese

Transport Tips

To transport and serve, pack the baking dish with the rice mixture into a casserole holder or wrap it in newspaper. Keep the thawed shrimp in the original packaging, and package along with the bacon and cheese in a cooler. Then combine everything in the dish and bake when you arrive.

1. Spray a 9" × 13" glass baking dish with nonstick cooking spray and set aside. In large deep skillet, fry bacon until crisp. Drain bacon on paper towels, crumble, and refrigerate. Drain bacon fat from skillet; do not wipe out.

2. Add butter and olive oil to skillet and place over medium heat. Add onion, leek, and garlic; cook and stir until vegetables are tender, about 6 minutes. Add rice and chicken broth to skillet; bring to a simmer. Cover and simmer until rice is almost tender, about 30 minutes.

3. Stir in Alfredo sauce and peas. Transfer to prepared baking dish. At this point you can take the dish to the party or continue with the recipe.

4. Stir in shrimp and bacon and sprinkle with cheese. Bake at 400°F for 25–35 minutes or until casserole is bubbly and cheese is melted.

Shrimp Dijon in Phyllo

*To save money, if you'd like to double this recipe, use 1 pound of shrimp
and 1 pound fish fillets, cubed, and mix them in the filling.*

EASILY DOUBLES

INGREDIENTS | SERVES 6

2 tablespoons butter

1 leek, chopped

3 cloves garlic, minced

1 teaspoon salt

⅛ teaspoon white pepper

1 pound raw medium shrimp

2 tablespoons lemon juice

⅓ cup Dijon mustard

1 (13-ounce) can evaporated milk

½ cup heavy cream

16 (9" × 15") sheets frozen phyllo, thawed

⅓ cup butter, melted

Nonstick butter-flavored cooking spray

½ cup grated Parmesan cheese

1 egg, beaten

1 tablespoon milk

Transport Tips

To transport this recipe, you can prepare the bundles completely, then brush with some melted butter instead of the egg mixture. Place in a baking pan and refrigerate up to 12 hours. When you get to the party, place bundles on a cookie sheet and bake as directed, adding about 10 minutes to the baking time.

1. In large skillet, melt 2 tablespoons butter over medium heat. Add leek and garlic; sprinkle with salt and pepper. Cook and stir until tender, about 7–8 minutes. Add shrimp and lemon juice; cook and stir until shrimp curl and turn pink.

2. Remove shrimp from skillet and set aside. Add mustard, evaporated milk, and heavy cream to skillet. Simmer over low heat until sauce is reduced by half.

3. Layer 8 sheets of phyllo dough on top of each other, alternately brushing with melted butter and spraying with cooking spray. Sprinkle cheese over each layer. Repeat with remaining sheets of dough, butter, spray, and cheese.

4. Preheat oven to 425°F. Return shrimp to sauce. Spread in center of each phyllo stack. Roll up, folding in ends. Place, seam side down, on cookie sheet. Combine egg with milk and brush on bundles.

5. Bake for 18–23 minutes or until phyllo dough is golden brown. Let stand for 5 minutes, then slice each into three sections to serve.

Crab and Potato Au Gratin

Tender potatoes help stretch the crab meat in this luscious comforting dish.

MAKE AHEAD

INGREDIENTS | SERVES 6

3 tablespoons butter

1 onion, chopped

2 cloves garlic, minced

3 tablespoons flour

1 teaspoon salt

¼ teaspoon white pepper

1 teaspoon dried thyme leaves

2 cups whole milk

1 cup shredded Cheddar cheese

1 cup shredded Havarti cheese

4 potatoes, thinly sliced

¾ pound lump crab meat, picked over

1 cup soft bread crumbs

3 tablespoons butter, melted

¼ cup grated Parmesan cheese

1. Preheat oven to 400°F. Spray a 2-quart casserole dish with nonstick cooking spray. In large saucepan, melt 3 tablespoons butter. Cook onion and garlic until tender, about 6 minutes. Add flour, salt, pepper, and thyme; simmer for 3 minutes.

2. Add milk, all at once, and cook and stir until thickened. Add Cheddar and Havarti cheeses; remove from heat and stir until smooth.

3. Place ⅓ of the potatoes in prepared baking dish and season to taste, then top with half of the crab meat. Pour one-third of the sauce over all. Repeat layers, ending with potatoes, and cover with rest of sauce. Cover and bake for 1 hour.

4. In small bowl, combine crumbs with 3 tablespoons melted butter and Parmesan cheese. Uncover casserole, sprinkle with bread crumb mixture, and bake for 25–35 minutes longer until potatoes are tender and crumbs are browned.

Sweet and Sour Fish

This sauce is a delicious complement to salmon or tuna.
Serve over hot cooked rice or couscous flavored with onion.

INEXPENSIVE

INGREDIENTS | SERVES 6

2 tablespoons butter

1 onion, chopped

1 onion, sliced

3 cloves garlic, minced

⅓ cup apple cider vinegar

½ cup brown sugar

1-¼ cups chicken or fish stock

1 teaspoon salt

⅛ teaspoon pepper

1 tablespoon minced ginger root

½ cup raisins

3 gingersnaps, crumbled

1 red bell pepper, chopped

1 green bell pepper, chopped

6 (6-ounce) fillets salmon or tuna

1. In large saucepan, melt butter over medium heat. Add onions and garlic; cook and stir until tender, about 7–8 minutes. Add vinegar, brown sugar, chicken stock, salt, pepper, ginger root, and raisins; bring to a simmer.

2. Add gingersnaps and simmer until the cookies dissolve. Add bell peppers and stir; place salmon fillets in skillet.

3. Cover and simmer for 15–20 minutes or until salmon flakes when tested with a fork. Serve the fish fillets with the sauce.

Transport Tips

To make this dish and take it to the host's house, make the sauce ahead of time, up to adding the gingersnaps. Refrigerate until cold, then package with the bell peppers and salmon in a cooler. Take it to the party, then reheat the sauce until simmering. Add the peppers and fish and continue with the recipe.

Seafood Casserole

You can make this dish ahead of time right up the baking point and refrigerate it.
Add another 10–15 minutes to the baking time.

MAKE AHEAD

INGREDIENTS | SERVES 6

1 cup wild rice
½ cup brown rice
3 cups chicken broth
2 tablespoons butter
1 onion, chopped
1 red bell pepper, chopped
2 cloves garlic, minced
1 (15-ounce) jar four-cheese Alfredo sauce
1 (12-ounce) bag frozen raw shrimp, thawed
1 pound lump crabmeat
1 cup shredded Gouda cheese
2 tablespoons lemon juice
⅓ cup chopped fresh basil
¼ cup grated Parmesan cheese

1. In large saucepan, combine wild and brown rice with chicken broth. Bring to a simmer over medium heat, reduce heat, cover, and simmer for 35–40 minutes until almost tender.

2. Meanwhile, in another large saucepan melt butter over medium heat. Add onion, bell pepper, and garlic; cook and stir until tender, about 5 minutes. Add Alfredo sauce and bring to a simmer.

3. Add shrimp; cook and stir until shrimp curl and turn pink, about 4–5 minutes. Remove pan from heat. Preheat oven to 400°F.

4. Stir in rice mixture, crabmeat, Gouda cheese, lemon juice, and basil. Turn into 2-quart casserole and sprinkle with Parmesan cheese. Bake for 20–25 minutes or until hot.

Spanish Salmon Loaf

The flavors of Spain add interest and delicious taste to a simple salmon loaf.

INEXPENSIVE

INTRODUCTION | SERVES 6

2 tablespoons butter

1 onion, minced

1 cup diced celery

3 cloves garlic, minced

½ cup soft bread crumbs

1 egg

¼ cup buttermilk

½ teaspoon salt

1 teaspoon paprika

⅛ teaspoon cayenne pepper

½ cup ground almonds, divided

½ cup shredded Manchego cheese

1 (15-ounce) can salmon, drained

1 green bell pepper, chopped

1 (8-ounce) can tomato sauce

½ cup sliced green olives

¼ cup chopped parsley

Party Fun

Salmon loaf is an old-fashioned recipe that is universally popular. You can decorate this recipe with sliced olives and almonds; make several "flowers" using the olives as the centers and the almonds as the petals. Not only is this pretty, but it also gives a hint as to what the recipe contains.

1. Preheat oven to 350°F. Spray a 9" × 5" loaf pan with nonstick baking spray containing flour and set aside.

2. In large saucepan, melt butter over medium heat. Add onion, celery, and garlic; cook and stir until tender, about 6–7 minutes. Remove pan from heat, then remove ½ cup of this mixture and place in large bowl; let cool for 10 minutes.

3. Add bread crumbs, egg, buttermilk, salt, paprika, cayenne pepper, ⅓ cup ground almonds, and cheese to mixture in bowl and mix. Then add salmon and stir until combined. Pour into prepared loaf pan and sprinkle with remaining almonds. Bake for 45–55 minutes until set.

4. About 15 minutes before salmon is done, return saucepan to heat. Add bell pepper, tomato sauce, and olives; bring to a simmer. Simmer until salmon is done.

5. Let salmon loaf stand for 5 minutes, then slice to serve. Serve with the sauce and sprinkle with parsley.

Seafood Crab Bake

Cheesy, creamy potatoes line the baking dish and are
topped with fish fillets and a creamy crab sauce in this special recipe.

EASY

INGREDIENTS | SERVES 6

1 (24-ounce) package prepared mashed potatoes

1 cup sour cream

½ cup grated Parmesan cheese

¼ cup chopped chives

6 (5-ounce) sole fillets

2 tablespoons lemon juice

1 teaspoon salt

½ teaspoon paprika

⅛ teaspoon pepper

1 (15-ounce) jar four-cheese Alfredo sauce

1 pound lump crabmeat or imitation crab flakes

1 green bell pepper, chopped

1 red bell pepper, chopped

⅓ cup chopped green onions

⅓ cup grated Parmesan cheese

¼ cup chopped parsley

1. Preheat oven to 400°F. Spray a 9" × 13" baking dish with nonstick cooking spray. In large bowl, place potatoes. Add sour cream, ½ cup Parmesan cheese, and chives and mix well. Spread in bottom and 1 inch up the sides of prepared baking dish.

2. Top with sole fillets; sprinkle with lemon juice, salt, paprika, and pepper.

3. In same large bowl, combine Alfredo sauce with crabmeat and bell peppers; mix gently. Spoon over fillets in baking dish. Top with green onions and ⅓ cup Parmesan cheese.

4. Bake for 40–50 minutes or until potatoes are browned around edges and fish flakes when tested with fork. Sprinkle with parsley and serve.

Slow-Cooked Wild Rice and Salmon

Wild rice pilaf is slowly cooked in the slow cooker,
then salmon fillets are added at the end to steam to perfection.

EASILY DOUBLES

INGREDIENTS | SERVES 6

1 tablespoon olive oil

1 tablespoon butter

1 onion, chopped

3 cloves garlic, minced

4 cups chicken broth

1 teaspoon salt

⅛ teaspoon pepper

½ teaspoon dried oregano leaves

2 cups wild rice

1 (16-ounce) package baby carrots

½ cup heavy cream

1 cup sour cream

¼ cup Dijon mustard

1 teaspoon dried basil leaves

6 (5-ounce) salmon fillets

Keep It Safe

Make sure that you add the salmon to the slow cooker when you're already at the party. The wild rice mixture will keep quite well in the slow cooker, even if you have to travel an hour to get to the party. Just plug the cooker in and let it cook for about 30 minutes, add the salmon, and dinner will be ready in about an hour.

1. In large saucepan, combine olive oil and butter over medium heat. Add onion and garlic; cook and stir until tender, about 6 minutes. Add chicken broth, salt, pepper, and oregano and remove from heat.

2. Rinse wild rice and drain; place in 4- or 5-quart slow cooker. Top with baby carrots and pour chicken broth mixture over all. Cover and cook on low for 7–8 hours or until wild rice is tender. Stir mixture in slow cooker and add cream.

3. In small bowl, combine sour cream, mustard, and basil. Spread over salmon fillets. Place salmon in slow cooker, layering with the wild rice mixture. Cover and cook on low for 40–55 minutes or until salmon flakes when tested with fork. Serve salmon with wild rice mixture.

Shrimp and Salmon Penne

Salmon and avocados are so delicious and so good for you too.

HEALTHY

INGREDIENTS | SERVES 12

½ cup butter
1 onion, chopped
5 cloves garlic, minced
1 pound salmon fillet
1 (16-ounce) package penne pasta
1 pound medium raw shrimp
1 teaspoon salt
⅛ teaspoon white pepper
⅓ cup lemon juice
3 tablespoons chopped parsley
2 avocados, peeled and diced
½ cup grated Romano cheese

Keep It Healthy

Use whole wheat pasta for even more nutrition in this simple recipe. There are some types available now that taste basically like white pasta. If you're still unsure, use half white pasta and half whole wheat. With all the other flavors going on in this recipe, no one will notice the swap!

1. Bring a large pot of water to a boil. In large saucepan, melt butter over medium heat. Add onion and garlic; cook and stir until tender, about 5 minutes.

2. Add salmon to skillet; cover and cook for 5–6 minutes until salmon flakes. Remove salmon from pan and set aside; flake.

3. Add penne to boiling water and cook according to package directions. Meanwhile, add shrimp to skillet along with onion and garlic; cook and stir until pink, about 3–4 minutes. Return salmon to pan; sprinkle with salt and pepper.

4. Add lemon juice and parsley to skillet with salmon and shrimp. Drain pasta, reserving ⅓ cup cooking water. Add pasta to skillet along with enough cooking water to make a sauce; cook and stir for 2–3 minutes. Sprinkle with avocado and cheese; toss and serve immediately.

Shrimp-Stuffed Green Peppers

Bell peppers are usually stuffed with a mixture of vegetables.
Using shrimp instead elevates this to a company dish.

EASILY DOUBLES

INGREDIENTS | SERVES 6

6 large green bell peppers
2 tablespoons butter
1 onion, chopped
3 cloves garlic, minced
½ cup long-grain white rice
1 cup chicken broth
½ teaspoon salt
⅛ teaspoon pepper
1 teaspoon dried thyme leaves
1 pound medium raw shrimp
1 (10-ounce) container refrigerated Alfredo sauce
1 cup grated Swiss cheese
2 cups water

1. Preheat oven to 350°F. Cut tops from bell peppers and scoop out seeds and membranes.

2. In medium saucepan, melt butter over medium heat. Add onion and garlic; cook and stir for 3 minutes. Add rice; cook and stir for 2 minutes. Add chicken broth, salt, pepper, and thyme; bring to a simmer.

3. Cover and simmer for 20 minutes until rice is almost tender. Stir in shrimp; cook just until shrimp turn pink. Remove saucepan from heat and stir in Alfredo sauce and cheese.

4. Stuff bell peppers with this mixture and place in glass baking dish. Pour water around peppers. Bake for 40–50 minutes or until peppers are tender when pierced with a knife.

Crab and Fish Casserole

Use mild white fish fillets in this easy casserole; orange roughy or cod would be perfect.

EASY

INGREDIENTS | SERVES 6

2 tablespoons butter

1 onion, minced

3 cloves garlic, minced

1 (16-ounce) jar Alfredo sauce

½ pound fish fillets

3 tablespoons orange juice

½ cup ground almonds

1 cup shredded Havarti cheese

½ pound crab meat

1 cup soft whole wheat bread crumbs

3 tablespoons grated Parmesan cheese

3 tablespoons butter, melted

Make It Ahead

This is an ideal casserole to make ahead of time. Prepare it through Step 3, then cover and refrigerate. Make the bread crumb and cheese topping and place in small plastic bag; refrigerate. Transport the casserole to the party in a cooler packed with ice, then sprinkle with the topping and bake, adding 10–15 minutes to the baking time.

1. Preheat oven to 350°F. Spray a 2-quart baking dish with nonstick cooking spray and set aside.

2. In large saucepan, melt butter over medium heat. Add onion and garlic; cook and stir for 5 minutes, until tender. Add Alfredo sauce and bring to a simmer. Add fish fillets; simmer for 4–5 minutes until fish flakes. Stir to break up fish.

3. Stir in orange juice and almonds and remove from heat. Add Havarti cheese and crab meat. Pour into casserole.

4. In small bowl, combine bread crumbs, Parmesan cheese, and 3 tablespoons melted butter; mix well. Sprinkle over casserole. Bake for 30–40 minutes until bread crumbs brown. Serve immediately.

Salmon Soufflé

A soufflé is always a wonderful party dish.
You could use tuna or shrimp or plain cooked fish fillets in place of the salmon if you'd like.

HEALTHY

INGREDIENTS | SERVES 6

5 tablespoons butter, divided

2 tablespoons grated Parmesan cheese

1 onion, chopped

3 cloves garlic, minced

¼ cup flour

½ teaspoon salt

⅛ teaspoon pepper

¼ cup orange juice

1¾ cups milk

3 egg yolks, beaten

1½ cups grated Swiss cheese

2 (12-ounce) pouches salmon, drained

1 cup frozen baby peas, thawed

2 tablespoons chopped parsley

3 egg whites

½ teaspoon cream of tartar

Party Fun

You could make this recipe in small ramekins or custard cups for individual servings. This could be a first course, or a main dish. Prepare the ramekins just as you would the soufflé dish. Bake at 375°F for 25–30 minutes or until the little soufflés are puffed and golden brown. These will wait a few minutes for guests.

1. Preheat oven to 375°F. Grease a 2-quart soufflé dish with 1 tablespoon butter and sprinkle with Parmesan cheese; set aside.

2. In large saucepan, melt remaining ¼ cup butter over medium heat. Add onion and garlic; cook and stir until tender, about 5 minutes. Add flour, salt, and pepper; cook and stir until bubbly, about 4 minutes.

3. Add orange juice and milk; cook and stir until thick. Stir a small amount of the hot milk mixture into egg yolks; return egg yolk mixture to pan. Cook and stir for 2 minutes.

4. Remove from heat and stir in cheese, salmon, peas, and parsley. In large bowl, beat egg whites with cream of tartar until stiff peaks form. Fold into salmon mixture and pour into prepared dish.

5. Bake for 45–50 minutes or until soufflé is puffed and golden brown. Serve immediately.

Apple-Poached Fish

Delicate fish is poached in apple juice, then the juice is used to make a cheese sauce that tops the fish and is broiled until golden.

EASILY DOUBLES

INGREDIENTS | SERVES 6

2 tablespoons olive oil

⅓ cup minced peeled apple

2 shallots, minced

3 cloves garlic, minced

6 (5-ounce) halibut or cod fillets

1 teaspoon salt

¼ teaspoon pepper

1 cup apple juice

2 tablespoons lemon juice

2 tablespoons cornstarch

½ cup heavy cream

½ cup shredded Swiss cheese

2 tablespoons grated Parmesan cheese

2 tablespoons ground walnuts

1. Preheat oven to 350°F. In a large ovenproof skillet, heat 2 tablespoons olive oil over medium heat. Add apple, shallots, and garlic; cook for 4 minutes. Sprinkle fish with salt and pepper and place in skillet.

2. Pour apple and lemon juices into skillet and bring to a simmer. Place skillet in oven and bake for 8 minutes, or until fish is just done. Remove skillet from oven. Remove fish from skillet and place on broiler pan. Turn oven to broil.

3. Return skillet on medium heat. In small bowl combine cornstarch and cream; stir into mixture in skillet and simmer until thickened. Stir in Swiss cheese and remove from heat.

4. Spoon sauce over fish and sprinkle with Parmesan cheese and walnuts. Broil for 2–3 minutes until cheese sauce bubbles and begins to brown. Serve immediately.

Breaded Walleye

You could use any mild white fish in place of the walleye:
flounder, cod, or orange roughy would work well.

EASY

INGREDIENTS | SERVES 6

6 (6-ounce) walleye fillets
1 teaspoon salt
1 teaspoon pepper
½ cup chicken broth
½ cup butter
1 onion, minced
3 cloves garlic, minced
2 tablespoons lemon juice
2 cups soft bread crumbs
¼ cup grated Parmesan cheese
2 tablespoons minced fresh dill

1. Preheat oven to 350°F. Place fish fillets on a baking dish and sprinkle with salt and pepper. Pour chicken broth into bottom of pan around fillets; set aside.

2. In medium saucepan, melt butter over medium heat. Add onion and garlic; cook and stir until tender, about 5–6 minutes. Remove from heat and stir in lemon juice. Then add bread crumbs, cheese, and dill.

3. Pat topping on the fillets to cover the top completely. Bake for 15–20 minutes until topping is golden brown and fish flakes when tested with fork. Serve immediately.

Keep It Healthy

Butter isn't bad for you—it contains vitamins and minerals and has no artificial trans fat. But if you would rather not use it, use ½ cup olive oil instead. The taste will be a bit different, but the topping consistency and final product will still be delicious. Or think about using half butter and half olive oil.

Hazelnut Crab Cakes

These crab cakes have a wonderful texture because of the hazelnuts;
which are a healthy nut.

EASILY DOUBLES

INGREDIENTS | SERVES 6

2 tablespoons butter
1 onion, finely chopped
3 cloves garlic, minced
1 cup ground hazelnuts, divided
½ cup dry bread crumbs, divided
2 eggs
3 tablespoons sour cream
2 tablespoons Dijon mustard
½ teaspoon Old Bay seasoning
½ teaspoon salt
⅛ teaspoon pepper
2 (6-ounce) cans crabmeat, drained
⅓ cup peanut oil

1. In large skillet, melt butter over medium heat. Add onion and garlic; cook and stir until very tender, about 7–8 minutes. Remove from heat and scrape mixture into a large bowl. Do not wipe out skillet.

2. Add ⅓ cup hazelnuts and 2 tablespoons bread crumbs to the onion mixture. Beat in eggs, sour cream, Dijon mustard, Old Bay, salt, and pepper until mixed. Stir in crab.

3. Chill mixture for 2–3 hours, then form into 8 patties. On plate, combine remaining hazelnuts and bread crumbs. Coat crab cakes in this mixture.

4. Heat oil in same skillet over medium-high heat. Sauté crab cakes for 3–5 minutes on each side, turning once, until crisp. Serve immediately.

Pesto Orange Roughy Packets

*These delicious packets can be made ahead of time, refrigerated,
and then baked when you want to eat.*

MAKE AHEAD

INGREDIENTS | SERVES 8

2 lemons, thinly sliced

8 (6-ounce) orange roughy fillets

1 teaspoon salt

⅛ teaspoon pepper

2 (3.5-ounce) small jars basil pesto

¼ cup mayonnaise

2 tablespoons lemon juice

⅓ cup grated Romano cheese

1 red onion, finely chopped

2 tomatoes, sliced

2 yellow summer squash, thinly sliced

Keep It Safe

Whenever you cook anything in a packet of
parchment paper or foil, heat and steam
builds up inside, and stays inside because
of the folds. So when the packet is opened,
a lot of steam will come streaming out.
Warn your guests to be careful of this
steam so they don't burn themselves.

1. Preheat oven to 400°F. Tear off eight 12" × 18" sheets of parchment paper and fold in half; crease edge and unfold.

2. Place lemon slices near center crease and top with fish fillets; sprinkle with salt and pepper. In small bowl, combine pesto, mayonnaise, lemon juice, and cheese and mix well.

3. Spread pesto mixture over fish fillets. Top with red onion, sliced tomatoes, and squash.

4. Fold top half of parchment over food. Seal by crimping the edges together. Place packets on two baking sheets. Bake for 16–22 minutes, rotating the sheets once during baking time, until fish is cooked.

CHAPTER 9

Healthy Vegetarian Choices

Oven Omelet

*This recipe can be served as the main dish for a Sunday brunch,
or as the centerpiece for a vegetarian luncheon.*

INEXPENSIVE

INGREDIENTS | SERVES 6–8

3 tablespoons butter, melted
18 eggs
1 teaspoon salt
⅛ teaspoon pepper
1 cup sour cream
1 cup whole milk
2 tablespoons Dijon mustard
1½ cups shredded Colby cheese
¼ cup grated Parmesan cheese

1. Preheat oven to 325°F. Pour melted butter into a 9" × 13" glass baking dish and spread on the bottom.

2. In large bowl, combine eggs with salt, pepper, and sour cream; beat with egg beater until mixed. Add milk and mustard and beat until blended.

3. Stir in Colby cheese and pour into prepared pan. Sprinkle with Parmesan cheese and bake for 35–45 minutes until eggs are puffed, set, and lightly browned.

Pierogies Casserole

*Pierogies are like large ravioli, usually stuffed with a seasoned potato mixture.
They're hearty and healthy, and easy to cook.*

EASY

INGREDIENTS | SERVES 8

2 (20-ounce) packages frozen vegetarian pierogies
1 (16-ounce) jar pasta sauce
1 (16-ounce) jar four-cheese Alfredo sauce
1 cup shredded mozzarella cheese
1 cup shredded Cheddar cheese

1. Preheat oven to 375°F. In 3-quart casserole, place pierogies. Pour over pasta sauce, then Alfredo sauce. Sprinkle with cheeses.

2. Cover with foil and bake for 45 minutes. Uncover and bake for 15–25 minutes longer until pierogies are hot and tender and cheese is melted and begins to brown.

Bean Bake

Baked beans can be baked again with no loss in flavor or texture.
The edamame, or soybeans, add an extra texture dimension to this dish.

HEALTHY

INGREDIENTS | SERVES 6

2 (28-ounce) cans baked beans, undrained

¼ cup molasses

1 onion, diced

4 cloves garlic, minced

1 (16-ounce) package frozen edamame, thawed

1 (15-ounce) can kidney beans, drained

½ cup ketchup

¼ cup chili sauce

¼ cup brown sugar

¼ cup Dijon mustard

⅛ teaspoon pepper

1. Preheat oven to 350°F. In 2½-quart baking dish, combine all ingredients and mix well.

2. Bake, covered, for 1 hour. Uncover, stir mixture, and bake for 50–60 minutes longer until mixture is thickened, hot, and bubbly.

Keep It Healthy

Make sure that the baked beans you use are labeled "vegetarian," especially if you're serving this as a vegetarian main dish. Read the label carefully to ensure that no animal products are used in the cans. Vegetarian baked beans are usually spicier than those made with pork or bacon to make up for that flavor loss.

Veggie Tacos

You can use your favorite frozen vegetable combo in this super-easy recipe.
Keep these ingredients on hand in case a recipe doesn't work and you need a quick substitute.

EASY

INGREDIENTS | SERVES 4–6

1 tablespoon olive oil

1 onion, chopped

1 (16-ounce) package stir-fry vegetables

1 (15-ounce) can black beans, drained

1 cup salsa

¼ cup tomato paste

8 crisp taco shells

½ cup sour cream

1 (4-ounce) can green chilies

1½ cups shredded pepper jack cheese

1. Preheat oven to 350°F. In large skillet, heat olive oil over medium heat. Add onion; cook and stir for 5 minutes. Add vegetables; cook and stir for another 4–5 minutes until vegetables are hot.

2. Add black beans, salsa, and tomato paste; bring to a simmer. Simmer for 4–5 minutes.

3. Place taco shells on cookie sheet and bake for 7–9 minutes until crisp. In small bowl, combine sour cream, chilies, and cheese.

4. Let guests assemble their own tacos using vegetable mixture, taco shells, and sour cream mixture.

Moussaka

Classic Moussaka is made vegetarian by using meatless protein crumbles instead of ground beef.

HEALTHY

INGREDIENTS | SERVES 10

2 eggplants, peeled
1 teaspoon salt
2 tablespoons olive oil
2 onions, chopped
4 cloves garlic, minced
1 (12-ounce) package meatless crumbles
1 (6-ounce) can tomato paste
1 (8-ounce) can tomato sauce
1 teaspoon dried oregano leaves
½ teaspoon cinnamon
1 teaspoon dried basil leaves
½ teaspoon salt
2 tablespoons butter
2 tablespoons flour
½ teaspoon salt
⅛ teaspoon white pepper
1½ cups milk
½ cup sour cream
2 eggs
1 cup grated Romano cheese
¼ cup grated Parmesan cheese
¼ cup dried bread crumbs

1. Slice eggplant ½ inch thick and sprinkle with salt. Let stand while preparing rest of recipe.

2. In large saucepan heat 2 tablespoons olive oil over medium heat. Add onions and garlic; cook and stir until tender, about 5 minutes. Stir in tomato paste and let brown for a few minutes. Stir in tomato sauce, oregano, cinnamon, basil, and ½ teaspoon salt; simmer over low heat for 30 minutes.

3. For cream sauce, in medium saucepan heat 2 tablespoons butter over medium heat. Add flour, ½ teaspoon salt, and white pepper; cook and stir until bubbly. Add milk and sour cream; cook and stir until thick. Remove from heat and beat in eggs and Romano cheese.

4. Rinse eggplant, pat dry, and broil for 7–8 minutes, turning once, until browned. Spray a 9" × 13" glass baking dish with nonstick cooking spray. Place a layer of eggplant in bottom, top with tomato sauce, and remaining eggplant.

5. Preheat oven to 350°F. Pour cream sauce over eggplants and top with a mixture of Parmesan cheese and bread crumbs. Bake for 40–50 minutes until top is golden brown. Cool for 10 minutes, then cut into squares to serve.

Eggs Emily in Puff Pastry

This elegant dish is totally made ahead of time.
All you have to do is assemble it and bake. It's perfect for a fancy brunch.

MAKE AHEAD

INGREDIENTS | SERVES 6

1 package puff pastry shells

8 eggs, beaten

1 (10-ounce) package refrigerated Alfredo sauce

2 tablespoons butter

1 cup shredded Havarti cheese

1 tablespoon olive oil

2 shallots, minced

3 tomatoes, chopped

½ teaspoon salt

⅛ teaspoon pepper

¼ cup chopped parsley

⅓ cup grated Parmesan cheese

Make-Ahead Tips

You can partially bake puff pastry ahead of time, cool it, then store it at room temperature to be filled and baked later. Since this preliminary baking is just to set the dough, the pastry will still be nice and flaky. Be sure to cook the eggs just until they're set. And then serve these little puffs right out of the oven.

1. Thaw and bake the pastry shells according to the package directions, except bake for 4 minutes less. Remove and cool on wire rack.

2. In large bowl, beat eggs with ½ cup Alfredo sauce. Melt butter·in large saucepan; add eggs and cook until just set but still moist.

3. Remove from heat and stir in remaining Alfredo sauce. Place in greased casserole dish and sprinkle with Havarti cheese. Cover and chill until ready to eat.

4. In small saucepan, heat olive oil over medium heat. Add shallots and tomatoes; sprinkle with salt and pepper. Cook, stirring, over medium heat until tender. Remove from heat and stir in parsley; chill until ready to eat.

5. Preheat oven to 400°F. Stir egg mixture gently until combined. Put a spoonful of the tomato mixture into each puff pastry shell and fill with egg mixture. Top with more tomato mixture and sprinkle with Parmesan cheese. Bake for 12–18 minutes until eggs are hot.

Cheese and Rice Soufflé

The rice helps give the soufflé structure so it won't fall as quickly as one made without.
This delicious recipe is easy to make too.

INEXPENSIVE

INGREDIENTS | SERVES 6

2 tablespoons grated Parmesan cheese
¼ cup butter
1 chopped onion
3 cloves garlic, minced
¼ cup flour
½ teaspoon salt
1 teaspoon dried basil leaves
⅛ teaspoon white pepper
1½ cups whole milk
5 eggs, separated
2 cups grated Colby cheese
1½ cups cooked cold rice
1 cup frozen baby peas, thawed
½ teaspoon cream of tartar

1. Preheat oven to 350°F. Grease the bottom only of a 2½-quart soufflé dish with unsalted butter; sprinkle with Parmesan cheese and set aside.

2. In large saucepan, melt butter over medium heat. Add onion and garlic; cook and stir until tender, about 6 minutes.

3. Add flour, salt, basil, and pepper; cook and stir until bubbly. Add milk and cook until thickened. Beat in egg yolks, one at a time, then add Colby cheese; stir until melted.

4. Remove from heat and add rice and peas; stir gently and set aside.

5. In medium bowl, combine egg whites with cream of tartar; beat until stiff peaks form. Stir a dollop into the rice mixture to lighten, then carefully fold in remaining egg whites.

6. Pour into prepared soufflé dish. Bake for 50–60 minutes or until soufflé is puffed and golden brown. Serve immediately.

Black-Eyed Pea Salad

This elegant salad can be served as the main dish for a vegetarian lunch along with some hot corn bread straight from the oven.

EASY

INGREDIENTS | SERVES 8

3 (15-ounce) cans black-eyed peas, drained
1 red onion, chopped
1 red bell pepper, chopped
1 yellow bell pepper, chopped
1 green bell pepper, chopped
2 cloves garlic, minced
½ cup honey mustard
½ cup honey mustard salad dressing
½ cup plain yogurt
¼ cup extra-virgin olive oil
¼ teaspoon salt
⅛ teaspoon pepper
½ teaspoon dried tarragon leaves

1. Rinse the peas and drain well. Combine in large bowl with onion, bell peppers, and garlic; toss gently and set aside.

2. In small bowl, combine remaining ingredients and mix well with wire whisk until blended. Pour over pea mixture and stir gently to coat. Cover and chill for 4–5 hours before serving.

Keep It Healthy

Black-eyed peas are legumes, just like kidney beans, chickpeas, and black beans. They provide incomplete protein, that is, they don't have all of the amino acids our bodies need. So serve it with another grain, like rice or corn bread, to make complete proteins. The hot corn bread is the perfect foil to the cool and creamy salad.

Black Bean Pizza

Think of this pizza as a big open taco, and top it with sliced avocados, sour cream, salsa, and chopped tomatoes. Yum.

INEXPENSIVE

INGREDIENTS | SERVES 12

2 tablespoons olive oil

1 onion, chopped

3 cloves garlic, minced

2 jalapeño peppers, minced

1 tablespoon chili powder

½ teaspoon ground cumin

½ teaspoon salt

¼ teaspoon cayenne pepper

1 (15-ounce) can refried beans

½ cup sour cream

1 cup salsa

2 Classic Pizza Crusts (page 70), prebaked

2 (15-ounce) cans black beans, drained

1½ cups shredded pepper jack cheese

2 plum tomatoes, diced

2 cups shredded Cheddar cheese

1. Preheat oven to 400°F. In large saucepan, heat olive oil over medium heat. Add onion, garlic, and jalapeños; cook and stir for 5–6 minutes until tender.

2. Add chili powder, cumin, salt, cayenne pepper, refried beans, and sour cream and salsa; bring to a simmer. Remove from heat.

3. Spread the refried bean mixture over the prebaked Crusts. Top each Crust with a can of rinsed and drained black beans, then sprinkle with pepper jack cheese, tomatoes, and Cheddar cheese.

4. Bake for 20–30 minutes or until cheese is melted and browned. Cut into wedges to serve.

Make It Easy

Instead of using a homemade pizza crust, you can buy commercial dough from a pizza parlor, use frozen bread dough, thawed and rolled out to 12-inch circles, or the canned pizza dough in the refrigerated section of the supermarket. You could also use those thick pizza crusts topped with cheese and seasonings.

Rice and Spinach Quiche

A quiche is welcome at any type of party. It's even good at room temperature!
But be sure to follow the 2-hour rule; eat it or refrigerate within 2 hours.

LAST MINUTE

INGREDIENTS | SERVES 8

1 tablespoon olive oil

1 tablespoon butter

1 onion, chopped

3 cloves garlic, minced

1 red bell pepper, chopped

1 cup cooked brown rice

1 (10-ounce) package frozen spinach, thawed and drained

4 eggs

1 cup sour cream

2 tablespoons Dijon mustard

½ teaspoon dried dill weed

1 cup shredded Swiss cheese

1 Make-Ahead Pie Crust (page 251)

1 cup shredded Gouda cheese

3 tablespoons grated Asiago cheese

1. Preheat oven to 375°F. In medium saucepan, heat olive oil and butter over medium heat. Add onion, garlic, and bell pepper; cook and stir until crisp-tender, about 5 minutes.

2. Add rice and spinach; cook and stir until moisture from spinach evaporates. Remove from heat and let cool for 15 minutes.

3. In large bowl, beat eggs with sour cream, mustard, and dill. Place Swiss cheese in bottom of Pie Crust. Top with rice mixture, then Gouda cheese.

4. Pour egg mixture into Crust, then top with Asiago cheese. Bake for 30–35 minutes or until quiche is puffed and top is golden brown.

Potluck Chickpea Curry

Cauliflower and curry powder is one of the best anticancer combinations in the food world. And it's delicious!

HEALTHY

INGREDIENTS | SERVES 6

1 onion, chopped

4 cloves garlic, minced

2 tablespoons minced ginger root

1 tablespoon curry powder

2 tablespoons olive oil

1 head cauliflower, cut into florets

½ teaspoon salt

⅛ teaspoon cayenne pepper

⅓ cup water

1 (14.5-ounce) can diced tomatoes, drained

1 (15-ounce) can chickpeas, drained

½ cup coconut milk

Keep It Healthy

Coconut milk sounds rich and decadent, but it's actually quite good for you. The oil in coconut milk is made up of medium-chain fatty acids, which the body burns easily for energy, so it doesn't accumulate in fat cells. This healthy recipe would be just as good without the coconut milk if you want to leave it out.

1. In large skillet over medium heat, cook onion, garlic, ginger root, and curry powder in olive oil for 4–5 minutes.

2. Add cauliflower, salt, pepper, and water. Bring to a simmer, cover, reduce heat to low, and simmer for 5–8 minutes until cauliflower is crisp-tender.

3. Add tomatoes, chickpeas, and coconut milk and bring back to a simmer. Simmer, uncovered, stirring frequently, for 5–8 minutes until mixture is blended.

Pesto Pasta Skillet

This super-easy skillet meal cooks the pasta right in the pan,
so you don't have to boil extra water to cook it.

LAST MINUTE

INGREDIENTS | SERVES 6

2 tablespoons olive oil

1 onion, chopped

2 cloves garlic, minced

1 red bell pepper, chopped

2¼ cups vegetable broth

1½ cups uncooked orzo pasta

1 cup sliced baby spinach leaves

4 plum tomatoes, chopped

½ cup basil pesto

½ cup grated Asiago cheese

Party Fun

This excellent and quick skillet recipe depends on small pasta, which cooks more quickly than larger thicker pasta like farfalle or gemelli. You could also use small shell pasta or alphabet pasta. Make several pans of this recipe for a vegetarian potluck; add different vegetables and cheeses to each.

1. In large skillet, heat olive oil over medium heat. Add onion and garlic; cook and stir until tender, about 6 minutes.

2. Add bell pepper and vegetable broth; bring to a boil. Stir in orzo; bring to a simmer. Cover and simmer for 8 minutes, stirring occasionally.

3. Uncover and add spinach and tomatoes; simmer for 3 minutes. Stir in pesto and cheese; remove from heat, cover, and let stand for 5 minutes. Stir and serve.

Barley Mushroom Casserole

Barley is a delicious, nutty, and mild grain that's very healthy.
Cooked with vegetables, it makes an excellent vegetarian main dish or side dish for grilled meats.

EASY

INGREDIENTS | SERVES 6

2 tablespoons butter
1 onion, chopped
3 cloves garlic, minced
2 cups sliced cremini mushrooms
1 cup sliced button mushrooms
1½ cups pearl barley
½ cup chopped celery
1 teaspoon salt
¼ teaspoon pepper
1 teaspoon dried thyme leaves
3½ cups vegetable broth
¼ cup chopped flat-leaf parsley
½ cup grated Parmesan cheese

1. Preheat oven to 350°F. Spray a 2½-quart casserole with nonstick cooking spray and set aside.

2. In large saucepan, melt butter over medium heat. Add onion and garlic; cook and stir until crisp-tender, about 4 minutes. Add mushrooms; cook and stir for 4 minutes longer.

3. Add barley; cook and stir for 5–6 minutes, stirring, until barley is lightly browned. Add celery, salt, pepper, thyme, and broth and bring to a simmer.

4. Pour mixture into casserole, cover, and bake for 50–65 minutes until barley is tender. Mix in chopped parsley and cheese and serve.

Cheese and Tomato Manicotti

This decadent and elegant dish is perfect for a main-dish vegetarian option.

MAKE AHEAD

INGREDIENTS | SERVES 8

1 cup part-skim ricotta cheese

1 cup mascarpone cheese

1 (3-ounce) package cream cheese, softened

1 egg, beaten

1 teaspoon dried Italian seasoning

¼ teaspoon white pepper

1 cup shredded part-skim mozzarella cheese

1 cup shredded provolone cheese

6 plum tomatoes, seeded and chopped

¼ cup chopped flat-leaf parsley

14 uncooked manicotti shells

1 (32-ounce) jar pasta sauce

1 (14.5-ounce) can diced tomatoes, undrained

⅓ cup grated Parmesan cheese

¼ cup grated Asiago cheese

Make-Ahead Tips

The pasta shells have to sit a while in the sauce to soften before baking, which is why the completed casserole is refrigerated for several hours. It's also easier to stuff uncooked manicotti! Those limp cooked noodles can be hard to handle. You can use a small iced-tea spoon to stuff the pasta, or put the filling in a pastry bag and use that.

1. In large bowl, combine ricotta, mascarpone, and cream cheese; beat until smooth and combined. Beat in egg, Italian seasoning, and pepper.

2. Add mozzarella, provolone, tomatoes, and parsley. Using a small spoon, stuff the manicotti shells with cheese mixture.

3. Spread 1 cup pasta sauce in bottom of 9" × 13" glass baking dish. Top with stuffed manicotti. Add tomatoes to remaining pasta sauce in jar and mix well; pour over manicotti.

4. Cover and chill for 8–12 hours. When ready to eat, preheat oven to 350°F. Bake the manicotti, covered, for 55 minutes. Uncover and sprinkle with Parmesan and Asiago cheese; bake for 15–25 minutes longer until manicotti is tender when tested with fork.

Black Bean Lasagna

No one will miss the meat in this rich and indulgent casserole.
It feeds a crowd easily.

MAKE AHEAD

INGREDIENTS | SERVES 12

2 tablespoons olive oil

1 onion, chopped

4 cloves garlic, minced

2 jalapeño peppers, minced

1 (15-ounce) can refried beans

2 (15-ounce) cans black beans, drained, divided

1 tablespoon chili powder

½ teaspoon cumin

¼ teaspoon cayenne pepper

1 cup sour cream

1 cup part-skim ricotta cheese

1 (4-ounce) can diced green chilies, drained

2 cups vegetable broth

3 cups salsa

12 dry lasagna noodles

2 cups shredded part-skim mozzarella cheese

½ cup grated Cotija cheese

1. In large skillet, heat olive oil over medium heat. Add onion, garlic, and jalapeño peppers; cook and stir until tender, about 6 minutes. Add refried beans, 1 can of black beans, chili powder, cumin, and cayenne pepper; simmer for 3 minutes.

2. Meanwhile, in medium bowl combine sour cream, ricotta cheese, green chilies, and remaining can of black beans; mix gently.

3. Combine broth and salsa in another bowl and mix. Place ½ cup broth mixture in bottom of greased 13" × 9" glass baking dish. Top with four of the lasagna noodles, one-third of the refried bean mixture, one-third of the sour cream mixture, and one-third of the mozzarella cheese. Repeat layers. Pour remaining salsa mixture over all.

4. Cover casserole and refrigerate for 12–24 hours. When ready to eat, preheat oven to 350°F. Bake for 1½ hours, then uncover and sprinkle with Cotija cheese. Bake for 10–15 minutes longer until casserole is bubbly and pasta is tender. Let stand for 15 minutes, then serve.

Sweet Potato Enchiladas

*Sweet potatoes add great flavor, nutrition, and fiber to
these wholesome and delicious enchiladas.*

MAKE AHEAD

INGREDIENTS | SERVES 8

2 tablespoons olive oil

1 onion, chopped

3 cloves garlic, minced

2 jalapeño peppers, minced

1 (15-ounce) can refried beans

1 tablespoon chili powder

1 teaspoon ground cumin

½ teaspoon salt

⅛ teaspoon pepper

3 tablespoons Dijon mustard

1 (20-ounce) can sweet potatoes,
drained and chopped

1½ cups salsa, divided

12 (10-inch) flour tortillas

2½ cups shredded Cheddar cheese,
divided

1 (18-ounce) can enchilada sauce

Transport Tips

This casserole is best baked at the party so
it can be served piping hot. If you're the
guest, make sure that the host knows that
you need a 375°F oven to finish your contri-
bution. Cover it well, using toothpicks or
wire picks to hold the foil away from the
dish, and bring the cheese along in a separate bag.

1. In large skillet, heat olive oil over medium heat. Add onions, garlic, and jalapeño pepper; cook and stir until tender, about 6 minutes.

2. Add refried beans, chili powder, cumin, salt, pepper, and mustard; bring to a simmer. Add sweet potatoes and ½ cup salsa and remove from heat.

3. Place tortillas on work surface. Divide sweet potato mixture among them; top each with 2 tablespoons Cheddar cheese. Roll up, enclosing filling.

4. Combine remaining 1 cup salsa with enchilada sauce and mix well. Place ½ cup in 13" × 9" glass baking dish. Top with enchiladas, then pour remaining sauce over. Cover and chill for 12–24 hours in refrigerator.

5. When ready to eat, preheat oven to 375°F. Uncover and top with remaining 1 cup Cheddar cheese. Bake for 45–55 minutes until casserole is hot and bubbling.

Greek Pasta Salad

White balsamic vinegar and Worcestershire sauce are used to keep the dressing light colored, so the colors of the food shine through.

MAKE AHEAD

INGREDIENTS | SERVES 8

1 clove garlic, peeled
½ teaspoon salt
¼ cup olive oil
2 tablespoons lemon juice
2 tablespoons white balsamic vinegar
1 teaspoon white Worcestershire sauce
½ teaspoon dried oregano
⅛ teaspoon white pepper
2 cups orzo pasta
2 cups sliced spinach
2 cups canned cannellini beans, drained
1 red bell pepper, chopped
¼ cup sliced green onion
½ cup minced red onion
4 plum tomatoes, seeded and chopped
½ cup crumbled blue cheese
1 cup walnut pieces, toasted
¼ cup grated Asiago cheese

1. In large bowl, combine garlic and salt; work together with back of spoon until a paste forms. Gradually whisk in olive oil until smooth. Add lemon juice, vinegar, Worcestershire sauce, oregano, and pepper and blend well.

2. Bring a large pot of salted water to a boil. Add orzo pasta; cook according to package directions until al dente. Drain well and immediately stir into dressing in bowl.

3. Add all remaining ingredients and toss well to coat. Serve immediately or cover and chill for 4–6 hours before serving.

Tomato Veggie Pizza

This pizza is served cold, so it's perfect to take to a potluck party.
It's also delicious as an appetizer, cut into smaller pieces.

MAKE AHEAD

INGREDIENTS | SERVES 8–10

1 recipe Make-Ahead Pie Crust (page 251)

1 (3-ounce) package cream cheese, softened

1 (8-ounce) package cream cheese, softened

½ cup ranch salad dressing

½ teaspoon seasoned salt

½ teaspoon dried oregano leaves

1 red onion, minced

3 stalks celery, chopped

2 red bell peppers, chopped

4 plum tomatoes, seeded and chopped

1 cup grated carrots

1 cup shredded Cheddar cheese

3 tablespoons grated Asiago cheese

1. Preheat oven to 400°F. Make the Pie Crust recipe for two crusts. Roll the crusts out on a cookie sheet into two 7" × 15" rectangles; crimp edges. Bake for 12–16 minutes until crusts are deep golden brown. Let cool on sheets.

2. Spread the 3-ounce package of cream cheese evenly over crusts. Work carefully. In small bowl, beat together 8-ounce package cream cheese, ranch salad dressing, seasoned salt, and oregano. Spread over cream cheese on crust.

3. Top with the chopped vegetables, then Cheddar and Asiago cheese. Cover and chill for 2–3 hours before cutting into squares to serve.

Party Fun

You could make this excellent recipe several different ways. Flavor the cream cheese mixture with your favorite salad dressing. Top the two crusts with different vegetable mixtures. And the way you serve the pizza can be varied too. Cut into strips across the whole rectangle, cut into triangles, or into small squares.

Classic Quiche

Three kinds of rich cheese are delicious in this simple and mild quiche.

INEXPENSIVE

INGREDIENTS | SERVES 6

¼ cup butter

1 onion, finely chopped

3 tablespoons flour

½ teaspoon salt

⅛ teaspoon pepper

Pinch nutmeg

1 cup light cream

¼ cup sour cream

4 eggs, beaten

1½ cups shredded Swiss

1 Make-Ahead Pie Crust (page 251), prebaked

3 tablespoons grated Asiago cheese

1. Preheat oven to 350°F. In large saucepan, melt butter over medium heat. Add onion; cook and stir until tender, about 6 minutes.

2. Add flour, salt, pepper, and nutmeg; cook and stir until bubbly. Add light cream; cook and stir until thick. Remove from heat.

3. Beat in sour cream, then add eggs, one at a time, beating well after each addition.

4. Place Swiss cheese into pie crust and pour egg mixture over. Sprinkle with Asiago cheese. Bake for 40–50 minutes or until quiche is puffed and golden brown. Let stand for 5 minutes and serve.

Curried Vegetable Quiche

Curry adds great flavor to mild vegetables in this easy quiche.

EASY

INGREDIENTS | SERVES 6

2 tablespoons butter

1 onion, chopped

2 cloves garlic, minced

1 green bell pepper, chopped

1 cup sliced mushrooms

1 tablespoon curry powder

½ teaspoon salt

⅛ teaspoon pepper

1 Make-Ahead Pie Crust (page 251), prebaked

1½ cups grated Swiss cheese

4 eggs, beaten

½ cup sour cream

¼ cup milk

3 tablespoons grated Parmesan cheese

Make-Ahead Hints

Quiches reheat beautifully, so you can make this recipe ahead of time. Just cool it at room temperature for about an hour, then cover and refrigerate until you're ready to eat. Preheat the oven to 350°F. Add the quiche, covered, and bake for 10–15 minutes. Uncover and bake another 5 minutes or so until it's hot.

1. Preheat oven to 350°F. In large skillet, melt butter over medium heat. Add onion and garlic; cook and stir until tender, about 5 minutes. Add bell pepper and mushrooms; cook and stir until liquid evaporates, about 6–7 minutes.

2. Add curry powder; cook and stir for 1–2 minutes longer. Add salt and pepper and remove from heat. Place in prebaked Pie Crust and top with Swiss cheese.

3. In medium bowl, beat eggs with sour cream and milk. Pour over cheese in Crust. Sprinkle with Parmesan cheese.

4. Bake quiche for 35–45 minutes until it's puffed and golden brown. Let stand for 5 minutes before slicing to serve.

CHAPTER 10

Side Dishes and Vegetables

Almond Barley Casserole

Barley is very good for you and it's delicious too.
The nutty flavor is accented by two kinds of almonds, onions, and garlic.

INEXPENSIVE

INGREDIENTS | SERVES 6–8

2 tablespoons butter

1 tablespoon olive oil

½ cup slivered almonds

1 onion, chopped

3 cloves garlic, minced

1 (8-ounce) package sliced mushrooms

1½ cups medium pearl barley

3 cups vegetable broth

½ cup sliced almonds

1. Preheat oven to 350°F. In large skillet, melt butter with olive oil over medium heat. Add slivered almonds; cook until toasted; remove with slotted spoon.

2. Add onion, garlic, and mushrooms to pan; sauté until crisp-tender, about 6–8 minutes. Add barley and stir until coated.

3. Add broth and toasted almonds to pan; bring to a simmer. Transfer to a 2½-quart baking dish and top with sliced almonds. Bake for 65–75 minutes or until barley is tender and broth is absorbed.

Mustard Sauce

This delicious sauce can be served with a spiral sliced ham,
with grilled salmon, or baked chicken.

EASY

INGREDIENTS | YIELDS 1 CUP; SERVES 6

2 tablespoons flour

½ cup honey

2 teaspoons dry mustard powder

1 cup light cream

3 egg yolks

½ cup Dijon mustard

⅓ cup apple cider vinegar

1. In small saucepan, combine flour, honey, mustard powder, cream, and egg yolks. Whisk well and add mustard; beat until blended.

2. Place over medium heat and slowly whisk in the vinegar. Bring to a boil; reduce heat and simmer for 3–4 minutes until thickened. Cool for 30 minutes, then refrigerate for up to 4 days.

Party Fun

This sauce can be dressed up by adding fresh chopped herbs. Basil, cilantro, parsley, tarragon, thyme, or oregano would all be good additions. Make several batches and offer them as sauces for grilled meats, or use as a dipping sauce for appetizers like crudités, hot cooked meatballs, or breadsticks.

Mustard and Garlic Carrots

This super easy dish infuses carrots with lots of flavor.
You could use 4 cups sliced carrots instead of the baby carrots; just cook for 10 minutes.

EASILY DOUBLES

INGREDIENTS | SERVES 6

1 (16-ounce) package baby carrots
1 cup water
3 tablespoons butter
3 cloves garlic, minced
¼ cup honey mustard
2 tablespoons honey
2 tablespoons brown sugar
2 tablespoons Dijon mustard
⅛ teaspoon pepper

1. Place carrots in large saucepan; add water. Bring to a simmer, reduce heat, and cook, covered, for 6–7 minutes until carrots are just tender.

2. When carrots are done, drain and set aside. In large skillet, melt butter over medium heat. Add garlic; cook and stir for 2–3 minutes until fragrant. Stir in honey mustard, honey, brown sugar, Dijon mustard, and pepper.

3. Add carrots; cook and stir over medium heat until carrots are glazed.

Pecan Green Beans

This simple yet elegant side dish is very last minute,
so it can be thrown together in a flash.

EASY

INGREDIENTS | SERVES 8

2 pounds fresh green beans, trimmed
1 tablespoon olive oil
2 tablespoons butter
½ cup chopped pecans
3 cloves garlic, minced
½ teaspoon salt
⅛ teaspoon white pepper
2 tablespoons white balsamic vinegar

1. Bring a large pot of water to a boil. Add green beans; bring to a boil. Reduce heat and simmer for 4–6 minutes until beans are crisp-tender. Drain well.

2. In large saucepan, combine olive oil and butter; melt over medium heat. Add pecans; cook and stir until fragrant. Remove pecans from saucepan.

3. Add garlic, salt, and pepper to saucepan; cook and stir until garlic is fragrant, about 2 minutes. Add green beans; cook and stir for 3–4 minutes until crisp-tender. Drizzle with balsamic vinegar, toss, then sprinkle with pecans and serve.

Grilled Vegetable Medley

*You could also skewer these foods onto soaked bamboo
or metal kabobs and grill for 3–5 minutes.*

EASY

INGREDIENTS | SERVES 8–10

2 cups small button mushrooms

2 cups cherry tomatoes

2 yellow summer squash, sliced

2 green bell peppers, sliced

2 tablespoons olive oil

1 teaspoon seasoned salt

1/8 teaspoon pepper

1 teaspoon dried Italian seasoning

1. Trim off the ends of the mushrooms and wipe with damp cloth to clean. Combine all vegetables in large bowl.

2. Drizzle with olive oil and sprinkle with salt, pepper, and seasoning. Toss gently to coat.

3. Place vegetables in a grill basket; close basket. Cook over medium direct heat for 7–10 minutes, turning basket frequently, until vegetables are tender. Can be served immediately, at room temperature, or cold.

Roasted Honey Mustard Potatoes

Roasted potatoes are a huge hit at any potluck party.

EASY

INGREDIENTS | SERVES 8–10

2 pounds small red potatoes

4 cloves garlic, minced

1/2 teaspoon salt

1/8 teaspoon white pepper

3 tablespoons butter, melted

1 tablespoon olive oil

1/4 cup honey mustard

2 tablespoons honey

1 tablespoon Dijon mustard

1 teaspoon dried thyme leaves

1. Preheat oven to 400°F. Scrub potatoes and cut them in half or in quarters if larger than 2 inches in diameter. Place in large roasting pan and sprinkle with garlic, salt, and pepper.

2. In small bowl, combine remaining ingredients and mix well. Drizzle over the potatoes and stir to coat.

3. Roast for 45–55 minutes, turning potatoes with spatula twice, until the potatoes are tender with golden brown edges. Serve immediately.

Rice and Cheese Balls

This old fashioned recipe is a great accompaniment to a grilled steak.

INEXPENSIVE

INGREDIENTS | SERVES 8

1 tablespoon olive oil
½ cup minced onion
1 tablespoon flour
½ teaspoon salt
½ teaspoon dried thyme leaves
⅛ teaspoon cayenne pepper
½ cup buttermilk
1½ cups shredded Muenster cheese
2 cups cold cooked rice
1 egg, beaten
¾ cup seasoned dry bread crumbs
1 cup peanut oil

1. In medium saucepan, heat olive oil over medium heat. Add onion; cook and stir until tender. Add flour, salt, thyme, and pepper; cook and stir until bubbly.

2. Add buttermilk; cook until thick. Then remove from heat and stir in shredded cheese. Add rice and mix well; chill for 4–8 hours.

3. Roll chilled rice mixture into 1½-inch balls. Dip into beaten egg and roll in bread crumbs to coat. At this point balls can be chilled again.

4. When ready to eat, heat peanut oil over medium heat in skillet. Add balls, about 6–7 at a time, and fry until golden brown. Drain on paper towels and serve. You can keep the balls warm in a 250°F oven until all are fried.

Curried Cauliflower

Cauliflower and curry powder together is one of the healthiest combinations of food on the planet. And it's delicious!

MAKE AHEAD

INGREDIENTS | SERVES 8–10

2 heads cauliflower
⅓ cup olive oil
1 onion, chopped
3 cloves garlic, minced
3 tablespoons apple cider vinegar
1 tablespoon curry powder
1 teaspoon salt
⅛ teaspoon pepper

1. Preheat oven to 400°F. Remove cauliflower florets from the heads; place in large roasting pan.

2. In medium skillet, heat 2 tablespoons olive oil over medium heat; add onion and garlic and cook until tender, about 5 minutes. Remove from heat and stir in remaining olive oil, vinegar, curry powder, salt, and pepper.

3. Drizzle this mixture over the cauliflower and stir to coat. Roast for 40–50 minutes or until cauliflower is tender and light brown. Serve immediately or cool and serve at room temperature.

Three-Bean Medley

Edamame are soybeans. They are very healthy and delicious too.
Tender and nutty, they combine well with garbanzo and lima beans in this simple recipe.

INEXPENSIVE

INGREDIENTS | SERVES 8–10

2 tablespoons olive oil

1 onion, chopped

3 cloves garlic, minced

1 (15-ounce) can garbanzo beans, drained

2 cups frozen edamame, thawed

2 cups frozen lima beans, thawed

1 (14-ounce) can diced tomatoes, drained

1 teaspoon dried basil leaves

$\frac{1}{8}$ teaspoon pepper

1. In large saucepan, heat olive oil over medium heat. Add onion and garlic; cook and stir until tender, about 6 minutes.

2. Rinse and drain garbanzo beans. Add with edamame, lima beans, tomatoes, basil, and pepper to saucepan. Bring to a simmer; reduce heat and simmer for 3–5 minutes until beans are hot. Serve immediately.

Scalloped Onions

Scalloped onions is an old-fashioned dish that is suave and satisfying.
It's perfect served next to a roasted chicken.

INEXPENSIVE

INGREDIENTS | SERVES 8–10

2 tablespoons butter

1 tablespoon olive oil

8 large onions, chopped

3 cloves garlic, minced

1 teaspoon salt

$\frac{1}{8}$ teaspoon pepper

1 teaspoon dried marjoram leaves

$\frac{1}{2}$ cup dried bread crumbs

$\frac{1}{2}$ cup grated Parmesan cheese

1 tablespoon dried parsley

1 cup whole milk

2 eggs, beaten

1. Preheat oven to 350°F. Spray a 3-quart casserole dish with nonstick cooking spray and set aside.

2. Melt butter and olive oil in very large skillet over medium heat. Add onion and garlic; cook and stir until onions are tender. Sprinkle with salt, pepper, and marjoram and remove from heat.

3. In small bowl combine bread crumbs, cheese, and parsley and mix well. In another small bowl, combine milk and eggs and beat until combined.

4. Place ¼ of the onions in prepared dish; top with ¼ of bread crumb mixture. Repeat layers, ending with bread crumb mixture. Pour milk mixture over all. Bake for 35–45 minutes until top is browned and casserole is set.

Green Rice

This could be the main dish for a vegetarian meal.
Serve with a fresh corn salad and some brownies for dessert.

EASY

INGREDIENTS | SERVES 6

2 tablespoons olive oil

1 onion, chopped

3 cloves garlic, minced

1 (10-ounce) package frozen chopped spinach, thawed and drained

3 cups cooked long-grain rice

1 cup light cream

2 eggs, beaten

⅓ cup chopped flat-leaf parsley

1 cup shredded Swiss cheese

½ teaspoon salt

⅛ teaspoon pepper

¼ cup grated Romano cheese

1. Preheat oven to 350°F. Spray a 2½ quart casserole dish with nonstick cooking spray and set aside.

2. In medium skillet, heat olive oil over medium heat. Add onion and garlic; cook and stir until tender, about 5 minutes. Add spinach; cook and stir until liquid evaporates.

3. Combine with remaining ingredients except Romano cheese in large bowl. Pour into prepared casserole dish and top with Romano cheese. Bake for 45–55 minutes until casserole is hot and bubbling.

Transport Tips

You can transport the casserole to the party either before or after it's baked. If you choose to bake it at home, wrap in lots of newspaper or place in an insulated container. Remember that the two-hour time limit for leaving perishable foods out of refrigeration starts at your house and continues through to the party.

Corn Pudding

When you stir this pudding halfway through cooking,
the browned bits get mixed into the casserole, adding lots of flavor.

EASY

INGREDIENTS | SERVES 8

2 tablespoons butter
1 onion, chopped
2 cloves garlic, minced
1 green bell pepper, chopped
2 tablespoons flour
½ teaspoon salt
⅛ teaspoon pepper
1 teaspoon dried thyme leaves
1 cup milk
1 (15-ounce) can cream-style corn
1½ cups frozen corn, thawed
2 eggs, beaten
1 cup shredded Gouda cheese

1. Preheat oven to 375°F. In large skillet, melt butter; cook onion, garlic, and bell pepper until tender. Add flour, salt, pepper, and thyme; cook and stir until bubbly.

2. Add milk; cook and stir until thickened. Remove from heat and beat in cream-style corn, frozen corn, eggs, and cheese.

3. Pour mixture into a greased 2-quart casserole dish. Bake for 30 minutes, then stir mixture, pulling the browned sides into the center. Return to oven and bake for 20–30 minutes longer until set and browned.

Creamy Cheesy Potatoes

Every potluck has to have a dish of creamy, cheesy potatoes.
Everyone will devour this one; make two!

EASILY DOUBLES

INGREDIENTS | SERVES 10

2 tablespoons butter

1 onion, chopped

1 (16-ounce) jar four-cheese Alfredo sauce

1 cup sour cream

1 cup plain yogurt

⅓ cup milk

1 (32-ounce) package frozen hash brown potatoes

1 cup shredded Cheddar cheese

1 cup shredded Havarti cheese

¾ cup grated Romano cheese, divided

Keep It Healthy

You can use low-fat versions of the Alfredo sauce, sour cream, yogurt, milk, and cheeses if you'd like. Just remember to combine low-fat and nonfat versions. No dish will turn out well if all of the ingredients are nonfat. And remember that low-fat cheeses won't melt as well as the full-fat versions.

1. Preheat oven to 375°F. In large skillet, melt butter over medium heat. Add onion; cook and stir until tender. Add Alfredo sauce and bring to a simmer.

2. Remove from heat and stir in sour cream, yogurt, and milk and mix well. Add potatoes, Cheddar, Havarti, and ½ cup Romano cheese; mix well.

3. Pour into prepared casserole dish and sprinkle with remaining ¼ cup Romano cheese. Bake for 55–65 minutes until top is golden brown.

Crisp Hash Brown Casserole

No, this isn't a healthy recipe, but it's fabulously delicious.
Everyone will love it.

MAKE AHEAD

INGREDIENTS | SERVES 8–10

2 tablespoons butter

2 tablespoons olive oil

1 onion, chopped

3 cloves garlic, minced

¼ cup chopped chives

1 (16-ounce) jar four-cheese Alfredo sauce

½ cup light cream

1 cup grated Swiss cheese

1 cup grated Cheddar cheese

1 (32-ounce) package frozen hash brown potatoes, thawed

1. Preheat oven to 375°F. In saucepan, melt butter with olive oil over medium heat. Add onion and garlic; cook and stir until tender, about 6 minutes.

2. Remove from heat and add chives, Alfredo sauce, cream, and cheeses; stir until combined.

3. Place hash browns in 13" × 9" baking dish; pour sauce over. Stir gently to mix. Bake for 20 minutes, then stir. Bake for 40–50 minutes longer, stirring twice to fold brown edges into the casserole, until tender and bubbly.

Party Fun

You could make one "light" version of this dish and one "indulgent" version. Use low-fat and nonfat products for the light version, or you could add more vegetables like mushrooms, bell peppers, peas, or corn. Experiment with this recipe because it's quite tolerant and will work as long as you follow the basic formula.

Three-Rice Pilaf

Three types of rice add interest to a classic pilaf recipe.
The mushrooms and tarragon add great flavor.

INEXPENSIVE

INGREDIENTS | SERVES 8–10

3 tablespoons butter
1 tablespoon olive oil
1 onion, chopped
3 cloves garlic, minced
1 cup chopped mushrooms
¾ cup long-grain brown rice
¾ cup wild rice
5 cups vegetable broth
½ cup long-grain white rice
½ teaspoon dried tarragon leaves
½ teaspoon salt
⅛ teaspoon pepper

1. In large saucepan, melt butter with olive oil over medium heat. Add onion, garlic, mushrooms, brown and wild rice; cook and stir until rice is lightly browned.

2. Add the broth and bring to a simmer. Cover and simmer for 20 minutes.

3. Uncover and add white rice, tarragon, salt, and pepper. Bring back to a simmer; cover and simmer for 20–30 minutes longer until all of the rice is tender. Let stand 10 minutes, then fluff to serve.

Keep It Healthy

Any time you use a large amount of vegetable, chicken, or beef broths, look for low-sodium versions. Many of these products have very high sodium content. The low-sodium broths also have more flavor. Look for boxed broths for the most long-simmered flavor. You can use part of the broths and just close the box and refrigerate the rest.

Mustard Cheese Fan Potatoes

These potatoes taste like something you'd find at a steak house,
yet they are very easy to prepare.

INEXPENSIVE

INGREDIENTS | SERVES 6

6 large russet potatoes

¼ cup butter

3 tablespoons olive oil

1 onion, minced

4 cloves garlic, minced

1 teaspoon dried thyme leaves

⅛ teaspoon pepper

3 tablespoons Dijon mustard

½ cup grated Romano cheese

Party Fun

Once you've learned how to cut potatoes into this fan shape, you can flavor them any way you'd like. Leave out the mustard and add some minced jalapeño peppers and diced tomatoes for Tex-Mex Potato Fans. Use finely diced Havarti cheese and add a bit of dried tarragon for French Potato Fans.

1. Preheat oven to 400°F. Scrub the potatoes and dry. Place potatoes, one at a time, between two handles of wooden spoons, so the long side of the potato is against the spoons. Cut down to the spoon handles, at ¼" intervals, making sure to not cut through to the bottom of the potato. The potato will hold together but the slices will fan out.

2. In small saucepan, melt butter and olive oil; cook onion and garlic until tender, about 6–7 minutes. Remove from heat and add thyme, pepper, mustard, and cheese; mix well.

3. Drizzle this mixture over the potatoes, making sure that some goes between the slices. Place potatoes, cut side up, on a baking dish. Bake for 55–65 minutes or until potatoes are tender and tops are golden brown.

Roasted Brussels Sprouts

Even Brussels sprouts haters will love these! They become sweet, nutty, slightly creamy, and crisp all at the same time.

EASY

INGREDIENTS | SERVES 8–10

2 pounds Brussels sprouts

2 tablespoons lemon juice

3 tablespoons olive oil

2 tablespoons butter

5 cloves garlic, minced

1 teaspoon salt

¼ teaspoon pepper

Make-Ahead Tips

This recipe, and the Curried Cauliflower (page 177), can be made ahead of time and reheated or served at room temperature. Because there's nothing perishable in the recipe, you don't have to be concerned about food safety. And there's something really nice about serving a room-temperature vegetable at a party; it's so relaxing!

1. Bring a large pot of water to a boil. Trim the ends off the Brussels sprouts and drop into the water. Bring back to a boil; simmer for 1 minute, then drain the Brussels sprouts.

2. Preheat oven to 400°F. Place the sprouts on a kitchen towel to dry. Then place in large roasting pan. Drizzle with lemon juice and toss to coat.

3. Melt together olive oil, butter, and garlic and drizzle over the sprouts. Sprinkle with salt and pepper and toss very well.

4. Roast the sprouts for 25–30 minutes, shaking pan occasionally and turning the sprouts twice with a spatula, until very deep brown on the outside. Serve immediately or cool and serve at room temperature. To reheat, bake at 350°F for 15–20 minutes.

Spanish Rice

Spanish rice is an excellent well-flavored pilaf. It can be served as an accompaniment to grilled meats, or as the centerpiece of a vegetarian meal.

INEXPENSIVE

INGREDIENTS | SERVES 6

3 tablespoons olive oil, divided

1¼ cups long-grain white rice

1 onion, chopped

3 cloves garlic, minced

2 jalapeño peppers, minced

1 green bell pepper, chopped

1 (14-ounce) can diced tomatoes, undrained

1½ cups vegetable broth

1½ teaspoons paprika

1 teaspoon dried thyme leaves

1 cup frozen baby peas, thawed

⅓ cup chopped flat-leaf parsley

1. In medium skillet, heat 1 tablespoon olive oil. Add rice; cook and stir until rice is browned, about 7–9 minutes, stirring frequently and watching constantly. Set aside.

2. In large saucepan, heat remaining 2 tablespoons olive oil over medium heat. Add onion, garlic, and jalapeño pepper; cook and stir until tender, about 5 minutes.

3. Add rice to onion mixture. Add remaining ingredients except peas and parsley; bring to a simmer. Cover and simmer for 20–30 minutes until rice is tender. Add peas; cook for 3 minutes longer.

4. Remove from heat, stir in parsley, let stand for 5 minutes, fluff with fork, and serve.

Party Fun

Offer several different flavors of rice pilaf when you serve any dish with a sauce. The pilaf can be simple, as with Three-Rice Pilaf (page 183), or more complicated, as in Spanish Rice or Green Rice (page 179). In fact, with some grilled chicken or pork chops and cheese sauce, you can offer a pilaf buffet.

Roasted Vegetables

This super-healthy and delicious dish is a perfect potluck recipe.
You can serve it hot out of the oven, at room temperature, or cold.

EASILY DOUBLES

INGREDIENTS | SERVES 8–10

5 carrots, cut into chunks
1 sweet potato, peeled and cubed
2 russet potatoes, cubed
1 onion, chopped
4 cloves garlic, minced
2 red bell peppers, sliced
2 yellow summer squash, sliced
2 cups sliced mushrooms
⅓ cup olive oil
¼ cup Dijon mustard
1 teaspoon salt
¼ teaspoon pepper
1 tablespoon fresh oregano leaves

1. Preheat oven to 400°F. In one large bowl, combine carrots, sweet potato, potatoes, onion, and garlic and toss. In another bowl, combine bell peppers, squash, and mushrooms.

2. In small bowl, combine remaining ingredients and mix well. Drizzle over both bowls of vegetables and mix gently to coat.

3. Place carrot mixture in large roasting pan. Roast for 25 minutes. Then add the bell pepper mixture and roast for 30–40 minutes longer, stirring twice during roasting time, until the vegetables are tender and light golden brown. Serve immediately or at room temperature.

Keep It Healthy

Roasted vegetables are one of the best healthy choices for any meal. And they are very popular. Choose a good combination of vegetables with different colors and flavors for more interest. Olive oil is a healthy choice for coating the vegetables to help keep them moist; the monounsaturated fat is heart healthy.

Orzo Pilaf

This rich "pilaf" uses orzo pasta instead of rice.
The pasta is shaped like rice.

QUICK

INGREDIENTS | SERVES 8

2 tablespoons butter

1 tablespoon olive oil

2 shallots, minced

4 cloves garlic, minced

1 (16-ounce) box orzo pasta

4 cups vegetable broth

1 red bell pepper, chopped

1 cup frozen baby peas

½ cup heavy cream

½ cup grated Havarti cheese

½ cup grated Parmesan cheese

Keep It Safe

This orzo dish is quite portable, but it does include perishable ingredients, so you have to use the 2-hour rule. Cover the pan with its cover, then wrap several times in heavy-duty foil. Wrap this in a blanket or place in an insulated carrier and bring to the party.

1. In large saucepan, melt butter with olive oil over medium heat. Add shallots and garlic; cook and stir until tender, about 4 minutes.

2. Add orzo; cook and stir until orzo begins to turn light brown around the edges. Remove from heat and add vegetable broth.

3. Return to heat and bring to a simmer. Cover and simmer for 7 minutes. Uncover and add bell pepper and peas; cover and cook for 4–5 minutes longer until pasta is tender and vegetables are hot.

4. Add cream and cheeses; cook and stir until cheeses melt. Serve immediately.

CHAPTER 11

Salads on the Side

Russian Salad Dressing

Russian dressing is creamy and slightly spicy.
If you like it really hot, add some cayenne pepper.

LAST MINUTE

INGREDIENTS | SERVES 8

¼ cup olive oil

¼ cup apple cider vinegar

¼ teaspoon salt

⅛ teaspoon pepper

2 tablespoons finely grated onion

1 clove garlic, minced

¼ cup ketchup

½ cup chili sauce

½ cup low-fat mayonnaise

¼ cup sugar

½ teaspoon paprika

Place all ingredients in a blender or food processor. Blend or process until smooth. Store in refrigerator for up to 5 days; shake dressing before serving.

Party Fun

Make a salad buffet for your party, even if the salad is just one course of the meal. Offer a selection of greens, including baby spinach, endive, butter lettuce, and red and green lettuces, along with several homemade salad dressings. For toppings, include croutons, crumbled cooked bacon, cheeses, and vegetables like mushrooms and green bell pepper.

French Bleu Salad Dressing

Your own homemade salad dressing adds a lot to even plain bagged salads.

INEXPENSIVE

INGREDIENTS | SERVES 6

½ cup olive oil

¼ cup minced onion

½ cup tomato sauce

½ cup ketchup

¼ cup sugar

½ teaspoon salt

⅓ cup apple cider vinegar

1 teaspoon paprika

½ cup crumbled bleu cheese

1. In blender or food processor, combine all ingredients except for bleu cheese. Blend or process until smooth. Store covered in refrigerator up to 5 days.

2. Stir in bleu cheese just before serving.

Fresh Cranberry Salad

Cranberries have a fresh, tart taste. When combined with lemon gelatin, pineapple, and marshmallows, they make a delightful salad.

INEXPENSIVE

INGREDIENTS | SERVES 8–10

4 cups fresh cranberries
1 cup sugar
½ cup heavy cream
½ cup miniature marshmallows
2 (3-ounce) packages lemon Jell-O
1 cup cranberry juice, heated
2 cups water
1 (8-ounce) can pineapple tidbits

1. Grind the cranberries in a food processor or blender and combine with sugar; set aside.

2. In small saucepan, heat heavy cream and add marshmallows; cook and stir until marshmallows melt. Place mixture in medium bowl and refrigerate until cold.

3. When cream mixture is cold, combine Jell-O with hot cranberry juice; stir until dissolved. Add water and pineapple tidbits; fold in cranberry mixture.

4. Beat cream mixture until fluffy; stir into cranberry mixture. Pour into 2-quart mold and chill for 4–6 hours until firm.

Make-Ahead Cabbage Salad

The large amount of sugar in this salad helps preserve it, so it will last for days in the refrigerator.

INEXPENSIVE

INGREDIENTS | SERVES 12

1 cup sugar
¾ cup vinegar
1 teaspoon salt
1 teaspoon celery seed
⅛ teaspoon white pepper
1 head green cabbage, shredded
1 head red cabbage, shredded
2 cups shredded carrot
1 green bell pepper, chopped

1. In medium saucepan, combine sugar, vinegar, salt, celery seed, and white pepper. Bring to a boil; boil for 1 minute, stirring frequently, until sugar dissolves.

2. Combine remaining ingredients in very large bowl. Pour hot sugar mixture over the cabbage mixture and stir gently. Cover and refrigerate for at least 6 hours before serving.

Keep It Safe

Salads like this one, which don't contain dairy products, eggs, cheeses, meats, or dressings that contain eggs, are the best choice for long trips. The salad will taste best cold, but it can sit out at room temperature for several hours. Pack it in an ice chest or a sturdy box and keep it in the car with you.

Overnight Spinach Pea Salad

This layered salad is pretty and healthy too. You could use other vegetables like canned mushrooms, chopped zucchini, or summer squash.

MAKE AHEAD

INGREDIENTS | SERVES 8

6 cups baby spinach leaves

1 (16-ounce) bag frozen baby peas, thawed and drained

½ cup chopped green onion

1 cup shredded Parmesan cheese, divided

1 cup chopped celery

1 red bell pepper, chopped

1 yellow bell pepper, chopped

¼ cup honey mustard

1 tablespoon honey

1 cup low-fat mayonnaise

1. Place spinach, peas, green onion, ¾ cup Parmesan cheese, celery, red bell pepper, and yellow bell pepper in glass salad bowl in order given.

2. In small bowl, combine honey mustard, honey, and mayonnaise and spoon over salad. Sprinkle with remaining ¼ cup Parmesan cheese. Cover with plastic wrap and chill overnight.

3. When ready to serve, gently toss salad and serve.

Lima Bean Salad

Lima beans are wonderfully nutty and tender. In this special salad, they're combined with grape tomatoes and avocado.

MAKE AHEAD

INGREDIENTS | SERVES 8

2 (16-ounce) packages frozen baby lima beans, thawed

¼ cup olive oil

1 red onion, chopped

1 garlic clove, grated

¼ cup apple cider vinegar

¼ cup minced fresh parsley

½ teaspoon salt

⅛ teaspoon pepper

½ cup low-fat sour cream

1 pint grape tomatoes

2 avocados, peeled and chopped

1 head red lettuce, torn

1. Drain the lima beans and place them in a large bowl. In small bowl, combine oil, onion, garlic, vinegar, parsley, salt, pepper, and sour cream; mix well.

2. Pour over lima beans and add tomatoes; stir gently. Cover and chill for 3–4 hours before serving. Add avocados just before serving; serve on bed of red lettuce.

Sugar Snap Spinach Salad

This easy and healthy salad has a wonderful combination of textures, colors, and flavors.

LAST MINUTE

INGREDIENTS | SERVES 8

6 cups baby spinach

1 (16-ounce) package frozen sugar snap peas, thawed

1 (8-ounce) package sliced mushrooms

⅓ cup sliced green onion

2 red bell peppers, chopped

⅔ cup Family-Style Salad Dressing (page 195)

Combine all ingredients except Dressing in large bowl and toss gently. Drizzle with the Dressing and toss; serve immediately.

Cottage Cheese Veggie Salad

This simple salad is colorful and delicious.
You can use low-fat cottage cheese if you'd like.

EASY

INGREDIENTS | SERVES 8

1 (16-ounce) container cottage cheese

¼ cup low-fat mayonnaise

⅛ teaspoon pepper

1 pint cherry tomatoes

2 tomatoes, chopped

2 cucumbers, peeled, seeded, and sliced

1 yellow bell pepper, chopped

1 red onion, chopped

1 cup diced Swiss cheese

1. In a medium bowl, combine cottage cheese, mayonnaise, and pepper and mix well. Add remaining ingredients and stir gently.

2. Cover and chill for 3–4 hours before serving, or serve immediately.

Avocado Salad Dressing

This rich and creamy salad dressing turns even plain lettuce into a gourmet treat.

EASILY DOUBLES

INGREDIENTS | SERVES 8
2 avocados, peeled and chopped
¼ cup lemon juice
¼ cup olive oil
1 tablespoon chopped fresh chives
¼ teaspoon garlic powder
½ teaspoon salt
⅛ teaspoon pepper
⅓ cup mayonnaise
½ teaspoon dry mustard

1. In blender or food processor, combine all ingredients. Blend or process until smooth.

2. Pour into small bowl and press plastic wrap directly onto the surface of the dressing. Cover and chill for 2–3 hours before serving.

Keep It Healthy

Avocados are very good for you. They are high in fat, true, but it's heart-healthy monounsaturated fat. Since the avocados turn brown very quickly due to an enzymatic process, you must include citrus juices in any recipe. That adds vitamin C as well. Serve this dressing over mixed greens and chopped vegetables.

Red Wine Vinaigrette

This simple vinaigrette has a lot of flavor. You can drizzle it over any salad, vegetable or green, or use it as a marinade for chicken or steak.

EASY

INGREDIENTS | SERVES 8
½ cup olive oil
½ cup red wine vinegar
¼ cup sugar
2 tablespoons honey
2 tablespoons Dijon mustard
½ teaspoon salt
½ teaspoon dried thyme leaves
⅛ teaspoon pepper

Combine all ingredients in small bowl and whisk well until the sugar dissolves. Store in refrigerator. Before serving, whisk again to blend ingredients.

Marinated Mushroom Salad

Mushrooms soak up lots of flavor in this super-easy recipe.
You could use a bottled vinaigrette if you'd like.

HEALTHY

INGREDIENTS | SERVES 8–10

1 (8-ounce) package button mushrooms
1 (8-ounce) package cremini mushrooms
1 red onion, chopped
1 clove garlic, minced
⅓ cup chopped flat-leaf parsley
⅔ cup Red Wine Vinaigrette (page 194)
8 cups butter lettuce

1. Wipe the mushrooms and trim off the bottom of the stem. Combine in medium bowl with red onion, garlic, and parsley.

2. Pour Vinaigrette over all and toss; cover and refrigerate for 4–6 hours, stirring occasionally.

3. When ready to serve, place lettuce on a serving platter and pour mushroom mixture over.

Keep It Healthy

Mushrooms are a good source of vitamin D, the B vitamin complex, and fiber. Don't rinse or wash them to clean; just brush with a damp cloth. Mushrooms are grown in sterile soil, so a little bit of dirt that clings to the mushrooms isn't going to hurt you. Just trim off the bottom and eat!

Family-Style Salad Dressing

This dressing has a bit of a kick from the mustard and chili sauce.
It's great served over any green salad.

INEXPENSIVE

INGREDIENTS | SERVES 12

½ cup sugar
⅓ cup apple cider vinegar
2 tablespoons Dijon mustard
1 tablespoons Worcestershire sauce
½ cup minced red onion
⅓ cup ketchup
⅓ cup chili sauce
½ cup olive oil

In small bowl, combine all ingredients and mix with wire whisk until the sugar dissolves. Cover and chill for 2–3 hours before serving. Can store in refrigerator for 5 days.

Make-Ahead Hints

Most homemade salad dressings can be kept in the refrigerator for 4–5 days and still be good. You can make this one and keep it for a couple of weeks if you leave out the red onion. Use ½ teaspoon onion powder instead, or add some minced red onion just before serving.

Frozen Cranberry Salad

This dual-layered salad has a wonderful fresh flavor. It's perfect for the holidays.

MAKE AHEAD

INGREDIENTS | SERVES 9

1 (16-ounce) bag fresh cranberries

1¾ cups sugar

1 cup apple juice

1 cup water

3 tablespoons lemon juice

1 envelope unflavored gelatin

1 teaspoon vanilla

1 cup chopped toasted pecans

1 cup heavy whipping cream

⅓ cup powdered sugar

¼ cup mayonnaise

½ cup chopped dried cranberries

Transport Tips

Frozen salads as well as frozen desserts will travel well to the party as long as you pack them carefully. Remove the food from the freezer at the last minute before you leave. Pack into an insulated container, or a sturdy cardboard box, with frozen gel packs or containers of ice cubes.

1. In large saucepan, combine cranberries with sugar, apple juice, and water. Cook over low heat, stirring frequently, until cranberries pop.

2. In small bowl, combine lemon juice with gelatin and let stand for 5 minutes. Stir into hot cranberry mixture until gelatin dissolves. Stir in vanilla and pecans.

3. Pour mixture into 9" × 9" glass baking dish and chill until firm.

4. In medium bowl, beat cream with powdered sugar until stiff peaks form. Fold in mayonnaise until blended, then fold in dried cranberries. Spread over cranberry mixture. Cover and freeze for 3–4 hours before serving.

Bing Cherry Fruit Salad

Gelatin salads are easy; just keep stirring until that gelatin and the sugar dissolve.

EASY

INGREDIENTS | SERVES 8

2 (0.25-ounce) packages unflavored gelatin

⅓ cup sugar

2 cups cherry juice

1 (15-ounce) can crushed pineapple, drained

1 (8-ounce) package cream cheese, softened

2 cups pitted, halved Bing cherries

1 cup chopped walnuts

Party Fun

This beautiful pink salad is gorgeous served as a large mold, but you can also make smaller molds to serve as individual salads. Place the individual salads on a bed of lettuce leaves on a beautiful platter to serve as the centerpiece for a luncheon, or set one salad at each place to serve as markers.

1. Place gelatin in large bowl along with sugar. Measure cherry juice and add enough of the juice from the drained pineapple to equal 3 cups.

2. Heat 1 cup of this liquid in the microwave until boiling; stir into gelatin mixture. Stir until gelatin and sugar dissolve. Add cream cheese and stir until melted.

3. Add remaining 2 cups liquid, then chill until mixture is syrupy. Beat with electric mixer until fluffy, then fold in the cherries, pineapple, and walnuts. Pour into 2-quart salad mold and chill until firm.

Cobb Salad

Cobb Salad is a delicious make-ahead main dish salad that you can change to suit your tastes.

EASY

INGREDIENTS | SERVES 8

1 head butter lettuce, chopped

2 cups baby spinach, chopped

1 bunch curly endive, chopped

5 hard-cooked eggs, sliced

12 slices crisply cooked bacon, crumbled

3 chopped tomatoes

4 Poached Chicken breasts (page 112), chopped

2 cucumbers, peeled, seeded, and chopped

1 cup ranch salad dressing

⅓ cup crumbled blue cheese

2 avocados, peeled and chopped

1. On a large platter, combine lettuce with spinach and toss; arrange in shallow layer.

2. Top with remaining ingredients except for salad dressing, blue cheese, and avacados, arranging ingredients in strips across the lettuce mixture.

3. Sprinkle with the blue cheese and drizzle with ranch dressing. Cover and chill for 3–4 hours before serving. Top with avocado and gently toss before serving.

Keep It Safe

Hard-cooked eggs must be refrigerated just like raw eggs. To hard-cook eggs, cover the eggs with cold water in a saucepan. Bring to a boil, then immediately remove from heat, cover, and let stand for 15 minutes. Run cold water into the pan until the eggs feel cold, then tap them against the sides of the pan and peel.

Mango Berry Cottage Cheese Salad

This old-fashioned recipe is so easy to make and it's delicious.
You could use your favorite fruits; just substitute 1 to 1.

HEALTHY

INGREDIENTS | SERVES 8

1 (16-ounce) container cottage cheese

1 cup low-fat mayonnaise

½ cup heavy whipping cream

2 tablespoons powdered sugar

1 cup miniature marshmallows

1 (16-ounce) jar sliced mangoes, drained

1 (8-ounce) can crushed pineapple, drained

2 cups blueberries

1 cup sliced strawberries

1 cup raspberries

1. In large bowl, combine cottage cheese with mayonnaise and mix well. In small bowl, beat cream with powdered sugar until stiff peaks form; fold into cottage cheese mixture.

2. Add marshmallows; let stand for 10 minutes. Meanwhile, cut mangoes into chunks.

3. Add drained pineapple, mangoes, blueberries, and strawberries to cottage cheese mixture; cover and chill for 4–5 hours before serving. When ready to serve, top with raspberries.

Keep It Healthy

You can substitute low-fat cottage cheese for the full-fat version, and substitute 1 cup nonfat frozen dairy whipped topping for the heavy cream and powdered sugar. But don't use all nonfat varieties of the creamy products in this recipe. You'll get better taste and texture if you combine low-fat and nonfat products.

Four-Bean Salad

*Combine canned and frozen beans to make a delicious
and healthy bean salad to accompany broiled or grilled chicken or steak.*

QUICK

INGREDIENTS | SERVES 10

1 (16-ounce) package green beans
1 (12-ounce) package frozen edamame
1 (15-ounce) can black beans, drained
1 (15-ounce) can yellow wax beans, drained
1 red onion, chopped
1 clove garlic, minced
½ cup apple cider vinegar
⅓ cup sugar
¼ cup olive oil
2 tablespoons Dijon mustard
¼ teaspoon salt
1 teaspoon celery seed
⅛ teaspoon pepper
1 teaspoon dried thyme leaves

1. Cook the green beans and edamame according to package directions and drain. Place in large bowl. Drain, rinse, and drain again the black beans and wax beans and add to bowl with red onion and garlic.

2. In small bowl, combine remaining ingredients and whisk with wire whisk until sugar dissolves and mixture is blended. Pour over bean mixture and stir gently. Cover and chill for 3–4 hours before serving.

Broccoli Bacon Salad

This twist on a classic salad will make even broccoli haters take second helpings! The trick is to make it at least 12 hours ahead of time, so the broccoli has a chance to soften in the dressing.

MAKE AHEAD

INGREDIENTS | SERVES 8–10

10 slices bacon

2 heads broccoli, cut into florets

½ cup chopped red onion

¼ cup chopped green onion

½ cup golden raisins

½ cup dried cranberries

½ cup toasted sliced almonds

1 cup diced Swiss cheese

⅓ cup sugar

1 cup low-fat mayonnaise

⅓ cup plain yogurt

2 tablespoons buttermilk

1 tablespoon apple cider vinegar

3 tablespoons grated Romano cheese

1. Cook bacon until crisp; drain on paper towels, crumble, and set aside. Cut broccoli into small florets. Combine in large bowl with bacon, red and green onion, raisins, cranberries, almonds, and cheese; toss gently.

2. In small bowl, combine remaining ingredients and mix well. Pour over broccoli mixture and stir well. Cover and chill for at least 12 hours before serving.

Candied-Walnut Mango Salad

This twist on a fruit and candied-almond salad is beautiful and a real treat.
Serve it with a grilled steak and some garlic bread.

EASY

INGREDIENTS | SERVES 8

¼ cup sugar

1 cup walnut pieces

4 cups baby spinach leaves

4 cups butter lettuce

⅓ cup sliced green onions

1 (16-ounce) jar mango slices, drained

¾ cup Red Wine Vinaigrette (page 194)

Make-Ahead Hints

You can make the candied almonds and the Vinaigrette ahead of time. When it's time to eat, toss the walnuts with the lettuce, green onions, and chopped mangoes, then toss with the Vinaigrette. Once the salad has been dressed, it has to be served immediately or the greens will start to wilt.

1. In small, heavy saucepan, combine sugar with the walnut pieces. Cook over low heat, stirring occasionally, until sugar melts and turns brown. Stir and turn the walnuts out onto a greased cookie sheet. Let cool and break into pieces.

2. When ready to eat, combine spinach, lettuce, and green onion in salad bowl. Chop the mango slices and add to salad along with candied walnuts. Drizzle Vinaigrette over all, toss, and serve.

Ranch Potato Salad

Potato salad is a must at any cookout.
This one has lots of flavor from the cheese and ranch salad dressing.

INEXPENSIVE

INGREDIENTS | SERVES 8–10

3 pounds russet potatoes

1 onion, chopped

4 cloves garlic, minced

2 tablespoons olive oil

½ teaspoon salt

⅛ teaspoon pepper

1 cup ranch salad dressing

½ cup mayonnaise

¼ cup buttermilk

½ cup grated Romano cheese

1 cup chopped celery

Party Fun

Make a collection of potato salads for your cookout. The same dressing can be used; just vary the flavorings. Instead of the ranch salad dressing, use French or Thousand Island. Add chopped bell peppers, crisply cooked bacon, or sliced mushrooms. The nice thing about potato salad is that it's so versatile.

1. Preheat oven to 400°F. Wash potatoes and cut into 1-inch chunks. Combine in large roasting pan with the onion and garlic. Drizzle with olive oil and sprinkle with salt and pepper.

2. Roast for 1 hour, turning with spatula after 30 minutes, until potatoes are tender with some brown crispy edges.

3. While potatoes are in oven, in large bowl combine salad dressing, mayonnaise, buttermilk, and cheese and mix well. Add hot potato mixture and celery and stir to mix. Cover and chill for 3–4 hours before serving.

Orange Fluff Salad

This pretty and fluffy salad can double as dessert. Kids love it!

MAKE AHEAD

INGREDIENTS | SERVES 8

2 (0.25-ounce) packages unflavored gelatin

⅓ cup sugar

3 cups orange juice

1 cup heavy whipping cream

3 tablespoons powdered sugar

1 teaspoon vanilla

2 (15-ounce) cans mandarin oranges, drained

1 (8-ounce) can crushed pineapple, drained

1. In large bowl, combine gelatin with sugar and mix well. Heat 1 cup orange juice until steaming, and add to gelatin mixture. Stir until gelatin and sugar dissolve. Add remaining orange juice and chill until syrupy.

2. In small bowl, beat cream with powdered sugar and vanilla until stiff peaks form. Using same beaters, beat the gelatin mixture until fluffy.

3. Fold in drained oranges and pineapple. Pile into serving bowl, cover, and chill until firm, about 4–6 hours.

CHAPTER 12

Hot and Cold Soups and Stews

Bean and Bacon Soup

*This hearty soup has the best flavor, and a wonderful rich texture.
Serve it with hot corn bread and a green salad for an inexpensive meal.*

INEXPENSIVE

INGREDIENTS | SERVES 8

8 slices bacon
2 onions, chopped
3 cloves garlic, minced
3 (15-ounce) cans kidney beans, drained
3 potatoes, peeled and diced
4 carrots, peeled and sliced
5 cups chicken broth
1 bay leaf
1 (14-ounce) can diced tomatoes, undrained
1 (8-ounce) can tomato sauce
¼ teaspoon pepper
1 teaspoon dried thyme leaves

1. In large soup pot, cook bacon until crisp. Drain on paper towels, crumble, and refrigerate. Drain fat from pan but do not wipe out.

2. Add onions and garlic to pot; cook and stir until crisp-tender, about 5 minutes. Add beans, potatoes, carrots, chicken broth, and bay leaf. Bring to a simmer.

3. Cover pot and simmer on low heat for 10–14 minutes until carrots and potatoes are tender. Add remaining ingredients and bring to a simmer. Mash some of the beans and potatoes.

4. Add bacon, simmer soup for 10–15 minutes until blended and slightly thickened. Remove bay leaf and serve.

Chilled Borscht

If you chill the beets beforehand, you can serve this easy and beautiful soup without chilling.

QUICK

INGREDIENTS | SERVES 4

1 (16-ounce) can beets
1 cup orange juice
2 tablespoons lemon juice
½ cup red onion, chopped
½ cup sour cream
¼ cup heavy cream
½ teaspoon salt
⅛ teaspoon white pepper
¼ teaspoon dried dill weed
¼ cup chopped green onions

1. Combine all ingredients except green onions in food processor or blender. Process or blend until smooth.

2. Cover and chill for 2–3 hours before serving. Garnish with chopped green onion.

Wedding Soup

The trick to this soup is using the best quality chicken broth you can find. Homemade is best, but one of the good boxed stocks is a quality second.

LAST MINUTE

INGREDIENTS | SERVES 8

1 tablespoon olive oil
1 onion, minced
2 cloves garlic, minced
1 teaspoon dried basil leaves
4 cups chicken broth
4 cups beef broth
2 cups water
1 (16-ounce) package tiny frozen cooked meatballs
1 cup orzo pasta
2 cups sliced baby spinach
⅓ cup grated Parmesan cheese

1. Heat olive oil in large pot on medium heat. Add onion and garlic; cook and stir until tender, about 6 minutes. Add basil, both types of broth, and water; bring to a simmer.

2. Add the meatballs; return to a simmer. Reduce heat to low, cover, and simmer for 10–15 minutes until meatballs are hot and tender.

3. Add pasta and spinach; bring back to a simmer. Simmer for 8–10 minutes until pasta is tender. Sprinkle with Parmesan cheese and serve.

Potato Cheese Chowder

You can make this easy soup vegetarian by omitting the bacon and using vegetable broth in place of the chicken broth.

EASY

INGREDIENTS | SERVES 8

6 slices bacon
2 tablespoons butter
2 onions, chopped
3 cloves garlic, minced
6 russet potatoes, peeled and chopped
4 cups chicken or vegetable broth
4 cups water
1 teaspoon salt
¼ teaspoon pepper
2 tablespoons cornstarch
2 cups light cream
1½ cups shredded Cheddar cheese

1. In large skillet, cook bacon until crisp. Drain on paper towels, crumble, and refrigerate. Drain skillet but do not wipe out. Add butter; cook onions and garlic until tender, about 5 minutes.

2. Place in 5-quart slow cooker along with potatoes, broth, water, salt, and pepper. Cover and cook on low for 8–9 hours until potatoes are tender. Using a potato mash, mash some of the potatoes.

3. In small bowl, combine cornstarch with cream and mix well. Stir into soup along with reserved bacon. Cover and cook on high for 20–30 minutes until thickened. Stir in cheese and serve.

Curried Chicken Stew

*Curry and chicken are natural partners
and are combined with orange in this gorgeous soup.*

EASY

INGREDIENTS | SERVES 6

4 boneless, skinless chicken breasts, cubed

3 tablespoons flour

1 teaspoon salt

⅛ teaspoon pepper

2 tablespoons olive oil

1 onion, chopped

2 cloves garlic, minced

1 green bell pepper, chopped

1 tablespoon curry powder

6 cups chicken broth

1 cup orange juice

½ cup mango chutney

½ cup heavy cream

1. Toss chicken breasts with flour, salt, and pepper. Heat olive oil in large saucepan. Add chicken; brown, stirring frequently, about 5 minutes. Remove chicken from saucepan.

2. Add onion, garlic, and bell pepper; cook and stir until crisp-tender, about 4 minutes. Add curry powder; cook and stir for 1 minute longer.

3. Add chicken, chicken broth, and orange juice. Bring to a simmer; cover, reduce heat to low, and simmer for 15–20 minutes until chicken is thoroughly cooked and vegetables are tender.

4. Stir in chutney and cream; heat through, but do not boil. Serve immediately.

Split Pea Chowder

*Buy a ham bone at those stores that sell spiral-sliced ham;
they are inexpensive with a lot of meat still on them.*

INEXPENSIVE

INGREDIENTS | SERVES 8

6 cups dried split peas, divided

1 ham bone

½ teaspoon salt

¼ teaspoon pepper

2 carrots, diced

1 onion, chopped

3 cloves garlic, minced

1 potato, peeled and diced

2 quarts chicken broth

3 cups water

1. Combine all ingredients except 2 cups of the split peas in a 5-quart slow cooker and mix well.

2. Cover and cook on low for 6 hours, then stir well. Add remaining 2 cups peas and cover again; cook on low for 3–4 hours longer until peas are tender.

3. Remove the ham bone and cut off meat; dice meat and return to slow cooker. Mash some of the peas and potatoes, leaving some whole, and stir. Serve immediately.

Meatball Chowder

This rich and thick chowder has the best combination of flavors and textures.

EASY

INGREDIENTS | SERVES 10–12

¼ cup olive oil

3 onions, chopped

4 cloves garlic, minced

4 stalks celery, sliced

3 carrots, sliced

½ cup long-grain brown rice

½ teaspoon salt

1 teaspoon dried marjoram leaves

6 cups beef broth

2 cups tomato juice

1 tablespoon sugar

2 bay leaves

1 (16-ounce) bag frozen cooked meatballs

1 (12-ounce) can evaporated milk

3 tablespoons cornstarch

1 cup shredded Swiss cheese

1. In large stock pot, heat olive oil over medium heat. Add onion and garlic; cook and stir for 5 minutes. Add celery and carrots; cook and stir for 3 minutes longer.

2. Add rice, salt, and marjoram; cook and stir for 2 minutes. Then add broth, tomato juice, sugar, and bay leaves; bring to a simmer. Reduce heat to low, cover, and simmer for 10 minutes.

3. Add meatballs; simmer for 10–15 minutes until meatballs are hot. In small bowl, combine milk with cornstarch; add to chowder along with cheese. Simmer, stirring frequently, until cheese melts and chowder is thickened. Remove bay leaves before serving.

Minestrone

Minestrone is a hearty vegetable soup that combines legumes with pasta.

EASILY DOUBLES

INGREDIENTS | SERVES 10

1 pound Italian sausage links, sliced

1 onion, chopped

4 cloves garlic, minced

1 cup sliced celery

1½ cups sliced carrots

6 cups beef broth

2 (14.5-ounce) cans diced tomatoes, undrained

½ teaspoon dried oregano

1 teaspoon dried Italian seasoning

½ cup chili sauce

1 (15-ounce) can kidney beans, drained

2 cups elbow macaroni

1 red bell pepper, chopped

1 green bell pepper, chopped

¼ cup minced fresh parsley

½ cup grated Parmesan cheese

1. In large stockpot, cook sausages with onion and garlic until meat is browned. Drain well, then add celery and carrots.

2. Cook and stir for 5 minutes longer. Stir in beef broth, tomatoes, oregano, Italian seasoning, and chili sauce; bring to a simmer. Simmer for 15–20 minutes until vegetables are tender.

3. Stir in kidney beans, macaroni, and bell peppers. Bring back to a simmer; cook for 6–9 minutes longer until macaroni is tender. Stir in parsley and serve with cheese.

Keep It Healthy

You can substitute vegetable broth for the beef broth, and omit the sausages to make this a vegetarian minestrone. Add a bit more of each vegetable, or add some chopped mushrooms to make up for the missing meat. You could also use whole wheat macaroni to add more fiber and B vitamins to this hearty soup.

Cold Tomato Soup with Pesto

For a hot day, this cold soup is a wonderful treat.
Serve with Spicy Apple Muffins (page 68) and some fresh fruit.

Serve with Spicy Apple Muffins (page 68) and some fresh fruit.

MAKE AHEAD

INGREDIENTS | SERVES 8

2 (14.5-ounce) cans diced tomatoes, undrained

3 ripe tomatoes, chopped

2 cups tomato juice

3 stalks celery, diced

¼ cup chopped green onions

1 red bell pepper, chopped

1 cucumber, peeled, seeded, and chopped

3 tablespoons lime juice

1 teaspoon sugar

½ teaspoon salt

½ teaspoon dried basil leaves

1 tablespoon Worcestershire sauce

½ cup prepared pesto

¼ cup grated Parmesan cheese

1 avocado, peeled and chopped

1. Combine all ingredients except pesto, cheese, and avocado in large bowl; mix well. Taste for seasoning, correct if necessary, then cover and chill for 3–4 hours.

2. When ready to serve, combine pesto, cheese, and avocado and mix well. Serve soup in chilled glass bowls; top with pesto mixture.

Party Fun

This soup is already beautiful, but you can garnish it in many different ways. Use edible flowers to add color and flavor to the soup. Edible flowers include nasturtiums, chive blossoms, basil blossoms, carnations, and fuchsia. Make sure that the flowers are pesticide free. Rinse gently before using.

Pumpkin Black Bean Soup

This beautiful soup, with its deep orange color and black beans dotting the surface,
would be ideal for a fall or Halloween potluck party.

QUICK

INGREDIENTS | SERVES 6

2 tablespoons olive oil

1 tablespoon butter

1 onion, chopped

3 cloves garlic, minced

1 (16-ounce) can solid pack pumpkin

4 cups chicken broth

1 teaspoon dried thyme leaves

2 (15-ounce) cans black beans, drained

½ teaspoon seasoned salt

⅛ teaspoon white pepper

½ cup heavy cream

½ cup sour cream

1. In large soup pot, heat olive oil and butter over medium heat. Add onion and garlic; cook and stir until tender, about 5 minutes.

2. Add pumpkin and 1 cup of the chicken broth; stir until pumpkin dissolves. Gradually add remaining broth, stirring constantly, until soup is smooth.

3. Add thyme, beans, salt, and pepper and bring to a simmer. Simmer for 10–15 minutes until soup is blended.

4. Add heavy cream and sour cream; heat until steam rises, but do not let soup boil. Serve immediately.

Keep It Healthy

Pumpkin and black beans both have a lot of fiber and vitamins, so this soup is very healthy. You can substitute 1 cup of low-fat evaporated milk for the heavy cream and sour cream mixture if you'd like. Also look for low-sodium broth to reduce the sodium count in this delicious soup.

Chilled Pea Soup

A cold soup is most appropriate on a hot day. This gorgeous one has a velvety texture.
The topping of soybeans, tomatoes, and mint is inspired.

MAKE AHEAD

INGREDIENTS | SERVES 6

2 tablespoons olive oil

2 shallots, minced

1 clove garlic, minced

1 (16-ounce) package frozen baby peas

6 cups vegetable broth

1 teaspoon dried thyme leaves

½ teaspoon dried mint leaves

1 teaspoon salt

⅛ teaspoon white pepper

⅓ cup heavy cream

½ cup sour cream

1 cup frozen edamame, thawed

1 cup chopped cherry tomatoes

¼ cup chopped fresh mint

Transport Tips

Cold soups are very easy to transport. Make sure they are placed in a leak-proof container, and place in an insulated carrier with frozen gel packs or bags of ice cubes. Be sure to put the soup into the refrigerator as soon as you arrive at the party. Serving is easy; just stir and serve.

1. In large pot, heat olive oil over medium heat. Add shallots and garlic; cook and stir until tender, about 3 minutes. Add peas; cook and stir for 3–4 minutes longer.

2. Add vegetable broth, thyme, dried mint, salt, and pepper and bring to a simmer. Simmer for 4–5 minutes until peas are tender.

3. Remove pan from heat, add heavy cream, and puree using an immersion blender. Stir soup well, pour into serving pitcher, cover, and chill for 4–6 hours.

4. Meanwhile, in small bowl combine sour cream, edamame, cherry tomatoes, and fresh mint; mix well, cover, and refrigerate.

5. When ready to serve, stir soup and pour into chilled bowls. Top with sour cream mixture and serve immediately.

Slow Cooker Stroganoff Soup

Beef stroganoff is a wonderful recipe for entertaining.
Turn it into a soup cooked in the slow cooker for an even easier version.

MAKE AHEAD

INGREDIENTS | SERVES 8

1½ pounds beef sirloin
1 teaspoon salt
⅛ teaspoon pepper
2 onions, chopped
4 cloves garlic, minced
1 bay leaf
1 teaspoon dried oregano leaves
6 cups beef broth
2 cups water
2 cups sliced carrots
½ cup sour cream
¼ cup light cream
2 tablespoons flour
2 cups egg noodles

1. Trim excess fat from sirloin; cut into 1-inch cubes. Place in 5–6 quart slow cooker; sprinkle with salt and pepper.

2. Add onions, garlic, bay leaf, and oregano and stir. Add beef broth, water, and carrots and cover. Cook on low for 8–9 hours. Remove bay leaf.

3. Turn slow cooker to high. In small bowl, combine sour cream, light cream, and flour and mix with wire whisk until smooth. Stir egg noodles and sour cream mixture into slow cooker. Cover and cook on high for 15–20 minutes until noodles are tender and soup has thickened slightly. Stir well and serve.

Chicken Risi Bisi Soup

Risi Bisi is a mixture of rice and tiny peas along with Parmesan cheese.
This soup takes this classic dish to a new level.

LAST MINUTE

INGREDIENTS | SERVES 6

3 boneless, skinless chicken breasts, cubed

2 tablespoons flour

1 teaspoon salt

⅛ teaspoon pepper

1 teaspoon dried thyme leaves

½ teaspoon dried Italian seasoning

2 tablespoons butter

1 tablespoon olive oil

1 onion, chopped

3 cloves garlic, minced

1 cup long-grain white rice

8 cups chicken broth

2 cups frozen baby peas, thawed

1 cup grated Parmesan cheese

Keep It Healthy

You could use brown or wild rice in place of the white rice, but it needs to be pre-cooked or the other ingredients will over-cook. Cover the rice with water and bring to a simmer. Simmer for 15 minutes, then drain and add to soup as directed. Simmer until the rice is tender and chicken is thoroughly cooked.

1. Toss cubed chicken with flour, salt, pepper, thyme, and Italian seasoning. In large pot, melt butter with olive oil over medium heat.

2. Add chicken; brown on all sides, about 5–7 minutes. Remove chicken from pot and set aside.

3. Add onion and garlic to pan; cook and stir to loosen pan drippings. Cook until crisp-tender, about 4 minutes. Add rice; cook and stir for another 4 minutes.

4. Return chicken to pot and add broth. Bring to a simmer; reduce heat, cover, and simmer for 20–25 minutes until rice is tender.

5. Stir in peas; heat through until rice is tender and chicken is cooked. Stir in Parmesan cheese and serve immediately.

Chicken Wild Rice Chowder

*An Alfredo sauce will add a wonderful richness to this easy soup,
and you don't even have to make a white sauce.*

EASY

INGREDIENTS | SERVES 8

6 boneless, skinless chicken thighs, cubed

3 tablespoons flour

1 teaspoon salt

⅛ teaspoon pepper

1 teaspoon dried thyme leaves

¼ cup butter

1 onion, chopped

1 (8-ounce) package sliced mushrooms

1½ cups wild rice

8 cups low-sodium chicken broth

2 cups water

1 (16-ounce) jar four-cheese Alfredo sauce

1 cup shredded Swiss cheese

1. Toss chicken with flour, salt, pepper, and thyme. Melt butter in large soup pot; add chicken thighs. Brown on all sides, about 5–6 minutes, stirring frequently. Remove chicken from skillet.

2. Add onion and mushrooms to pot; cook and stir to loosen pan drippings. Return chicken to skillet along with wild rice, chicken broth, and water. Bring to a simmer, reduce heat, cover, and simmer for 35–45 minutes until rice is tender and chicken is thoroughly cooked.

3. Stir in Alfredo sauce and bring to a simmer again. Then add cheese. Stir over low heat until cheese melts and soup is slightly thickened.

Keep It Healthy

You can find low-fat versions of bottled Alfredo sauce in the grocery store. And you can use low-fat Swiss cheese in place of the regular. Just don't use all nonfat products, because this can change the texture of the finished recipe. A blend of low-fat and nonfat products works best.

Succotash Chowder

Succotash is a mixture of lima beans, corn, and other vegetables.
Turn it into a hearty and healthy soup with this easy recipe.

HEALTHY

INGREDIENTS | SERVES 8–10

1 onion, chopped

3 cloves garlic, minced

1 tablespoon grated ginger root

2 tablespoons olive oil

1 teaspoon salt

¼ teaspoon pepper

2 russet potatoes, peeled and diced

2 cups frozen baby lima beans

2 cups frozen edamame

2 cups sliced carrots

2 cups frozen corn

8 cups vegetable broth

1 (14.5-ounce) can diced tomatoes, undrained

2 tablespoons cornstarch

½ cup sour cream

2 cups shredded sharp Cheddar cheese

1. In large soup pot, cook onions, garlic, and ginger root in olive oil over medium heat. Add salt and pepper and potatoes; cook and stir for 5 minutes longer.

2. Stir in remaining ingredients except tomatoes, cornstarch, sour cream, and cheese. Bring to a simmer; simmer, covered, for 20–25 minutes until vegetables are tender. Stir in tomatoes.

3. In small bowl, combine cornstarch and sour cream. Blend in 1 cup of the hot soup liquid, then return sour cream mixture to pot along with cheese. Cook and stir for a few minutes until soup thickens and cheese melts. Serve immediately.

Transport Tips

To transport this soup, cook it through Step 2, then either pack it as a hot item or chill it in the refrigerator and pack it as a cold item. When you get to the party, reheat it to a simmer, then add the sour cream mixture and cheese; cook and stir until the soup is creamy and blended.

Best Beer Cheese Soup

Be sure to use a beer that you like in this easy recipe,
because you can taste it in the soup.

INEXPENSIVE

INGREDIENTS | SERVES 6

¼ cup butter
1 cup finely chopped onion
2 cloves garlic, minced
1 cup finely chopped carrot
1 cup finely chopped mushrooms
1 (12-ounce) can beer
1 quart chicken broth
2 tablespoons Dijon mustard
½ cup light cream
2 tablespoons cornstarch
2 cups shredded Colby cheese
1 cup diced American cheese
4 cups popped cheese-flavored popcorn

1. In large pot, melt butter over medium heat. Add onion and garlic; cook and stir until tender, about 6 minutes. Add carrot and mushrooms; cook and stir for another 4 minutes.

2. Add beer and chicken broth; bring to a simmer. Cover, reduce heat to low, and simmer for 15–20 minutes until vegetables are tender.

3. In small bowl, combine mustard, cream, and cornstarch and mix well. Add to soup along with both types of cheese. Cook and stir until soup is hot and creamy and cheese is melted. Serve immediately with popcorn for topping.

Party Fun

This soup is very filling, so if you're serving it as part of a buffet, make sure to advise small portions. It can easily be the main dish of a fall supper after a high school football game. Serve it in warmed soup bowls or mugs along with a spinach salad, a gelatin salad, and some hot scones fresh from the oven.

Gouda Vegetable Soup

This easy soup is delicious and full of vegetables.
Serve it as the main dish for a vegetarian lunch, or as part of a larger buffet.

QUICK

INGREDIENTS | SERVES 8

2 tablespoons butter
2 tablespoons olive oil
2 onions, chopped
4 cloves garlic, minced
2 russet potatoes, peeled and chopped
3 cups small cauliflower florets
4 carrots, sliced
3 tablespoons flour
½ teaspoon salt
1 teaspoon dried thyme leaves
⅛ teaspoon pepper
8 cups vegetable broth
1½ cups frozen baby peas, thawed
2 tablespoons cornstarch
1½ cups shredded Gouda cheese
½ cup shredded provolone cheese

1. In large soup pot, melt butter with olive oil over medium heat. Add onions and garlic; cook and stir until crisp-tender, about 5 minutes.

2. Add potatoes; cook and stir for 4 minutes. Add cauliflower and carrots; cook and stir for 3–4 minutes longer.

3. Stir in flour, salt, thyme, and pepper; cook and stir until bubbly. Then add broth. Bring to a simmer; reduce heat, cover, and simmer until vegetables are tender, about 15–20 minutes. Add peas; simmer for 3–4 minutes longer.

4. In small bowl, combine cornstarch with both types of cheese. Add to soup; cook, stirring, until cheese melts and soup is slightly thickened. Serve immediately.

Sour Cream Vegetable Soup

*This bright soup is quick and easy to make. Just chop the vegetables,
and the soup will be ready in about half an hour.*

QUICK

INGREDIENTS | SERVES 6

3 tablespoons olive oil
1 onion, chopped
3 cloves garlic, minced
2 cups sliced carrots
1 cup chopped celery
1 teaspoon salt
⅛ teaspoon pepper
1 teaspoon dried basil leaves
4 cups vegetable broth
1 cup instant mashed potato flakes
1½ cups milk
2 cups baby frozen peas, thawed
½ cup sour cream
1 tablespoon lemon juice
1 tablespoon cornstarch
¼ teaspoon dried dill weed

Make-Ahead Hints

While this soup can be made at the last
minute, you can also make it ahead of time.
Stop at the end of Step 2. The soup can
stand for 2 hours at room temperature or
can be refrigerated longer. Then just
reheat the soup and continue with the
recipe.

1. In large soup pot, heat olive oil over medium heat.
   Add onion and garlic; cook and stir for 3 minutes. Add
   carrots; cook and stir for 3 minutes longer.

2. Add celery, salt, pepper, basil, and broth; bring to a
   simmer. Cover and simmer for 10–15 minutes until
   vegetables are tender.

3. Add potato flakes, milk, and peas; cook and stir over
   medium heat until soup thickens.

4. In small bowl, combine remaining ingredients. Stir
   into soup; heat through, stirring frequently, until soup
   is thickened and blended.

Butternut Squash Soup

With a gorgeous golden color, this flavorful soup is perfect for a fall meal.
Serve with a green salad, some bread hot from the oven, and a fruit salad.

HEALTHY

INGREDIENTS | SERVES 6

1 butternut squash
2 tablespoons butter, melted
2 tablespoons olive oil
1 onion, chopped
1 apple, peeled and diced
1 tablespoon grated fresh
ginger root
2 cloves garlic, minced
1 tablespoon curry powder
½ teaspoon salt
⅛ teaspoon pepper
4 cups low-sodium chicken broth
1 (8-ounce) package cream cheese,
softened

1. Preheat oven to 375°F. Cut the squash in half lengthwise and remove seeds. Brush cut side with melted butter and place, cut side down, on cookie sheet. Roast for 45–55 minutes until squash is tender. Let cool for 30 minutes.

2. Remove flesh from skin and cut squash into 1-inch pieces; set aside.

3. In large soup pot, heat olive oil over medium heat. Add onion, apple, ginger root, garlic, and curry powder; cook and stir for 5 minutes.

4. Add cubed squash along with salt, pepper, and chicken broth. Bring to a simmer; reduce heat, cover, and simmer for 20–25 minutes until vegetables are tender.

5. In food processor, combine cream cheese with 3 cups of the soup; process until smooth. Return to pot; mash with potato masher or blend using immersion blender. Heat through but do not boil.

Chilled Pesto Gazpacho

*This very fresh recipe has a nice bit of spice because of the vegetable cocktail juice.
Look for low-sodium versions.*

HEALTHY

INGREDIENTS | SERVES 6

6 plum tomatoes, seeded and chopped
1 cucumber, peeled and seeded
1 red onion, finely chopped
1 green bell pepper, chopped
4 cups vegetable cocktail juice
¼ cup red wine vinegar
2 tablespoons lemon juice
½ cup basil pesto
¼ teaspoon Tabasco sauce
2 cloves garlic, minced
½ cup chopped fresh basil
⅓ cup grated Parmesan cheese
1 avocado, peeled and diced

1. In large bowl, combine all ingredients except basil, cheese, and avocado and mix well. Cover and chill for 3–4 hours.

2. When ready to serve, stir in basil and cheese. Top with diced avocado and serve immediately.

Party Fun

You can serve gazpacho or other cold soups in lots of fun ways. Hollow out some bell peppers and spoon in the soup. Or serve the soup in chilled mugs with iced tea spoons. Garnish these fresh-tasting soups with croutons, sprigs of fresh herbs, or diced tomato or avocado.

CHAPTER 13

Cookies, Brownies, and Candies

Chewy Cherry Bars

These chewy bars are very easy to make and serve.
Chop the cherries to make sure there are no pits in them.

INEXPENSIVE

INGREDIENTS | YIELDS ABOUT 3 DOZEN BARS

4 eggs
½ cup brown sugar
1¼ cups granulated sugar
2 teaspoons vanilla
1½ cups flour
Pinch salt
1 teaspoon baking powder
1 cup dried cherries, chopped
1 cup flaked coconut
1 cup chopped walnuts
1 cup powdered sugar

1. Preheat oven to 375°F. Spray a 9" × 13" pan with nonstick cooking spray and set aside.

2. In large bowl, beat eggs with brown sugar and sugar until light colored and thick. Beat in vanilla, then stir in flour, salt, and baking powder.

3. Add dried cherries, coconut, and walnuts. Spread into prepared pan. Bake for 30–40 minutes or until bars are golden brown and set. Cool completely on wire rack.

4. Cut bars into 1" × 3" bars and roll on all sides in powdered sugar. Store at room temperature in airtight container.

Best Fudge

You have to stir the sugar and milk mixture constantly so it doesn't burn.
Small brown bits may appear; that's okay, it adds a depth of flavor to the fudge.

QUICK

INGREDIENTS | YIELDS 36 PIECES

1½ cups sugar
1 cup brown sugar
1 (13-ounce) can evaporated milk
2 (12-ounce) packages semisweet chocolate chips
¼ cup light corn syrup
3 tablespoons butter
2 teaspoons vanilla

1. Grease a 9-inch square pan with unsalted butter and set aside. In large heavy saucepan, combine sugar, brown sugar, and evaporated milk. Cook over medium heat, stirring constantly with wire whisk, until mixture comes to a boil.

2. Reduce heat to low. Cook for 10 minutes longer, stirring constantly. Then remove from heat and stir in chocolate chips, corn syrup, butter, and vanilla.

3. Beat until chocolate is melted and fudge is smooth. Spread into prepared pan and chill until firm.

Peanut Butter Fudge Brownies

These rich brownies feed a crowd.
They must be cut into small pieces because they're so rich.

EASY

INGREDIENTS | YIELDS 36 BROWNIES

1 cup butter

1¼ cups peanut butter, divided

1 square unsweetened chocolate, chopped

1 cup sugar

¾ cup brown sugar

¼ cup cocoa

4 eggs

2 teaspoons vanilla

1 cup flour

¼ teaspoon salt

½ teaspoon baking powder

1 (12-ounce) package semisweet chocolate chips

1. Preheat oven to 350°F. Spray a 9" × 13" baking pan with nonstick baking spray containing flour and set aside.

2. In large saucepan, combine butter, ¼ cup peanut butter, and unsweetened chocolate. Melt over medium heat until smooth.

3. Remove from heat and stir in sugar, brown sugar, and cocoa; beat well. Beat in eggs, one at a time, then add vanilla.

4. Add flour, salt, and baking powder and mix just until combined. Spread into prepared pan. Microwave ½ cup peanut butter for 30 seconds, stir, and then drop by spoonfuls over batter; swirl with knife.

5. Bake for 25–35 minutes or just until brownies are set. Do not overbake.

6. For frosting, melt remaining ½ cup peanut butter with the chocolate chips in small skillet until smooth. Pour over warm brownies, spread to cover, then cool completely.

Angel Cookies

Traditional meringue cookies usually have just nuts and chopped dates inside.
This twist on the classic is lighter and delicious.

HEALTHY

INGREDIENTS | YIELDS 4 DOZEN COOKIES

4 egg whites

¼ teaspoon cream of tartar

¼ teaspoon salt

½ cup sugar

1½ cups powdered sugar

1 teaspoon vanilla

1 cup cornflakes cereal, crushed

1 cup chopped dried apricots

½ cup chopped cashews

Keep It Healthy

These little cookies are sweet and chewy, and very low in fat. You could make them even lower by substituting ½ cup chopped dates or dried cherries for the cashews. To make them more decadent and still healthy, top them with a drizzle of dark or bittersweet chocolate after they've cooled.

1. Preheat oven to 325°F. Line cookie sheets with parchment paper or Silpat liners. In large bowl, combine egg whites, cream of tartar, and salt; beat until foamy. Gradually add ½ cup sugar; beat until soft peaks form.

2. Gradually beat in powdered sugar until stiff peaks form, then add vanilla. Fold in remaining ingredients.

3. Drop mixture by teaspoons onto cookie sheets. Bake for 12–16 minutes or until cookies are set and light golden brown. Let cool for 3 minutes, then remove to wire racks to cool completely.

Lemon Meringue Bars

*A sweet-and-sour meringue tops a sweet and sour crust
in these special and different bar cookies.*

INEXPENSIVE

INGREDIENTS | YIELDS 24 BARS

½ cup butter, softened

1 tablespoon grated lemon zest

½ cup powdered sugar

2 egg yolks

1 cup flour

2 egg whites

2 tablespoons lemon juice

½ cup sugar

⅓ cup finely crushed hard lemon candies

1. Preheat oven to 350°F. Spray a 9" × 13" pan with nonstick baking spray and set aside. In medium bowl, combine butter with zest and powdered sugar; beat well. Add egg yolks and flour and mix until a dough forms.

2. Press dough evenly in prepared pan. Bake for 8–9 minutes until very light golden brown. Remove from oven and set aside.

3. In large bowl, combine egg whites with lemon juice; beat until soft peaks form. Gradually add sugar, beating until stiff peaks form. Fold in candies.

4. Spread meringue mixture on base. Bake for 20–30 minutes longer until meringue is light golden brown. Cool completely, then cut into bars.

Almond Biscotti

Slivered almonds work best for grinding, because they don't have any skins.

MAKE AHEAD

INGREDIENTS | YIELDS 24 BISCOTTI

½ cup butter, softened

1 cup brown sugar

2 eggs

½ teaspoon almond extract

¼ cup buttermilk

¼ cup sour cream

⅔ cup ground almonds

3 cups flour

1 cup sliced almonds

Keep It Healthy

Butter isn't bad for you! Of course, it's smart to eat everything in moderation, but butter isn't a bad choice for your diet, especially in baked goods. Butter contains no artificial trans fat, and it has vitamins and minerals. Plus, it's a natural food. With all the information about artificial foods coming out, it's best to eat natural.

1. Preheat oven to 300°F. In large bowl, combine butter and brown sugar; beat until light and fluffy. Beat in eggs, one at a time, and add almond extract.

2. Combine buttermilk and sour cream. Combine ground almonds and flour. Alternately add flour mixture and buttermilk mixture to butter mixture, beginning and ending with dry ingredients.

3. You may have to add more flour to form a workable dough. Divide dough into thirds. Press into three logs, 3" × 10", and smooth edges. Bake for 40 minutes.

4. Let logs cool for 5 minutes, then cut into 1-inch slices. Press the cut sides of slices into sliced almonds and place, cut side up, on cookie sheets.

5. Reduce heat to 275°F. Bake cookies for 15 minutes, then turn and bake for 15 minutes longer, until light browned and crisp. Cool completely on wire racks.

Meringue-Filled Chocolate Cookies

These little cookies are very special. A chocolate meringue is encased in a chocolate cookie, all dressed up with a chocolate drizzle.

MAKE AHEAD

INGREDIENTS | YIELDS 6 DOZEN COOKIES

3½ cups flour

¼ cup cornstarch

1 teaspoon salt

½ cup cocoa

1 cup powdered sugar

1 cup butter

1 cup sour cream

¼ cup milk

2 egg yolks

2 teaspoons vanilla

2 egg whites

¼ teaspoon salt

½ cup sugar

1¼ cups pecans, ground

1 cup semisweet chocolate chips

½ cup milk chocolate chips

1. The day before, sift flour with cornstarch, salt, cocoa, and powdered sugar into a large bowl. Cut in butter until particles are fine.

2. In small bowl, combine sour cream, milk, egg yolks, and vanilla and mix well. Stir into flour mixture until a dough forms. You may need to add more flour or milk to make a soft but workable dough. Cover and chill for 24 hours.

3. When you want to bake the cookies, beat egg whites with salt in medium bowl until foamy. Add sugar gradually, beating until stiff peaks form. Fold in ground pecans and chocolate chips.

4. In two batches, roll out dough to 1/8" thickness on work surface dusted with powdered sugar. Cut into 2-½" squares. Place a teaspoon of the meringue filling in center of each square. Fold two opposite corners together to meet in middle. Preheat oven to 350°F.

5. Bake cookies for 18–23 minutes until dough is set. Cool on wire racks. In small saucepan, combine 1 cup semisweet chocolate chips with the milk chocolate chips. Melt over low heat, then drizzle over cooled cookies.

Mocha Date Treats

If you can find Medjool dates, use those; they are bigger, sweeter, and more tender than regular packaged dates

EASILY DOUBLES

INGREDIENTS | YIELDS 36 CANDIES

¾ cup chocolate icing

½ teaspoon instant coffee powder

½ cup chopped pecans

36 pitted dates

2 tablespoons cocoa powder

¼ cup powdered sugar

1 teaspoon instant coffee powder

1 cup semisweet chocolate chips

½ cup milk chocolate chips

Party Fun

These elegant little candies are fun to make and eat. Your guests will think they're eating some generic chocolate-covered candy, but they bite into a sweet date stuffed with nuts and other goodies. You could coat some of the dates in white chocolate, some in almond bark, and some in the semisweet chocolate for a nice selection.

1. In small bowl, combine icing, ½ teaspoon coffee powder, and pecans; mix well. Using small spoon or pastry bag, spoon or pipe mixture into the dates. In sifter, combine cocoa powder, powdered sugar, and 1 teaspoon coffee powder; sift onto plate. Roll dates into cocoa mixture to coat.

2. In microwave glass measuring cup, place chocolate chips. Microwave on 50% power for 2 minutes; stir until melted. Add milk chocolate chips; stir constantly until chocolate is melted and mixture is smooth.

3. Place dates on a fork and dip, one at a time, into chocolate mixture. Tap fork on side of cup to remove excess chocolate. Place on waxed paper–lined cookie sheets. Let stand until firm. Store, covered, at room temperature.

Toffee Rocky Road Drops

*Dried cranberries and toffee baking bits add a
sophisticated twist to traditional Rocky Road candies.*

MAKE AHEAD

INGREDIENTS | YIELDS 4 DOZEN
CANDIES

1 (12-ounce) package semisweet
chocolate chips

1 (11.5-ounce) package milk chocolate
chips, divided

1 (1-ounce) square unsweetened baking
chocolate

1 cup dried cranberries

2 cups chopped walnuts

1 cup toffee baking bits

2 cups salted peanuts

3 cups miniature marshmallows

1. In medium saucepan, combine semisweet chocolate chips and 1½ cups milk chocolate chips with baking chocolate. Melt together over low heat, stir until smooth.

2. Remove from heat and stir in remaining ½ cup milk chocolate chips, stirring constantly, until smooth.

3. Stir in remaining ingredients just until mixed. Drop by tablespoons onto waxed paper–lined cookie sheets. Let stand until firm.

Party Fun

This is another candy recipe you can vary by using different types of chocolate. Also think about mixing it up by drizzling the set candies with contrasting chocolate. If you use white chocolate chips for the base of the candy, drizzle the finished creations with dark chocolate, and vice versa.

Eight-Layer Cookie Bars

*This bar is perfect for the non-cook. Vanilla wafer crumbs, dried cranberries,
and toffee bits dress up a classic bar cookie.*

EASY

INGREDIENTS | YIELDS 24 BAR COOKIES

1½ cups vanilla wafer crumbs

½ cup butter, melted

1 (14-ounce) can sweetened condensed milk

1 cup semisweet chocolate chips

1 cup milk chocolate chips

1 cup chopped dried cranberries

½ cup English toffee baking bits

½ cup chopped pecans

Party Fun

These bars are so easy to vary. Instead of the vanilla wafer crumbs, try crushing chocolate sandwich cookies, oatmeal cookies, or chocolate chip cookies. The sweetened condensed milk has to be used each time, but try different types of chocolate chips, dried fruit, and nuts to make the recipe your own.

1. Preheat oven to 350°F. Line a 9" × 13" pan with heavy-duty foil, making sure the foil extends past the pan edges. Spray foil with nonstick baking spray containing flour.

2. In small bowl, combine crumbs with melted butter and mix well. Place in prepared pan; press down evenly to form crust.

3. Drizzle with half of the sweetened condensed milk, as evenly as possible. Top with remaining ingredients in order listed. Drizzle with the rest of the sweetened condensed milk. Press down gently with the back of a spoon.

4. Bake bars for 25–35 minutes until light golden brown. Cool completely, then cut into bars.

Lemon Meringue Cookies

A crisp shortbread oatmeal cookie is bordered with a lemon meringue,
then filled with a creamy lemon curd. These are special cookies for a special occasion.

INEXPENSIVE

INGREDIENTS | YIELDS 6 DOZEN COOKIES

⅔ cup butter, softened
1 cup sugar
1 egg
1 teaspoon grated lemon zest
1 teaspoon baking soda
½ teaspoon salt
1¾ cups flour
2 tablespoons cornstarch
¾ cup quick-cooking oatmeal
3 eggs, separated
1½ cups sugar, divided
½ cup lemon juice, divided
1 tablespoon butter
2 tablespoons sour cream

1. In large bowl, beat butter with 1 cup sugar until fluffy. Add egg and lemon zest; beat well. Add baking soda, salt, flour, cornstarch, and oatmeal.

2. Form mixture into two rolls about 1½ inches in diameter and wrap in waxed paper; chill until firm.

3. For lemon filling, in small saucepan, combine 3 egg yolks with ¾ cup sugar and 6 tablespoons lemon juice; cook, stirring, until mixture boils and thickens. Remove from heat and add 1 tablespoon butter and sour cream. Cool for 15 minutes, then chill in refrigerator.

4. When ready to bake, preheat oven to 300°F. Slice the cookie dough $1/8$-inch thick and place 2 inches apart on cookie sheets. Refrigerate while preparing meringue.

5. In small bowl, beat 3 egg whites with 2 tablespoons lemon juice until soft peaks form; gradually beat in ¾ cup sugar until stiff peaks form. Place in pastry bag. Pipe a circle of meringue on the outside edge of each cookie.

6. Bake for 11–14 minutes until meringue is set. Cool on wire racks, then fill each with lemon filling. Store in refrigerator.

Chinese Chews

A crumbly crust is topped with a soft and chewy mixture that's full of fruit and nuts. Yum.

EASILY DOUBLES

INGREDIENTS | YIELDS 36 COOKIES

1 cup butter, softened
¼ cup brown sugar
1½ cups flour
4 eggs, separated
1 cup brown sugar
1 cup chopped pecans
½ cup finely chopped dried apricots
½ cup flaked coconut
½ cup granulated sugar
⅓ cup lemon juice
1½ cups powdered sugar
3 tablespoons butter, melted

Make-Ahead Hints

These bar cookies can be made up to 24 hours in advance, but not much longer. The creamy filling tends to melt into the crust as the bars stand. You can make the crust a few days ahead of time, then prepare and add the filling, bake, and frost the day of your party.

1. Preheat oven to 325°F. In medium bowl, combine 1 cup butter with ¼ cup brown sugar and flour; mix until crumbly. Press into 9" × 13" pan. Bake for 10 minutes, then remove and cool.

2. In same medium bowl, beat egg yolks with 1 cup brown sugar until light and fluffy. Add pecans, apricots, and coconut. In small bowl, beat egg whites with ½ cup granulated sugar until stiff peaks form. Fold into egg yolk mixture.

3. Spoon and spread onto baked layer. Bake for 30–35 minutes until mixture is set and golden brown. Cool on wire rack.

4. In small bowl, combine lemon juice, powdered sugar, and 3 tablespoons melted butter; mix well with wire whisk. Pour over bars, then let cool. Store covered in cool dry place.

Best Brownies

*These rich, fudgy brownies are topped with chocolate fudge.
There's nothing better!*

MAKE AHEAD

INGREDIENTS | YIELDS 36 BROWNIES

1 cup butter

1 square unsweetened chocolate, chopped

1½ cups brown sugar

1¼ cups granulated sugar

1 tablespoon vanilla

4 eggs

¾ cup cocoa powder

¼ teaspoon salt

1½ cups flour

1 cup milk chocolate chips

1 (13-ounce) can sweetened condensed milk

1 (12-ounce) package semisweet chocolate chips

1. Preheat oven to 325°F. Spray a 9" × 13" pan with nonstick baking spray containing flour; set aside.

2. In large saucepan, combine butter and unsweetened chocolate; melt over low heat, stirring until smooth. Beat in brown sugar and granulated sugar, then add vanilla. Remove from heat.

3. Beat in eggs, one at a time, beating until smooth after each addition. Add cocoa powder, salt, and flour; mix until combined. Stir in milk chocolate chips.

4. Spread into prepared pan. Bake for 40–45 minutes until brownies are just set. Cool completely on wire rack.

5. For frosting, in microwave-safe bowl, combine sweetened condensed milk and chocolate chips. Microwave on 50% power for 2–3 minutes, stirring twice during cooking time, until mixture is smooth. Pour over brownies, cool completely, then cut into bars.

Blueberry Oatmeal Cookies

These deliciously chewy oatmeal cookies have the sweet tart flavor of dried blueberries and crunchy nuts as special additions.

HEALTHY

INGREDIENTS | YIELDS 48 COOKIES

½ cup butter, softened
½ cup oil
1 cup sugar
¾ cup brown sugar
2 teaspoons vanilla
1 teaspoon cinnamon
2 tablespoons honey
2 eggs
2 tablespoons milk
1½ cups flour
½ cup whole wheat flour
1½ teaspoons baking soda
½ teaspoon salt
2 cups quick-cooking oatmeal
1 cup dried blueberries
½ cup chopped walnuts

1. Preheat oven to 350°F. In large bowl, combine butter, oil, sugar, brown sugar, vanilla, cinnamon, and honey and mix well.

2. Beat in eggs and milk until blended. Stir in flour, whole wheat flour, baking soda, and salt, and mix well. Stir in oatmeal, blueberries, and walnuts.

3. Drop by teaspoonfuls onto Silpat-lined cookie sheets about 2 inches apart. Bake for 11–14 minutes until cookies are light golden brown. Cool for 5 minutes, then remove to wire racks to cool completely.

French Lace Cookies

Lace cookies are thin and crisp and can be formed into lots of different shapes.

INEXPENSIVE

INGREDIENTS | YIELDS 36 COOKIES
1 cup butter, softened
⅔ cup brown sugar
⅔ cup granulated sugar
⅔ cup dark corn syrup
⅓ cup honey
2 cups all-purpose flour
½ cup ground oatmeal
1½ cups finely chopped almonds
2 teaspoons vanilla

Party Fun

You can shape these cookies in many different ways. When they're still pliable, press into greased muffin cups or on the greased outsides of custard cups. Or you can roll the warm cookies around a rolling pin, or around a cone form. Fill the cups or cylinders or cones with pudding, ice cream, or cheesecake filling.

1. Preheat oven to 350°F. Line cookie sheets with foil or parchment paper, or use Silpat liners.

2. In large saucepan, combine butter, brown sugar, granulated sugar, corn syrup, and honey over medium heat. Bring to a boil, stirring occasionally.

3. Meanwhile, combine flour, ground oatmeal, and almonds and mix well. Stir into the butter mixture and bring to another boil.

4. Remove from heat and stir in vanilla. Drop mixture by teaspoons onto prepared cookie sheets, leaving at least 3 inches around each cookie to allow for spreading.

5. Bake cookies for 6–10 minutes until golden brown and bubbly. Let cookies stand for 1 minute, then remove from sheet and shape. If not shaping, let the cookies cool on the pan for 2–3 minutes, then place on wire racks to cool.

S'Mores Bars

Wow—these decadent bars taste like a S'Mores to the tenth power.
Cut them in small squares because they're rich.

MAKE AHEAD

INGREDIENTS | YIELDS 48 BAR COOKIES

¾ cup butter, softened
1¼ cups brown sugar
1 egg
1 tablespoon vanilla
1 cup flour
1¼ cups graham cracker crumbs
1 teaspoon baking powder
¼ teaspoon salt
3 cups miniature marshmallows
1 cup milk chocolate chips
¼ cup butter
⅓ cup milk
1 cup semisweet chocolate chips
1 (3-ounce) package cream cheese
3 cups powdered sugar
1 teaspoon vanilla

1. Preheat oven to 350°F. Spray a 9" × 13" pan with nonstick baking spray containing flour and set aside.

2. In large bowl, combine ¾ cup butter with 1¼ cups brown sugar; beat until fluffy. Add egg and vanilla and mix well. Stir in flour, graham cracker crumbs, baking powder, and salt. Spoon and spread into prepared pan.

3. Bake for 25–35 minutes until cookie is just set and light golden brown. Immediately sprinkle with marshmallows and milk chocolate chips. Return to oven; bake for 2–4 minutes longer until marshmallows puff.

4. While bars are in oven for the first time, in large saucepan combine ¼ cup butter, milk, semisweet chocolate chips, and cream cheese. Cook over low heat, stirring frequently, until chocolate is melted and mixture is smooth. Remove from heat and stir in powdered sugar and 1 teaspoon vanilla.

5. When bars come out of oven with puffed marshmallows on top, pour frosting evenly over the marshmallows. Marble with a knife, then let stand until cool.

Orange-Mint Sugar Cookies

These easy crisp and sweet cookies have a wonderful orange-mint flavor.

INEXPENSIVE

INGREDIENTS | YIELDS 48 COOKIES

1 cup butter, softened
½ cup granulated sugar
½ cup brown sugar
2 eggs
2¾ cups flour
¼ cup cornstarch
1 teaspoon baking soda
1 (6-ounce) can frozen orange juice concentrate, thawed
2 tablespoons minced fresh mint leaves
½ cup granulated sugar
½ teaspoon mint extract

Make-Ahead Hints

Any sugar cookie dough can be made ahead of time and baked straight from the refrigerator. You can even divide the dough into balls and freeze it, or form the dough into two long rolls, wrap in waxed paper, then freeze wrap, and freeze it. Bake the balls just as they are, adding a few minutes to the baking time. Slice the rolls and bake.

1. Preheat oven to 400°F. In large bowl, combine butter, ½ cup granulated sugar, and brown sugar and beat until light and fluffy. Beat in eggs, one at a time, beating until light and fluffy.

2. Sift together flour, cornstarch, and baking soda. In small bowl, combine half of the thawed concentrate with mint leaves. Add flour mixture alternately with the orange juice to the butter mixture.

3. Place mixture on ungreased cookie sheets in ½ tablespoon measures. Bake for 8–9 minutes until light golden brown. Meanwhile, combine ½ cup granulated sugar with the mint extract and mix well.

4. Remove cookies to wire rack. Immediately brush with the remaining thawed concentrate and sprinkle with the mint sugar. Let cool completely.

Fresh Apple Bar Cookies

The taste of apples and cinnamon is complemented with a rich browned butter frosting in these classic and simple bars.

EASY

INGREDIENTS | YIELDS 36 COOKIES

½ cup butter

1 cup dark brown sugar

½ teaspoon salt

1 teaspoon cinnamon

¼ teaspoon nutmeg

1 egg

2 teaspoons vanilla

1½ cups flour

½ cup whole wheat flour

1 teaspoon baking powder

1 cup very finely chopped peeled apple

1 cup chopped walnuts

½ cup apple juice, divided

½ cup butter

3 cups powdered sugar

¼ cup apple juice

1. Preheat oven to 350°F. Spray a 9" × 13" pan with nonstick baking spray containing flour.

2. In large bowl, cream butter with sugar and salt until light and fluffy. Add cinnamon, nutmeg, egg, and vanilla and mix well.

3. Sift together flour, whole wheat flour, and baking powder. Add half of the flour mixture to the butter mixture and mix well. Beat in apples, nuts, and ¼ cup apple juice, then stir in remaining flour mixture.

4. Spread in prepared pan. Bake for 25–35 minutes until bars are golden brown. Cool completely on wire rack.

5. For frosting, melt ½ cup butter in heavy saucepan. Cook over medium-low heat until butter turns brown. Immediately remove from heat and beat in powdered sugar and apple juice. Frost cooled bars.

Layered Ginger Bars

*For this bar cookie, you make a crumbly mixture for the top,
then add ginger and sour cream to the remaining crumbs for an easy filling.*

INEXPENSIVE

INGREDIENTS | YIELDS 25 BAR COOKIES

2 cups brown sugar

2 cups flour

½ cup butter

1 egg

1 teaspoon ground ginger

¼ teaspoon nutmeg

1 cup sour cream

1 teaspoon baking soda

½ cup chopped walnuts

¼ cup butter, melted

2 cups powdered sugar

½ teaspoon ground ginger

2–4 tablespoons light cream

1. Preheat oven to 350°F. Spray a 9-inch square pan with nonstick baking spray containing flour and set aside.

2. In large bowl, combine brown sugar and flour and mix well. Cut in butter until particles are fine. Pat half of this mixture into bottom of prepared pan.

3. Add egg, ginger, nutmeg, sour cream, baking soda, and walnuts to remaining crumb mixture in bowl and beat well. Pour over crust.

4. Bake for 30–40 minutes until bars are set. Cool completely on wire rack.

5. For frosting, combine melted butter with powdered sugar, ½ teaspoon ground ginger, and enough light cream for desired spreading consistency. Spread over bars and cool completely.

Pineapple Squares

This old-fashioned recipe is delicious cut into squares,
topped with some sweetened whipped cream.

MAKE AHEAD

INGREDIENTS | YIELDS 18 BARS

½ cup butter

¾ cup brown sugar

2 egg yolks

24 graham crackers, crushed

1 teaspoon baking powder

½ teaspoon baking soda

½ cup chopped pecans

1 cup milk

1¼ cups sugar, divided

1 (15-ounce) can crushed pineapple, undrained

2 tablespoons powdered sugar

Transport Tips

Cookies are the easiest foods to transport. Regular cookies should be placed in a tin or plastic container, layers separated by waxed paper. Take bar cookies to the party in their original pan. Cut them into squares at the party. Candies should be layered in tins with waxed paper or foil separating the layers.

1. Preheat oven to 350°F. Spray a 9" × 13" pan with nonstick baking spray containing flour and set aside.

2. In large bowl, combine butter and brown sugar and beat until light and fluffy. Add egg yolks, one at a time, beating well after each addition.

3. In small bowl, combine graham cracker crumbs with baking powder, baking soda, and pecans. Add alternately with milk to the butter mixture.

4. In small bowl, beat egg whites with ¼ cup sugar until stiff peaks form. Fold into graham cracker mixture and spread in prepared pan. Bake for 35–45 minutes until golden brown and set. Place on wire rack.

5. In small saucepan, combine 1 cup sugar with undrained pineapple. Cook over low heat, stirring frequently, until mixture is thick. Spread over warm bars, then cool completely. Sprinkle with powdered sugar before serving.

Chocolate Cheesecake Cookies

Chocolate cheesecake in a bar cookie is a nice treat.
The crumbly topping also forms the crust, then the finished bars are drizzled with melted chocolate.

EASY

INGREDIENTS | YIELDS 16 BAR COOKIES

⅓ cup brown sugar

1 cup flour

3 tablespoons cocoa powder

½ cup chopped pecans

½ cup butter, melted

1 (8-ounce) package cream cheese

¼ cup brown sugar

1 (1-ounce) square unsweetened chocolate, melted

2 tablespoons cocoa powder

1 egg

2 tablespoons heavy cream

2 teaspoons vanilla

1 cup semisweet chocolate chips

2 tablespoons butter

1. Preheat oven to 350°F. Spray a 9-inch square pan with nonstick baking spray containing flour and set aside.

2. In medium bowl, combine ⅓ cup brown sugar, flour, 3 tablespoons cocoa, and pecans and mix well. Add ½ cup melted butter and mix until crumbly. Reserve ¾ cup of this mixture for topping. Press remainder into pan.

3. Bake crust for 12–16 minutes until it's just set. Place on wire rack to cool while preparing filling.

4. In medium bowl, beat cream cheese until smooth and fluffy. Add brown sugar, melted chocolate, and cocoa powder and beat until smooth. Add egg, heavy cream, and vanilla and mix well. Pour over crust and sprinkle with reserved crumbs.

5. Bake cookies for 22–27 minutes until filling is just set. Place on wire rack to cool. Combine chocolate chips with 2 tablespoons butter in microwave-safe glass measuring cup. Microwave on 50% power for 2 minutes, then stir until smooth. Drizzle over bars, then let stand until set.

CHAPTER 14

Pies and Cakes

Caramel Cream Cheese Frosting

Regular caramel frosting can be very sweet.
Cream cheese tempers the sweetness and adds a rich mouthfeel.

EASY

INGREDIENTS | YIELDS 3 CUPS FROSTING

1 (8-ounce) package cream cheese, softened

⅓ cup butter, softened

¼ cup brown sugar

⅓ cup caramel ice cream topping

2 teaspoons vanilla

Pinch salt

4 cups powdered sugar

1. In large bowl, combine cream cheese with butter and beat until fluffy. Add brown sugar; beat until sugar dissolves, about 4 minutes.

2. Add the ice cream topping, vanilla, and salt and beat well. Gradually add powdered sugar, beating until desired consistency.

Decadent Chocolate Frosting

This frosting is just like a chocolate truffle, except you get to eat more of it on a cake!

EASY

INGREDIENTS | YIELDS 3 CUPS FROSTING

1 pound milk chocolate, chopped

½ pound semisweet chocolate, chopped

1 cup heavy whipping cream

½ cup light cream

2 teaspoons vanilla

1. In large saucepan, combine all ingredients except vanilla and melt over low heat, stirring constantly.

2. When mixture is melted and smooth, remove from heat and add vanilla. Pour into large bowl and refrigerate until firm, about 5–6 hours.

3. When ready to frost cake, remove mixture from refrigerator and beat with electric mixer until light and fluffy. Frost cake.

Party Fun

Make different types of this frosting: one all milk chocolate, one with dark chocolate, and one with white chocolate. Prepare the recipe up to the stage where they are refrigerated. For dessert, have a cupcake bar: whip these frostings and offer a selection of cupcakes for your guests.

Date Pecan Pie

*Dates are high in fiber and B vitamins, and they are naturally sweet,
with only 23 calories per date. And they're delicious!*

HEALTHY

INGREDIENTS | SERVES 8–10

1 cup finely chopped dates
2 egg yolks
½ cup sugar
½ cup brown sugar
Pinch salt
¼ cup heavy cream
¼ cup butter, melted
1 teaspoon vanilla
2 egg whites
½ cup chopped pecans
1 Make-Ahead Pie Crust (page 251), unpricked

1. Preheat oven to 350°F. In medium bowl, combine dates, egg yolks, sugar, brown sugar, salt, cream, butter, and vanilla and mix well.

2. In small bowl, beat egg whites until stiff peaks form. Fold into date mixture along with pecans.

3. Pour into Pie Crust. Bake for 30–40 minutes or until pie is deep golden brown. Cool completely, then cut into wedges to serve.

Brown Butter Frosting

*It can seem like the butter takes forever to brown, but it will happen.
Watch the butter carefully, since it can go from browned to burned in a few seconds.*

EASY

INGREDIENTS | YIELDS 3 CUPS
FROSTING

1 cup butter
5–6 cups powdered sugar
1 teaspoon corn syrup
3–5 tablespoons heavy cream
2 teaspoons vanilla

1. In large saucepan, over low heat, melt butter. Keep butter on heat, swirling pan occasionally, until the butter starts to turn golden brown. Remove from heat and immediately add 2 cups powdered sugar; beat well.

2. Add corn syrup, then enough powdered sugar and heavy cream alternately until desired spreading consistency. Beat in vanilla. You may need to add more cream while you're frosting the cake.

Make-Ahead Hints

You can make this frosting ahead of time to let your guests frost cookies, cupcakes, or cakes when they arrive, or in a cupcake bar. Just cover it well and keep it at cool room temperature. You may need to add a bit more cream and beat it again for the best spreading consistency.

Decadent Brownie Pie

This pie is so decadent it has to be cut into tiny pieces.
You can make the shell ahead of time, then at the party, have guests make the brownie cream filling.

EASY

INGREDIENTS | SERVES 12

3 egg whites

Pinch salt

½ cup granulated sugar

¼ cup brown sugar

2 teaspoons vanilla, divided

1 cup crushed chocolate sandwich cookies

8 (2-inch) squares Best Brownies (page 235)

1 cup heavy whipping cream

2 tablespoons powdered sugar

2 tablespoons cocoa powder

1. Preheat oven to 300°F. Grease a 9-inch pie plate with solid shortening and sprinkle with a bit of cocoa powder; set aside.

2. In medium bowl, beat egg whites and salt until foamy. Gradually add granulated sugar, beating until stiff peaks form. Beat in brown sugar and 1 teaspoon vanilla until mixed. Fold in crushed cookies.

3. Spread into prepared pie plate. Bake for 35–40 minutes or until the crust is lightly browned. Cool completely.

4. Cut Brownies into ½-inch pieces. In large bowl, beat cream with powdered sugar, cocoa, and 1 teaspoon vanilla until thick. Fold in Brownies, and pile on top of pie. Cover and chill for 1–2 hours before serving.

Raspberry Dream Cake

*Dream Whip is a dry whipped topping mix that makes
the cake layers very light and fluffy.*

MAKE AHEAD

INGREDIENTS | SERVES 16

1 (18-ounce) box white cake mix

1 envelope Dream Whip topping mix

1 cup cold water

6 egg whites

1 (8-ounce) package cream cheese, softened

2 tablespoons butter, softened

3 cups powdered sugar

½ cup fresh raspberries, crushed

2–4 tablespoons heavy cream

⅓ cup raspberry preserves

Make-Ahead Hints

Make the cake ahead of time, and also prepare the frosting, omitting the raspberries. When guests start to arrive, have them fill the cake with preserves, then add the raspberries to the frosting and beat until creamy. You may need to add more powdered sugar. Then tell them to frost the cake, and it will be waiting for you!

1. Preheat oven to 350°F. Spray two 9-inch round cake pans with nonstick baking spray containing flour and set aside.

2. In large bowl, combine cake mix, Dream Whip, water, and egg whites; beat until blended. Then beat for 4 minutes at medium speed. Batter will increase in volume. Pour into prepared cake pans.

3. Bake for 25–30 minutes, until cake is golden brown and starts to pull away from sides of pan. Cool in pans for 5 minutes, then turn out onto baking racks to cool, top side up; cool completely.

4. In large bowl, beat cream cheese with butter until mixed. Add half of the powdered sugar, then all of the raspberries; beat well. Add enough remaining powdered sugar and cream for desired spreading consistency.

5. Place one cake layer on serving plate. Top with preserves. Top with second layer, then frost top and sides with raspberry frosting. Store covered at room temperature.

Carrot Cupcakes

Carrot cake is a delicious and pretty healthy recipe.
Carrot cupcakes are more fun to make, serve and eat!

HEALTHY

INGREDIENTS | YIELDS 24 CUPCAKES

½ (16-ounce) package baby carrots
1 (8-ounce) can crushed pineapple
½ cup vegetable oil
¼ cup butter, softened
¼ cup applesauce
1 cup sugar
1 cup brown sugar
2 eggs
2 teaspoons vanilla
2 cups flour
½ cup whole wheat flour
2 teaspoons baking soda
½ teaspoon salt
1 teaspoon cinnamon
⅛ teaspoon ground ginger
1½ cups coconut, divided
1 recipe Caramel Cream Cheese Frosting (page 246)

1. Preheat oven to 350°F. Spray 24 muffin tins with nonstick baking spray containing flour and set aside.

2. Place baby carrots in food processor; process until very finely chopped. Set aside. Drain pineapple, leaving some juice with the fruit; set aside.

3. In large bowl, combine oil, butter, applesauce, sugar, brown sugar, eggs, and vanilla and beat until smooth. Add flour, whole wheat flour, baking soda, salt, cinnamon, and ginger and mix well.

4. Add grated carrots, pineapple, and ½ cup coconut and mix. Spoon batter into prepared muffin tins, filling each about ⅔ full.

5. Bake cupcakes for 18–23 minutes or until tops spring back when lightly touched with finger. Cool completely on wire racks. Fold remaining 1 cup coconut into the Frosting and frost cupcakes. Store covered at room temperature.

Make-Ahead Pie Crust

This homemade pie crust mix is delicious and versatile;
you can use it for sweet and savory pies.

EASY

INGREDIENTS | MAKES 6 PIE CRUSTS

5 cups flour
1 cup whole wheat pastry flour
1 tablespoon salt
1 tablespoon sugar
1 cup solid vegetable shortening
1 cup butter
½ cup coconut oil

Make It Healthy

You can now find solid shortening that is trans fat free; use that in this recipe. The coconut oil is solid at room temperature, so is easy to cut in along with the other ingredients. And coconut oil is good for you; it has medium-chain fatty acids that are easily metabolized, along with antifungal properties.

1. In large bowl, combine flour, pastry flour, salt, and sugar and mix with wire whisk.

2. In food processor, combine shortening, butter, and coconut oil; mix until combined, scraping down sides twice. Cut into flour mixture until crumbs form; store covered in refrigerator.

3. To make a pie crust, scoop out 1¼ cups of the mix and place in medium bowl. Add 1 teaspoon orange juice and 1–2 tablespoons cold water; toss with a fork until mixture holds together.

4. Roll out between sheets of waxed paper to 11-inch circle. Place in pie plate, fold edges over and flute. If baking before filling, prick with fork and bake at 400°F for 8–10 minutes until browned. If filling before baking, do not prick and use as directed in recipe.

Chocolate Peppermint Pie

Marshmallows melted with milk and peppermint candies make the base for a lovely, fluffy pie with the best flavor.

INEXPENSIVE

INGREDIENTS | SERVES 8–10

1 cup semisweet chocolate chips

¼ cup butter

1 Make-Ahead Pie Crust (page 251), baked and cooled

¾ cup milk

½ cup crushed peppermint candies, divided

½ teaspoon peppermint extract

1 (10-ounce) package regular marshmallows

1 cup heavy whipping cream

2 tablespoons powdered sugar

1 cup hot fudge sauce

1. In small saucepan, melt chocolate chips with butter; stir until combined. Spread over Pie Crust and set aside to cool.

2. In large saucepan, combine milk and ¼ cup of the crushed candies; stir over low heat until candies melt. Add peppermint extract and marshmallows; cook and stir over low heat until marshmallows melt and mixture is smooth.

3. Chill marshmallow mixture until thickened. Beat cream with powdered sugar; using same beaters, beat marshmallow mixture. Fold together the whipped cream and marshmallow mixture; pour into pie crust.

4. Cover and chill until firm, about 4–5 hours. Serve with warmed hot fudge sauce.

Chocolate Caramel Frozen Pie

This elegant recipe can be varied in several ways.
Use all caramel or all chocolate toppings, or try strawberry for a nice change of pace.

MAKE AHEAD

INGREDIENTS | SERVES 10–12

1 (8-ounce) package cream cheese, softened

1 (14-ounce) can sweetened condensed milk

1 cup heavy cream

2 tablespoons brown sugar

1 teaspoon cornstarch

1 teaspoon vanilla

1 cup chocolate ice cream topping

1 cup caramel ice cream topping

1 cup crushed chocolate-covered toffee

2 (9-inch) prepared chocolate cookie pie crusts

1. In large bowl, beat cream cheese until fluffy. Gradually beat in the sweetened condensed milk until fluffy; set aside.

2. In small bowl, beat cream with brown sugar, cornstarch, and vanilla until stiff peaks form. Fold into cream cheese mixture.

3. Layer the cream cheese mixture, both types of topping, and crushed toffee in the two pie crusts. Cover and chill or freeze for 4–6 hours before serving.

Keep It Healthy

You can use low-fat cream cheese and nonfat sweetened condensed milk in this recipe. Never use all nonfat ingredients; a blend of low-fat and nonfat gives the best result. In place of the cream mixture, use frozen nonfat whipped topping, thawed. Add a bit of brown sugar to the cream cheese mixture to keep the flavor the same.

Graham Cracker Cupcakes

Kids will love these easy cupcakes that have a rich graham flavor.
They're inexpensive too.

INEXPENSIVE

INGREDIENTS | YIELDS 24 CUPCAKES

1 cup butter, softened
¾ cup brown sugar
¾ cup sugar
3 eggs
1¾ cups flour
¼ cup whole wheat flour
1 teaspoon baking powder
1 teaspoon baking soda
1 teaspoon cinnamon
¼ teaspoon nutmeg
1 cup orange juice
1 recipe Caramel Cream Cheese Frosting (page 246)

1. Preheat oven to 350°F. Line 24 cupcake tins with paper liners and set aside.

2. In large bowl, combine butter with brown sugar and sugar; beat until fluffy. Add eggs, one at a time, beating well until combined.

3. In medium bowl, combine flour, whole wheat flour, baking powder, baking soda, cinnamon, and nutmeg and mix. Add alternately with orange juice to butter mixture, beginning and ending with dry ingredients.

4. Spoon batter into prepared cupcake tins, filling each about ⅔ full. Bake for 17–23 minutes or until cupcakes spring back when lightly touched with finger. Remove to wire rack to cool. Frost with Frosting; store covered at room temperature.

Chocolate Walnut Toffee Pie

This pie is similar to pecan pie, but it's more complicated, with a firmer texture.
All of the different kinds of chocolate make it a winner.

QUICK

INGREDIENTS | SERVES 10

1½ cups walnut pieces
2 cups brown sugar
⅓ cup cocoa powder
3 eggs
2 teaspoons vanilla
½ cup light cream
¼ cup butter, melted
½ cup milk chocolate chips
½ cup English toffee bits
½ recipe Easy Paste Pastry (page 266), unbaked
½ (8-ounce) milk chocolate candy bar, melted

1. Preheat oven to 325°F. Spread walnuts on a cookie sheet and toast in oven for 8–10 minutes until golden brown. Cool completely.

2. In large bowl, combine brown sugar, cocoa, eggs, vanilla, cream, and butter and beat well with eggbeater until smooth. Stir in walnuts, chocolate chips, and toffee bits.

3. Pour mixture into an unpricked pie shell. Bake for 40–50 minutes or until pie is set but still slightly soft in center. Cool completely on wire rack. Drizzle with melted chocolate, then let stand until set.

Make-Ahead Tips

Don't try to assemble the filling for this pie ahead of time. The combination just doesn't hold well, even in the refrigerator. You have to make the entire pie ahead of time. You could give someone the job of melting the candy bar and drizzling it over the pie; that's a good task for the non-cook.

Peach Praline Pie

Peaches and pralinees are a natural combination.
This elegant pie is perfect when fresh peaches are in season.

MAKE AHEAD

INGREDIENTS | SERVES 10–12

3½ cups peeled, chopped peaches
2 tablespoons lemon juice
¼ cup sugar
3 tablespoons brown sugar
2 tablespoons flour
Pinch salt
1 cup flour
½ cup brown sugar
1 tablespoon lemon juice
½ cup butter, melted
½ cup toffee baking bits
½ cup chopped almonds
1 Make-Ahead Pie Crust (page 251), unpricked

1. Preheat oven to 425°F. In large bowl, combine peaches, 2 tablespoons lemon juice, sugar, 3 tablespoons brown sugar, 2 tablespoons flour, and a pinch of salt; mix well.

2. In medium bowl, combine 1 cup flour and ½ cup brown sugar and mix well. Add 1 tablespoon lemon juice and melted butter; mix until crumbly. Stir in toffee bits and chopped almonds.

3. Place ½ cup of the almond mixture in bottom of unbaked Pie Crust. Top with peach mixture, then remaining almond mixture.

4. Bake for 10 minutes, then reduce heat to 350°F and bake for 25–35 minutes longer until peaches are bubbling in center of pie and top is golden brown. Let cool completely, then serve.

Caramel Ginger Cake

If you love gingerbread, this cake is for you.
The smooth and rich caramel frosting is the perfect finishing touch.

INEXPENSIVE

INGREDIENTS | SERVES 16

1 cup butter, softened
1 cup brown sugar
¾ cup light molasses
2½ cups all purpose flour
2 teaspoons baking soda
1 tablespoon ground ginger
1 teaspoon cinnamon
½ teaspoon allspice
¼ teaspoon salt
1¼ cups buttermilk
4 eggs
2 teaspoons vanilla
½ cup toffee baking bits
1 recipe Caramel Cream Cheese
Frosting (page 246)

1. Preheat oven to 325°F. Spray a 9" × 13" baking pan with nonstick baking spray containing flour and set aside.

2. In large bowl, combine butter with sugar; beat until light. Stir in molasses. In medium bowl, combine flour, baking soda, ginger, cinnamon, allspice, and salt. Add alternately with buttermilk to butter mixture.

3. Beat in the eggs, one at a time, beating until thoroughly incorporated. Then beat in vanilla. Pour into prepared pan. Bake for 55–65 minutes or until toothpick inserted in center comes out clean. Cool completely on wire rack.

4. Stir baking bits into Frosting and frost cooled cake.

Transport Tips

Sheet cakes are the easiest types of cakes to transport to another person's house. All you need to do is cover the pan tightly with a double layer of foil. Also, some pans come with a cover. These are usually made of heavy plastic and snap onto the top of the pan. The frosting will be perfectly undisturbed.

White Chocolate Almond Lemon Fluff Pie

A praline brown sugar mixture nestles below a fluffy lemon filling,
topped with a white chocolate drizzle. Wow!

EASY

INGREDIENTS | SERVES 8–10

½ cup chopped almonds
2 tablespoons brown sugar
1 tablespoon butter, softened
1 Easy Paste Pastry (page 266), unpricked
1 cup sugar
2 tablespoons butter, softened
3 egg yolks
2 tablespoons flour
Pinch salt
1 cup milk
½ cup lemon juice
2 teaspoons grated lemon zest
3 egg whites
1 cup white chocolate chips
3 tablespoons heavy cream
2 teaspoons corn syrup

1. Preheat oven to 400°F. In small bowl, combine almonds, 2 tablespoons brown sugar, and 1 tablespoon butter; mix well. Press into bottom of pie shell; bake for 5 minutes, then place on wire rack.

2. In large bowl, combine sugar and 2 tablespoons butter; mix well. Stir in egg yolks and beat well. Add flour and salt and beat again.

3. Stir in milk, lemon juice, and zest; set aside. In small bowl, beat egg whites until stiff peaks form. Fold into egg yolk mixture and spoon into pie shell.

4. Bake for 10 minutes, then reduce temperature to 325°F. Bake for 30–40 minutes or until top is deep golden brown.

5. Place pie on wire rack. In small saucepan, melt chocolate chips, cream, and corn syrup, stirring until smooth. Drizzle over pie, then let cool completely. Store in refrigerator.

Fudge Cake

Brown Butter Frosting adds depth of flavor to a simple and fudgy chocolate cake in this excellent recipe.

INEXPENSIVE

INGREDIENTS | SERVES 16

½ cup boiling water

3 squares unsweetened chocolate, chopped

2 cups all purpose flour

2 tablespoons cornstarch

1 cup sugar

⅓ cup brown sugar

1 teaspoon baking soda

½ teaspoon cream of tartar

½ teaspoon salt

⅓ cup butter, softened

⅔ cup milk

2 teaspoons vanilla

4 egg whites

1 recipe Brown Butter Frosting (page 247)

Transport Tips

If you have one, a cake holder is the best way to transport a layer cake to a party. If not, find a large bowl that will fit over the cake. Use foil to wrap over and around the bowl and the stand to keep the two pieces together. Place the cake on the floor of the car, and surround it with sweaters or jackets so it won't slide around during the trip.

1. Preheat oven to 350°F. Spray two 8-inch round cake pans with nonstick baking spray containing flour; set aside.

2. In small bowl, combine boiling water with chocolate; stir until chocolate melts. Set aside.

3. In large bowl, combine flour, cornstarch, sugar, brown sugar, baking soda, cream of tartar, and salt; mix with wire whisk.

4. Add butter, milk, and vanilla; beat for 2 minutes on medium speed. Add unbeaten egg whites and beat for 1 minute longer. Then stir in the chocolate mixture until smooth.

5. Divide mixture among cake pans. Bake for 25–35 minutes until cakes start to pull away from sides of pan. Let cool for 5 minutes, then remove from pans and cool completely on racks. Fill and frost with Brown Butter Frosting.

Apple Cake with Creamy Frosting

The creamy frosting on this rich and flavorful apple cake is very special.
It makes a thin frosting, but it soaks into the cake as it cools.

INEXPENSIVE

INGREDIENTS | SERVES 16

3 eggs

¾ cup sugar

1 cup brown sugar

¾ cup canola oil

6 tablespoons butter, melted

2 teaspoons vanilla

2½ cups flour

1 teaspoon cinnamon

1 teaspoon baking soda

½ teaspoon salt

5 medium apples, peeled and chopped

½ cup chopped walnuts

½ cup sugar

¼ cup buttermilk

½ cup butter

1 tablespoon corn syrup

1 teaspoon vanilla

¼ teaspoon baking soda

1. Preheat oven to 325°F. Spray a 9" × 13" cake pan with nonstick baking spray containing flour and set aside.

2. In large bowl, beat eggs with sugar and brown sugar for 4 minutes. Add oil, 6 tablespoons melted butter, and vanilla and mix.

3. Add the flour, cinnamon, baking soda, and salt and beat well; batter will be thick. Fold in the apples and walnuts and spread in prepared pan. Bake for 50–60 minutes or until cake springs back when lightly touched in center.

4. When cake comes out of oven, make frosting. In large saucepan, mix ½ cup sugar, buttermilk, ½ cup butter, and 1 tablespoon corn syrup. Bring to a boil; boil and stir for 5 minutes. Remove from heat, stir in vanilla and baking soda, and then pour over hot cake. Cool completely.

Grasshopper Pie

Melted marshmallows make a decadent pie filling again!
It's a gorgeous pie perfect for any celebration.

EASILY DOUBLES

INGREDIENTS | SERVES 10

20 mint-flavored chocolate sandwich cookies, crushed

¼ cup butter, melted

2 cups mint chocolate chip ice cream

24 large marshmallows

⅔ cup whole milk

3 tablespoons crème de menthe liqueur

¼ teaspoon mint extract

1 cup heavy whipping cream

1 tablespoon powdered sugar

6 chocolate mint candies, chopped

Make It Healthy

Well, as healthy as this recipe can get! You can find nonalcoholic crème de menthe at the grocery store, or ask for it as a special order there or at the liquor store. If you can't find it, substitute ¼ cup heavy cream with ¼ teaspoon peppermint extract and ½ teaspoon mint extract.

1. In medium bowl, combine crushed cookies with butter; mix well. Press into bottom and up sides of 9-inch pan. Freeze for 10 minutes.

2. Slightly soften the ice cream and spread in bottom of crushed cookie pie crust. Freeze while preparing filling.

3. In large microwave-safe bowl, combine marshmallows with milk. Microwave on 100% power for 2 minutes, then remove and stir. Continue microwaving for periods of 30 seconds until marshmallows are melted and mixture is smooth. Stir in crème de menthe and mint extract; set aside.

4. In small bowl, beat cream with powdered sugar until stiff peaks form. Fold into the marshmallow mixture and spoon on top of ice cream. Garnish with chopped candies and freeze 4–6 hours until solid.

Apple Oatmeal Crumb Pie

Yum. This recipe is like apple crisp in a pie crust.
You could use toffee baking bits for the walnuts if you'd like.

INEXPENSIVE

INGREDIENTS | SERVES 8

2 tablespoons lemon juice

2 teaspoons vanilla

6 Granny Smith apples, peeled and thinly sliced

½ cup brown sugar

2 tablespoons flour

1 teaspoon cinnamon

⅛ teaspoon cardamom

1 Make-Ahead Pie Crust (page 251), unpricked

1 cup flour

1 cup quick-cooking oatmeal

½ cup chopped walnuts

1 cup brown sugar

½ cup butter, melted

1. Preheat oven to 375°F. In small bowl, combine lemon juice and vanilla; mix well. Thinly slice the apples into a large bowl; as you work, sprinkle with the lemon juice mixture.

2. In same small bowl, combine ½ cup brown sugar, 2 tablespoons flour, cinnamon, and cardamom; mix well. Sprinkle over apples and toss to coat. Place apples in the unbaked Pie Crust.

3. In same large bowl, combine 1 cup flour, oatmeal, walnuts, and 1 cup brown sugar; mix well. Add melted butter and mix until crumbly. Sprinkle on top of pie.

4. Bake for 50–60 minutes, covering pie with a sheet of foil if it starts browning too quickly. Cool completely on wire rack before serving.

Cream-Filled Chocolate Cupcakes

It's fun to bite into these cupcakes and discover the chocolate cream hidden inside.
These cakes are perfect for any type of party, from kids to adult.

EASILY DOUBLES

INGREDIENTS | YIELDS 12 CUPCAKES

1-⅓ cups flour

2 tablespoons cornstarch

2 tablespoons cocoa

½ cup brown sugar

¼ cup sugar

1 teaspoon baking soda

¼ teaspoon salt

2 tablespoons butter, melted

1 cup buttermilk

1 (1-ounce) square unsweetened baking chocolate, melted

1 cup heavy whipping cream

¼ cup powdered sugar

2 tablespoons cocoa

1 teaspoon vanilla

½ recipe Decadent Chocolate Frosting (page 246)

Party Fun

Part of the fun of these cupcakes is making them. Prepare the cupcakes and the Frosting ahead of time. Make the cream filling when you want to assemble them, then make an assembly line with your guests.

1. Preheat oven to 350°F. Spray 12 muffin tins with nonstick baking spray containing flour; set aside.

2. In large bowl, combine flour, cornstarch, cocoa, brown sugar, sugar, baking soda, and salt and mix with wire whisk.

3. In small bowl, combine butter and buttermilk and mix well. Stir into flour mixture along with melted chocolate; beat until smooth. Spoon mixture into prepared muffin tins, filling each about ¾ full. Bake for 15–20 minutes until tops spring back when touched with finger. Remove from muffin tins and cool completely on wire rack.

4. In small bowl, beat cream with powdered sugar, cocoa, and vanilla until stiff peaks form. Cut a slice from the top of the cupcakes, and scoop out center of cake. Fill with cream, replace tops, and then frost with Frosting. Store in refrigerator.

Meringue-Topped Devil's Food Cake

This super-moist and dark chocolate cake is topped with a
brown sugar meringue that's filled with dried fruit and nuts.

INEXPENSIVE

INGREDIENTS | SERVES 16

½ cup boiling water

½ cup cocoa

1½ teaspoons baking soda

⅔ cup butter, softened

1½ cups brown sugar, divided

1¼ cups granulated sugar, divided

1 egg

2 egg yolks

2¼ cups flour

¼ cup cornstarch

½ teaspoon salt

¾ cup buttermilk

2 teaspoons vanilla

2 egg whites

¼ teaspoon cream of tartar

1 teaspoon vanilla

½ cup chopped dried cranberries

¼ cup chopped pecans

1. Preheat oven to 350°F. Spray a 9" × 13" pan with nonstick baking spray containing flour. In small bowl, combine water, cocoa, and baking soda; mix well and set aside.

2. In large bowl, beat butter with 1 cup brown sugar and ¾ cup granulated sugar until fluffy. Add cocoa mixture and blend well. Then add egg and egg yolks and beat until smooth.

3. Sift together flour, cornstarch, and salt. Add alternately with buttermilk to creamed mixture, beginning and ending with dry ingredients, then beat in vanilla. Pour into prepared pan.

4. Bake cake for 35–40 minutes until cake springs back when touched lightly with finger but is still moist on top. While cake is in oven, prepare topping.

5. In small bowl, beat egg whites with cream of tartar until soft peaks form. Gradually add ½ cup granulated sugar, beating until stiff peaks form. Then beat in ½ cup brown sugar. Beat in vanilla, then fold in cranberries and pecans.

6. When cake is done, remove from oven and immediately spread with meringue mixture. Return to oven and bake for 10–14 minutes longer until meringue is light brown. Cool completely on wire rack.

Marshmallow Cake

This unusual cake is velvety and light.
The chocolate frosting is the perfect complement.

INEXPENSIVE

INGREDIENTS | SERVES 16

1¾ cups all-purpose flour

3 tablespoons cornstarch

1¾ cups sugar, divided

1 cup hot water

6 egg whites

1 teaspoon cream of tartar

¼ teaspoon salt

2 teaspoons baking powder

2 teaspoons vanilla

1 recipe Decadent Chocolate Frosting (page 246)

Party Fun

This reliable cake can be baked in many different shapes. Bake it in two 9-inch round cake pans for about 30–35 minutes, then fill and frost with your favorite frosting. Make cupcakes with it: you should get about 24 cupcakes. Offer several different frostings and make a cupcake bar. Or try a Bundt cake: bake for 45–55 minutes until golden brown.

1. Preheat oven to 350°F. Spray a 9" × 13" baking pan with nonstick baking spray containing flour and set aside.

2. Sift flour and cornstarch into a medium bowl. Stir in 1 cup sugar. Stir in hot water and mix until smooth; set aside.

3. In large bowl, beat egg whites with cream of tartar and salt until soft peaks form. Gradually beat in remaining ¾ cup sugar along with baking powder and vanilla until stiff peaks form.

4. Stir a dollop of the egg white mixture into the flour mixture and stir to lighten. Fold flour mixture into egg white mixture.

5. Spoon into prepared pan. Bake for 40–50 minutes until cake starts to pull away from sides of pan. Cool completely on wire rack, then frost with Frosting.

Easy Paste Pastry

This unusual method of making a pie crust is foolproof.
Be sure to cut the shortening into the flour until thoroughly blended.

EASY

INGREDIENTS | 2 PIE CRUSTS
2 cups flour
½ teaspoon salt
3 tablespoons water
1 tablespoon milk
½ cup solid shortening
3 tablespoons butter

1. Place flour and salt in a medium bowl and mix well. Remove ⅓ cup of this mixture to a small bowl and add water and milk; stir and set aside.

2. Cut shortening and butter into flour mixture in medium bowl until particles are the size of small peas. Add the flour/water mixture and stir vigorously with a fork until the dough comes together.

3. Divide dough in half and chill. Roll out each half for a 9-inch pie crust. Bake as directed in recipe, or for prebaked crust, bake at 400°F for 12–17 minutes until light golden brown.

CHAPTER 15

Sumptuous, Easy Desserts

Individual Cherry-Apple Trifles

A slight apple flavor and lots of cherries make this easy recipe special.
Save the rest of the cake to make Chocolate Peanut Butter Tiramisu (page 283).

EASILY DOUBLES

INGREDIENTS | SERVES 8

½ recipe Marshmallow Cake (page 265), unfrosted

⅓ cup brown sugar

2 tablespoons cornstarch

1 cup apple juice

½ cup water

½ cup cherry preserves

½ teaspoon grated lemon rind

4 cups pitted Bing cherries, cut in half

1 cup heavy whipping cream

3 tablespoons powdered sugar

1 teaspoon vanilla

1. Prepare Marshmallow Cake and let cool. Meanwhile, in large saucepan combine brown sugar, cornstarch, apple juice, water, and cherry preserves. Cook over medium heat, stirring frequently, until mixture comes to a boil and thickens.

2. Remove from heat and stir in lemon rind and cherries. Let cool. When ready to eat, whip cream with powdered sugar and vanilla until stiff peaks form.

3. Cut Cake into 8 pieces. Cut each piece in half crosswise. Place one cake bottom on each serving plate, cover with cherry sauce and top of cake; more cherry sauce and whipped cream. Serve immediately.

Chocolate Ice Cream Cake

This dessert resembles those expensive ice cream cakes you see in bakeries,
but it's much less expensive. And fun to make!

EASY

INGREDIENTS | SERVES 10–12

30 crumbled almond macaroons, divided

⅓ cup chopped toasted pecans

⅓ cup butter, melted

5 cups chocolate swirl ice cream

5 cups fudge brownie ice cream

1½ cups Best Chocolate Fudge Sauce (page 271), cooled

3 (4-ounce) chocolate-covered English toffee bars, crushed

1. In large bowl, combine macaroons with pecans and butter; mix until coated. Press half of this mixture into the bottom of a 9-inch springform pan.

2. Soften ice cream slightly. Spread the chocolate swirl ice cream over the macaroons in an even layer. Top with remaining macaroon mixture.

3. Top with fudge brownie ice cream. Freeze for 1 hour. Then top with the Chocolate Sauce, spreading to coat. Sprinkle with crushed toffee bars. Freeze for 4–6 hours before serving.

Frozen Yogurt Squares

Strawberries and chocolate are made for each other.
This easy recipe is light and refreshing.

INEXPENSIVE

INGREDIENTS | SERVES 16

24 filled chocolate cookies, crushed
½ cup ground walnuts
⅓ cup butter, melted
2 cups strawberry yogurt
1 cup frozen strawberries, thawed
½ cup strawberry preserves
1 (16-ounce) container frozen whipped topping, thawed
2 cups Best Chocolate Fudge Sauce (page 271)

1. In medium bowl, combine cookies, walnuts, and butter; mix until combined. Press into bottom of 13" × 9" pan and set aside.

2. In food processor or blender, combine 1 cup yogurt with the strawberries and process or blend until combined. Pour into large bowl. Stir in remaining yogurt and preserves, then fold in the whipped topping.

3. Pour mixture over crust and freeze for 2 hours until firm. Pour Chocolate Sauce over and freeze for 2–4 hours until firm. Cut into squares to serve.

Brownie Ice Cream Torte

This elegant torte is very easy to make; it's a good recipe to assign to non-cooks.
Tell them they can use any chocolate fudge ice cream topping in place of the Fudge Sauce.

EASY

INGREDIENTS | SERVES 16

1 recipe Best Brownies (page 235), unfrosted
1 recipe Best Chocolate Fudge Sauce (page 271)
2 cups vanilla ice cream
2 cups chocolate swirl ice cream
2 cups fudge brownie ice cream

1. Spray 9" × 13" glass baking dish with nonstick cooking spray; set aside. Cut Brownies into 2-inch squares and, in two batches, pulse in a food processor until crumbly.

2. Press half of Brownie crumbs into the glass baking dish. Drizzle with half of the Fudge sauce, then top with scoops of vanilla, chocolate swirl, and fudge brownie ice cream. Gently press ice cream into an even layer.

3. Drizzle with remaining Fudge sauce, then with remaining Brownie crumbs; press into an even layer.

4. Cover and freeze until firm, about 3–4 hours. To serve, let stand at room temperature for 10 minutes, then cut into squares.

Peach Torte

The base of meringue that is made with saltine crackers plays into the sweet/salty combination that is so popular in desserts now. The peaches are the perfect addition.

EASY

INGREDIENTS | SERVES 8

3 egg whites
½ teaspoon cream of tartar
½ teaspoon salt
1 cup sugar
1 tablespoon lemon juice
12 saltine crackers, crushed
2 teaspoons vanilla
⅔ cup chopped almonds
4 peaches, peeled and sliced
2 tablespoons lemon juice
1 cup heavy whipping cream
2 tablespoons brown sugar

1. Preheat oven to 350°F. Spray a 9-inch pie plate with nonstick baking spray containing flour and set aside. In large bowl, beat egg whites with cream of tartar and salt until soft peaks form. Gradually beat in sugar and lemon juice until stiff peaks form.

2. Fold in cracker crumbs, vanilla, and almonds until combined. Spread into prepared pie plate. Bake for 25–30 minutes or until mixture is light golden brown. Cool completely.

3. When ready to eat, combine peaches with lemon juice; fill pie. In small bowl, beat cream with brown sugar until stiff peaks form. Pile on top of peaches, then slice to serve.

Angel Rum Sticks

This unusual recipe is a great way to use up leftover angel food cake, or to fancy-up a store-bought cake.

INEXPENSIVE

INGREDIENTS | SERVES 14

1 loaf purchased angel food cake
½ cup butter
3 cups powdered sugar
¼ cup light cream
½ cup rum
2 cups crushed vanilla sandwich cookies
1 cup ground pecans
½ cup crushed toffee baking bits

1. Cut cake into 14 slices, then cut each slice in half lengthwise to make long slender pieces. In large bowl, beat butter with powdered sugar and cream until blended.

2. Slowly add rum, beating until smooth. You may need to add more sugar or cream until a soft spreading consistency is reached.

3. On plate, combine crushed cookies, pecans, and toffee bits. Frost the angel food pieces on all sides with the rum mixture, then roll in pecan mixture to coat.

4. Place on waxed paper-lined cookie sheet; cover and chill or freeze until ready to serve.

Best Chocolate Fudge Sauce

*Use this spectacular sauce to top ice cream layered in a glass pan,
or serve it as part of an ice cream sundae bar.*

MAKE AHEAD

INGREDIENTS | YIELDS 4 CUPS SAUCE

⅓ cup butter

2 cups chocolate chips

1 cup milk chocolate chips

1 (12-ounce) can evaporated milk

¼ cup heavy cream

3½ cups powdered sugar

1 teaspoon vanilla

1. Combine all ingredients except vanilla in large heavy saucepan. Place over medium heat and bring to a boil, stirring frequently with wire whisk.

2. Reduce heat to low. When sauce boils and can't be stirred down, cook for 8 minutes, stirring every minute, until smooth and thick.

3. Let sauce cool at room temperature, stirring occasionally, until very thick, about 2–3 hours. Stir in vanilla and store in refrigerator. Can warm in the microwave as needed. Sauce does not freeze hard; it will become slightly chewy when frozen.

Chocolate Caramel Rice Pudding

This decadent recipe is a great combination of comfort food and elegance.

INEXPENSIVE

INGREDIENTS | SERVES 8

4 cups water

2 cups milk

½ teaspoon salt

½ cup brown sugar

1 cup long-grain white rice

1 cup semisweet chocolate chips

1 cup heavy cream

2 tablespoons powdered sugar

2 teaspoons vanilla

½ cup caramel ice cream topping

1. In large saucepan, bring water, milk, salt, and sugar to a boil. Stir in rice. Bring to a simmer, then cover and cook over low heat for 40–50 minutes until rice is very soft. Stir gently twice during cooking time. Stir in chocolate chips until melted, then transfer to large bowl and chill until cold.

2. In small bowl, beat cream with powdered sugar and vanilla. Fold into rice mixture and place in serving cups. Drizzle with caramel ice cream topping. Chill for 2–3 hours before serving.

Curried Fruit Crisp

*All these fruits are complemented beautifully
by the curry powder and the crunchy topping.*

HEALTHY

INGREDIENTS | SERVES 12

1 (15-ounce) can sliced peaches, drained

1 (15-ounce) can pineapple tidbits, drained

1 (15-ounce) can apricot halves, drained

2 tablespoons lemon juice

1¼ cups melted butter, divided

1½ tablespoons curry powder

½ cup brown sugar

2 cups dark brown sugar

1½ cups flour

2 cups quick-cooking oatmeal

1 teaspoon cinnamon

Pinch salt

1. Preheat oven to 375°F. Arrange all the drained fruit in a 9" × 13" glass baking dish. In small bowl, combine lemon juice, ¼ cup butter, curry powder, and ½ cup brown sugar; mix well. Spoon this mixture over the fruit; stir gently to coat.

2. In large bowl, combine 2 cups dark brown sugar, flour, oatmeal, cinnamon, and salt. Add remaining 1 cup melted butter and mix until crumbly. Press this mixture over the fruit.

3. Bake for 50–60 minutes or until the topping is dark golden brown and crisp. Let cool for 30 minutes, then serve warm with ice cream.

Transport Tips

You could bake this dish and take it immediately to the party. It will cool down in the car and while you're eating dinner. Or you could assemble the whole thing and bake it at the party. There's nothing in the recipe that requires refrigeration, so you don't need to worry about keeping it cool.

Pots de Crème

These dense little puddings are full of chocolate.
You must serve this in tiny cups with demitasse spoons.

INEXPENSIVE

INGREDIENTS | SERVES 6

3 eggs

½ cup brown sugar

2 squares unsweetened chocolate, chopped

1 cup heavy cream

1 cup milk

Pinch salt

2 teaspoons vanilla

1 cup milk chocolate chips

¼ cup caramel ice cream topping

1. In top of double boiler, beat eggs until foamy. Add sugar and beat again. Add chocolate; place over simmering water. Cook and stir until chocolate melts.

2. Add cream, milk, and salt; cook, stirring with wire whisk, until mixture becomes thick and reaches 140°F.

3. Remove from heat and stir in vanilla. Let cool for 15 minutes, then stir in chocolate chips and pour into 6 demitasse cups. Cover and chill for 3–4 hours. Top with a drizzle of caramel ice cream topping before serving.

Party Fun

These little desserts are really the perfect end to almost any meal. The portion is small because the dessert is very rich. Decorate them so they match the scheme of your party. Use decorative custard or demitasse cups, or top each one with a candied violet before serving. A dollop of flavored whipped cream is also a perfect finish.

Frozen Fruitcake

This frozen dessert is an old-fashioned treat.
Drizzle it with some chocolate sauce before serving if you'd like.

MAKE AHEAD

INGREDIENTS | SERVES 9

1 (8-ounce) can crushed pineapple, drained

1½ cups whole milk

½ cup sugar

¼ cup flour

⅛ teaspoon salt

3 eggs, beaten

2 teaspoons vanilla

1 cup chopped dates

1 cup pecan pieces

2 cups crumbled coconut macaroons

1 cup heavy whipping cream

2 tablespoons powdered sugar

1. Drain pineapple, reserving juice. Add enough whole milk to the juice to equal two cups. In large saucepan, heat milk mixture until bubbles form around the edge. In small bowl, combine sugar, flour, and salt; add half of the milk mixture and stir until smooth. Return to saucepan with remaining milk mixture. Cook for 8 minutes, stirring frequently, until thick.

2. Beat eggs in small bowl until light; gradually beat in ½ cup of the hot milk mixture. Return egg mixture to saucepan, then simmer for 2 minutes, stirring with wire whisk. Remove from heat and stir in vanilla; cool for 30 minutes.

3. Add dates, drained pineapple, pecans, and macaroons. In small bowl, beat cream with powdered sugar until stiff peaks form. Fold into fruitcake mixture.

4. Place in 9-inch glass baking dish and freeze until firm. To serve, cut into squares.

Biscuit Tortoni

*The combination of crumbled macaroons with
chocolate ice cream and cream is just scrumptious.*

MAKE AHEAD

INGREDIENTS | SERVES 12

1 quart chocolate ice cream

1 cup heavy whipping cream

⅓ cup powdered sugar

2 tablespoons rum, if desired

½ cup chopped toasted almonds

1 cup crumbled almond macaroons

1 cup chocolate fudge ice cream topping

Party Fun

Make this recipe with lots of different ice cream and ice cream topping flavors. You could also use coconut macaroons in place of the almond macaroons. Try strawberry ice cream with coconut macaroons and strawberry ice cream topping. Or use a flavored sherbet with coconut macaroons and chocolate ice cream topping.

1. Line 12 muffin tins with paper liners and set aside. Place ice cream in large bowl; let stand while you beat cream with powdered sugar and rum.

2. Beat the cream mixture into the ice cream. Fold in almonds, and crumbled macaroons until blended, then fold in topping to marble.

3. Spoon mixture into prepared muffin cups. Cover and freeze until frozen solid, about 5–6 hours. To serve, let stand at room temperature for 10 minutes before eating.

Apple Cashew Toffee Crisp

*Cashews and toffee bits add fabulous flavor and texture
to the candy-like topping of this classic crisp recipe.*

INEXPENSIVE

INGREDIENTS | SERVES 12

7 Granny Smith apples, peeled and sliced

2 tablespoons lemon juice

¼ cup apple juice

½ cup sugar

½ cup brown sugar

2 tablespoons flour

1 teaspoon cinnamon

¼ teaspoon nutmeg

2 cups quick-cooking oatmeal

2 cups flour

2 cups brown sugar

½ teaspoon baking soda

1 cup butter, melted

1 cup English toffee bits

½ cup chopped cashews

1. Preheat oven to 350°F. Peel and slice apples. Place the apples in a bowl with the lemon juice and apple juice as you work; toss to coat apples. Sprinkle with ½ cup sugar, ½ cup brown sugar, 2 tablespoons flour, 1 teaspoon cinnamon, and nutmeg and toss.

2. In large bowl, combine oatmeal, 2 cups flour, brown sugar, and baking soda and mix well. Add melted butter and mix until crumbs form. Stir in toffee bits and cashews.

3. Place half of the oatmeal mixture in a 13" × 9" pan. Top with apple mixture, then remaining crumb mixture. Bake for 45–55 minutes or until topping is browned and apples are tender when pierced with a fork. Let cool for 1 hour, then serve.

Party Fun

You can use different types of apples in this easy dessert recipe. But make sure that you choose apples that hold their shape after baking. Those apples include Cortland, Empire, Golden Delicious, Granny Smith, Jonathan, McIntosh, and Winesap. Also try different nuts—chopped walnuts or pecans would be delicious.

Apricot Alaska

Pasteurized egg whites take a while to form peaks; just keep beating!

MAKE AHEAD

INGREDIENTS | SERVES 8

1 quart vanilla ice cream, slightly softened

1 cup frozen nondairy whipped topping, thawed

½ cup apricot preserves

1 tablespoon lemon juice

1 Make-Ahead Pie Crust (page 251), baked and cooled

1 cup miniature marshmallows

1 tablespoon apricot preserves

2 pasteurized egg whites

¼ teaspoon cream of tartar

⅓ cup sugar

1. In large bowl, combine ice cream with whipped topping, ½ cup preserves, and lemon juice; beat until smooth. Place into Pie Crust and freeze until firm, about 4 hours.

2. In small microwave-safe bowl, combine marshmallows with 1 tablespoon preserves. Heat on 100% power until marshmallows melt, about 1–3 minutes. Stir until smooth; set aside.

3. In large bowl, beat egg whites with cream of tartar until foamy. Gradually add sugar, beating until stiff peaks form. Beat in the marshmallow mixture.

4. Use this mixture to top the pie, sealing the meringue to the edges of the pie. Freeze for 4–6 hours.

5. When ready to serve, heat oven to 425°F. Bake pie for 2–5 minutes until meringue is lightly browned. Serve immediately.

Citrus Meringue Torte

*The completed recipe has to chill for a few hours so
the filling has time to soften the meringue a bit.*

INEXPENSIVE

INGREDIENTS | SERVES 8

3 egg whites
1 teaspoon lemon juice
Pinch salt
1½ cups sugar, divided
3 tablespoons flour
⅛ teaspoon salt
½ cup orange juice
½ cup lemon juice
3 egg yolks
2 tablespoons butter
1 cup heavy whipping cream
2 tablespoons powdered sugar
1 teaspoon vanilla

Party Fun

Make the meringue shell ahead of time,
then make the filling up to the point where
the cream is folded in. Whip the cream and
assemble the pie as part of the fun while
dinner is cooking, then chill it until you are
ready to eat dessert. This recipe can also
be made in tartlet pans for cute individual
desserts.

1. Preheat oven to 275°F. Spray a 9-inch pie pan with nonstick baking spray containing flour; set aside.

2. In large bowl, beat egg whites with lemon juice and salt until soft peaks form. Gradually add ¾ cup sugar, beating until stiff peaks form and sugar dissolves. Spread into pie pan. Bake for 1½ hours, then turn off oven and open door; let crust cool completely.

3. In large saucepan, combine ¾ cup sugar, flour, salt, orange juice, and lemon juice. Cook and stir over medium heat until mixture comes to a boil. Boil and stir for 1 minute.

4. Remove from heat and stir some of the mixture into egg yolks, then return egg yolk mixture to saucepan. Bring to a boil; boil for 1 minute. Remove from heat and stir in butter. Cover and chill.

5. In small bowl, beat cream with powdered sugar and vanilla until stiff; fold into cooled orange juice mixture. Pile into meringue shell, cover, and chill for 1–2 hours.

Ice Cream Roll

*Sponge cake is rolled up with strawberry sorbet
and drizzled with lemon sauce in this excellent recipe.*

HEALTHY

INGREDIENTS | SERVES 8

4 eggs, separated

½ teaspoon cream of tartar

⅛ teaspoon salt

1 cup sugar, divided

2 teaspoons vanilla

1 tablespoon lemon juice

1 teaspoon grated lemon zest

¾ cup flour

2 tablespoons cornstarch

6 cups strawberry sorbet, softened

½ cup purchased lemon curd

3 tablespoons heavy cream

Make It Healthy

When you shop for the strawberry sherbet, be sure to read labels. Some of the strawberry sherbets or sorbets available provide a good amount of vitamin C per serving, some up to 25% of recommended daily allowance. As long as you're going to eat dessert, you might as well get some nutrition from it!

1. Preheat oven to 350°F. Grease a 15" × 10" jelly roll pan with solid shortening, line with parchment paper; grease the parchment paper and set aside.

2. In large bowl, place egg whites. Add cream of tartar and salt and beat until soft peaks form. Gradually beat in ½ cup sugar until stiff peaks form.

3. Using same beaters, in small bowl beat egg yolks with vanilla, lemon juice, lemon zest, and remaining ½ cup sugar. Beat until mixture is pale yellow. Sift together the flour and cornstarch.

4. Fold the egg yolk mixture and the flour mixture into the egg whites. Spread into prepared pan. Bake for 12–17 minutes or until the cake is light brown and springs back when lightly touched.

5. While cake is in oven, heavily sprinkle a kitchen towel with powdered sugar. Invert cake onto towel and remove parchment paper. Roll up cake in towel, starting with short side; let cool.

6. Unroll cake and spread with sorbet. Roll up, wrap in waxed paper, and freeze until firm, 4–6 hours. To serve, unwrap and slice into 1-inch pieces. Combine lemon curd with cream; drizzle over slices and serve.

Éclair Torte

This dessert tastes just like an éclair, but it serves a crowd.
Make it the same day you want to eat it.

MAKE AHEAD

INGREDIENTS | SERVES 20

1 cup water

½ cup butter

¼ cup sugar

¼ teaspoon salt

1 cup flour

4 eggs

2 teaspoons vanilla

2 (16-ounce) cans prepared chocolate frosting

1 (8-ounce) package cream cheese, softened

3 cups cold milk

2 (4-ounce) packages French vanilla pudding mix

1½ cups heavy whipping cream

½ cup powdered sugar

1 teaspoon vanilla

2 (6-ounce) milk chocolate bars, grated

½ cup caramel ice cream topping

1 cup toffee baking bits

1. Preheat oven to 400°F. Spray a 10" × 15" jelly roll pan with nonstick baking spray containing flour and set aside.

2. In large saucepan, combine water, butter, sugar, and salt over high heat. Bring to a hard rolling boil. Stir in flour all at once and beat hard until mixture forms a ball and cleans sides of pan.

3. Remove from heat and beat in eggs, one at a time, until smooth and shiny. Beat in 2 teaspoons vanilla and spread in prepared pan. Bake for 18–24 minutes until puffy and deep golden brown. Cool completely on wire rack.

4. Spread the chocolate frosting evenly on the crust. In large bowl, beat cream cheese until fluffy. Gradually beat in ½ cup milk until smooth; beat in pudding mix, then gradually add remaining milk. Spread over frosting.

5. In medium bowl, beat cream with powdered sugar and 1 teaspoon vanilla. Spread over pudding mixture. Top with grated chocolate bars, drizzle with ice cream topping, and sprinkle with baking bits. Cover and chill for 2–3 hours before serving.

Grapefruit Alaska

This beautiful recipe can be served as a dessert,
or as part of an elegant Sunday brunch.

HEALTHY

INGREDIENTS | SERVES 6

3 large red grapefruit

3 cups low-fat vanilla ice cream

4 egg whites

½ teaspoon cream of tartar

⅛ teaspoon salt

1 (7-ounce) jar marshmallow creme

Make It Easy

Cream of tartar is not tartar sauce! It's made from grapes. It's used to lower the acidity of the egg whites while they are being beaten so the protein structure of the egg whites is strengthened. Then it can hold on to the air in the tiny bubbles that make the meringue light and fluffy.

1. Cut grapefruits in half. Remove and retain the flesh, then use a spoon to scrape and remove the membranes. Cut a tiny slice off the bottom of each grapefruit half so they will stand upright.

2. Chop the grapefruit and mix with the ice cream. Fill grapefruit halves with this mixture and place in freezer.

3. Place egg whites in large bowl with cream of tartar and salt. Beat until soft peaks form. Gradually add the marshmallow creme, beating until stiff peaks form.

4. Spread this mixture over the grapefruit, making sure to seal to the edges. Make peaks and swirls with the meringue. Return to freezer; freeze until firm, about 4–6 hours.

5. Preheat oven to 400°F. Place grapefruits on cookie sheet. Bake for 8–12 minutes until the meringue is golden brown. Serve immediately.

Chocolate Berry Cups

These beautiful little cups have such a rich and complex flavor.
You could use blueberries or blackberries for the strawberries or raspberries.

EASILY DOUBLES

INGREDIENTS | SERVES 6

6 (9" × 15") sheets frozen phyllo dough, thawed

⅓ cup butter, melted

½ cup semisweet chocolate chips, finely ground

2 cups pitted Bing cherries, halved

2 tablespoons flour

½ cup sugar

⅛ teaspoon salt

1 tablespoon lemon juice

1 cup chopped strawberries

1 cup raspberries

1 cup white chocolate chips

1 cup semisweet chocolate chips

½ cup heavy cream

Transport Tips

Bake the cups completely, then place back into muffin tins. Cover with heavy-duty foil, crimping the foil to the edges of the pan. Bring along the unprepared strawberries, raspberries, chocolate chips, and cream. At the party, top the cups with the berries and make the two sauces.

1. Preheat oven to 350°F. Place one sheet phyllo dough on work surface; brush with 1 tablespoon butter. Sprinkle with 1 tablespoon ground chocolate. Repeat layers.

2. Cut into six 4½" × 5" pieces. Line six muffin tins with the dough, pressing to the bottom. Bake for 10 minutes.

3. While cups are baking, combine cherries, flour, sugar, salt, and lemon juice in medium bowl; toss well. Remove cups from oven and divide cherry mixture among them. Bake for another 25–30 minutes until pastry is golden brown.

4. Let cups cool for 5 minutes, then remove to wire rack to cool completely.

5. When ready to serve, combine strawberries and raspberries in small bowl and toss; spoon into cups on top of cherries.

6. Then place white chocolate chips in one microwave-safe bowl and semisweet chocolate chips in another. Place ¼ cup cream in each bowl. Microwave each bowl on medium for 1–2 minutes, stirring, until chocolate melts and mixture is smooth. Drizzle both types of chocolate over each cup and serve.

Chocolate Peanut Butter Tiramisu

This elegant tiramisu is easy to make and,
if you leave out the liqueur, will appeal to kids.

MAKE AHEAD

INGREDIENTS | SERVES 20

½ recipe Marshmallow Cake (page 265), unfrosted

½ cup Frothy Hot Chocolate (page 28), cooled

2 tablespoons chocolate liqueur, if desired

1 (8-ounce) package cream cheese, softened

½ cup peanut butter

½ cup brown sugar

1 cup heavy whipping cream, divided

2 tablespoons powdered sugar

1 teaspoon vanilla

1 (4-ounce) chocolate bar with peanuts, chopped

1 cup chopped salted peanuts

1. Cut Cake into 2-inch pieces. Place in 13" × 9" glass baking dish, cut side down, to fill the pan. Combine Hot Chocolate and chocolate liqueur in small bowl; blend well. Drizzle over cake and set aside.

2. In large bowl, beat cream cheese with peanut butter until smooth. Add brown sugar; beat until sugar dissolves, about 5 minutes. Beat in ¼ cup of the cream.

3. In small bowl, combine remaining cream with powdered sugar and vanilla; beat until stiff peaks form. Fold into cream cheese mixture. Spoon and spread over Cake.

4. Top with chocolate bar and salted peanuts. Cover and chill for 4–6 hours before serving.

Make It Easy

You can use a purchased white or yellow cake, a chocolate cake, or a pound cake in place of the Marshmallow Cake if you'd like. Cupcakes would also be an easy substitution. Chocolate syrup combined with chocolate liqueur or even cooled strong coffee could be substituted for the Hot Chocolate.

Cherry Bonbons

These little bonbons are delicious and pretty too.
Be sure that the cherries have the pits removed; check each one.

EASY

INGREDIENTS | YIELDS 48 BONBONS

1 cup chopped pecans
½ cup butter, softened
½ cup brown sugar
2 eggs, separated
1 teaspoon vanilla
Pinch salt
¾ cup flour
3 tablespoons cornstarch
¼ teaspoon baking powder
48 pitted canned cherries, drained
Powdered sugar, for rolling

Make-Ahead Hints

You can make these little bonbons up to 2 days ahead of time. Store them in an airtight container at room temperature. You can freeze them for longer storage, but don't roll in powdered sugar. To thaw, let stand in refrigerator overnight, then at room temperature for 1 hour. Roll in powdered sugar before serving.

1. Preheat oven to 350°F. Spray 48 miniature muffin tins with nonstick baking spray containing flour. Divide pecans among the tins, using 1 teaspoon for each tin, and set aside.

2. In medium bowl, combine butter with brown sugar and beat until fluffy. Add egg yolks, one at a time, beating after each addition. Then add vanilla and salt.

3. Add flour, cornstarch, and baking powder and mix well. Beat egg whites in small bowl until stiff peaks form; fold into butter mixture.

4. Place a generous 1 teaspoon of batter on the nuts and press a cherry into the batter. Bake for 8–10 minutes until golden brown and set. Let cool for 5 minutes, then remove from tins and roll in powdered sugar. Cool on wire racks. When cool, roll again in powdered sugar to coat.

Raspberry Mint Dessert

You have to start this dessert two days ahead of time.
It sounds improbable, but it's really delicious, and it feeds a crowd.

MAKE AHEAD

INGREDIENTS | SERVES 16

1 (10-ounce) package miniature marshmallows

2 (10-ounce) packages frozen raspberries, thawed

1 (3-ounce) package raspberry Jell-O

2 cups flour

1 cup brown sugar

1 cup oatmeal

¾ cup butter, melted

1 (8-ounce) container low-fat nondairy frozen whipped topping, thawed

1 (8-ounce) package yellow butter mints, crushed

1 cup fresh raspberries

1. Two days before the party, combine marshmallows, thawed raspberries, and Jell-O in a large bowl. Stir well and cover; refrigerate overnight.

2. The next day, preheat oven to 375°F. In 9" × 13" pan, combine flour with brown sugar and oatmeal and mix well. Stir in butter until crumbs form. Spread evenly in pan and bake for 10–15 minutes, stirring once, until crumbs are light brown.

3. Remove 1 cup of the crumb mixture and set aside. Using the back of a spoon, press remaining crumb mixture into pan. Let cool completely.

4. Remove marshmallow mixture from refrigerator and stir well. Fold in whipped topping, butter mints, and fresh raspberries until blended. Pour over crumb mixture; top with reserved crumbs. Freeze for 6–8 hours until firm. Remove from freezer 15 minutes before serving to let soften slightly.

Suggested Menus

These menus for potluck parties are very flexible. Be sure to think about color, temperature, taste, and texture when planning a menu. Build a colorful plate, and your meal will be well balanced.

COMFORT FOOD PARTY

Fruity Sangria

Spanish Salmon Loaf

Meatball Chowder

Broccoli Bacon Salad

Ham Loaf with Mustard Sauce

Mocha Date Treats

Stuffed Meatloaf Pinwheels

Bing Cherry Fruit Salad

Decadent Brownie Pie

Caramelized Onion Scones

ADULT'S BIRTHDAY PARTY

Mango Margaritas

Shrimp and Salmon Penne

Ginger Turkey Meatballs

Chocolate Caramel Rice Pudding

Layered Ginger Bars

Chilled Pea Soup

Raspberry Dream Cake

Overnight Spinach Pea Salad

Avocado-Stuffed Pork Tenderloin

Mini Whole Wheat Cheesy Breads

BABY SHOWER

Fruited Tea Punch

Sugar Snap Spinach Salad

Thyme Cream Scones

Bacon-Stuffed Tomatoes

Chilled Pesto Gazpacho

Apple Cake with Creamy Frosting

Salmon Soufflé

Pineapple Bars

HOLIDAY MENU

Coconut Eggnog

Slow-Cooked Wild Rice and Salmon

Flaky Pâté Rolls

Chicken in Phyllo

Best Beer Cheese Soup

Marshmallow Cake

Parmesan Bread

Chewy Cherry Bars

Frozen Cranberry Salad

Chocolate Ice Cream Cake

Shrimp Pizzettes

POTLUCK PICNIC

Orange Wine Coolers

Cold Tomato Soup with Pesto

Cream-Filled Chocolate Cupcakes

Ranch Potato Salad

Chicken Salpicon

Eight-Layer Cookie Bar

LUNCH ON THE PORCH

Cheese Muffins

Spicy Apple Muffins

Gouda Vegetable Soup

Peach Praline Pie

Greek Pasta Salad

Frozen Yogurt Squares

CARDS AT EIGHT

Salmon-Stuffed Mushrooms

Spiced Nut Mix

Rice and Spinach Quiche

Curried Fruit Crisp

Sour Cream Vegetable Soup

Dinner-Size Herbed Popovers

Broccoli Bacon Salad

Easy Baked Pork Kiev

Brie Meatloaf Seafood Crab Bake

Caramel Ginger Cake

SUNDAY BRUNCH

Easy Walnut Boule

Banana Almond Muffins

Peach Torte

Potato Salmon Pie

Meringue-Topped Devil's Food Cake

Oven Omelet

Chicken-Stuffed Apples

COZY NIGHT WITH FRIENDS

Frothy Hot Chocolate

Potato Puffs

Honey Walnut Pork Chops

Bacon Blue Cheese–Stuffed Chicken

Spinach Salad Fudge Cake

Apricot Alaska Curried Meatballs

Split Pea Chowder

FAMILY REUNION

Glazed Pretzel Mix

Pumpkin Black Bean Soup

Old-Fashioned Meatball Casserole

Refrigerator Rolls

Green Salad with Avocado Salad Dressing

Graham Cracker Cupcakes

Smothered Steak

Apple Cashew Toffee Crisp

Potluck Bacon Chicken

APPETIZER PARTY

Tipsy Meatballs

Bacon Potato Skins

Mini Mexican Pizzas

Hazelnut Crab Cakes

Chocolate Cheesecake Cookies

Super-Easy Pineapple Cheese Balls

Meringue-Filled Chocolate Cookies

DESSERT PARTY

Chicken Wild Rice Chowder

Peanut Butter Fudge Brownies

Orange Mint Sugar Cookies

Chocolate Walnut Toffee Pie

Carrot Cupcakes

Chocolate Peanut Butter Tiramisu

Best Fudge

Pots de Crème

Lemon Meringue Bars

COOKOUT POTLUCK

Edamame Guacamole

Grilled Herb Cheese Breadsticks

Lip-Smackin' Ribs

Grilled Red Snapper with Fruit Salsa

Cottage Cheese Veggie Salad

Cherry Bonbons

Lima Bean Salad

Best Brownies

Teriyaki Steak

VEGETARIAN POTLUCK PARTY

Chilled Borscht

Fresh Cranberry Salad

Fresh Apple Bar Cookies

Marinated Mushroom Salad

Citrus Meringue Torte

Apple Oatmeal Crumb Pie

Cheese and Tomato Manicotti

Black Bean Lasagna

Resources

Books

Park Avenue Potluck by The Society Of Memorial Sloan Kettering And Florence Fabricant (Rizzoli)

Elegant recipes from New York City's most famous hostesses.

The New Potluck by *Taste Of Home* Editors (Reader's Digest)

Elegant and easy recipes perfect to take to potluck parties. Many recipes submitted by readers; all tested by the *Taste of Home* test kitchens.

The Church Potluck Supper Cookbook by Elaine Robinson (Adams Media)

Lots of recipes for potluck parties; information about safely serving a crowd.

The Big Book Of Potluck by Maryana Vollstedt (Chronicle Books)

Guidelines for throwing a potluck party, along with hundreds of recipes, especially hors d'oeuvres and casseroles.

What Can I Bring? by Anne Byrn (Workman Publishing)

By the author of *The Cake Mix Doctor*, lots of great recipes for potluck parties.

The Gourmet Potluck by Beth Hensperger (Ten Speed Press)

Recipes focus on fresh ingredients put together in gourmet recipes.

Websites

Entertaining At About.com

www.entertaining.about.com

Site provides lots of menus, recipes, and tips for holding parties. Special section on potluck parties.

Food Network

www.foodnetwork .com/food/et_pa_potluck_dinners

Recipes, tips, and information about how to throw the best potluck party. Recipes divided by category.

Party 411
www.party411.com
Information about party giving. Party planning ideas and guides.

Chowhound
www.chow.com/stories/10422
How to feed a crowd: recipes, tips, and shortcuts.

Magazines and Newsletters

Cooking Light
Lots of no-fail potluck recipes that are lighter, with fat content usually no more than 30 percent of total.

Familyfun
Magazine put out by the Disney company; offers lots of entertaining and party ideas and recipes.

BH&G
Magazine focuses on decorating and entertaining, with lots of recipes and party ideas.

Taste of Home
www.tasteofhome.com
Mostly recipes; submitted by readers, then vetted by the magazine's test kitchen.
List of potluck showstoppers; tried-and-true recipes to take to potluck parties.

All Party Ideas
www.allpartyideas.com/potluck-party.shtml
Lots of party menus and recipes, plus guidelines on giving an easy and relaxing potluck party.

The Party Planner
www.party-planner.fimark.net/potluck-party.html
Step-by-step guide to planning a dinner, with a timeline you can adjust to your own needs. Recipes and food preparation tips.

Allrecipes.com
www.allrecipes.com/HowTo/ Potluck-Show-Stoppers/Detail.aspx

Index

Note: Page numbers in **bold** indicate recipe category lists.